Matthew Condon is a prize-winning Australian novelist and journalist. He began his journalism career with the *Gold Coast Bulletin* in 1984 and subsequently worked for leading newspapers and journals including the *Sydney Morning Herald*, the *Sun-Herald*, Melbourne's *Sunday Age* and the *Courier-Mail*. He has written ten books of fiction, including *The Trout Opera*, and is the author of the best-selling true-crime series about Queensland crime and corruption – *Three Crooked Kings* (2013), *Jacks and Jokers* (2014), *All Fall Down* (2015) and *Little Fish are Sweet* (2016).

THE
NIGHT
DRAGON

MATTHEW
CONDON

UQP

First published 2019 by University of Queensland Press
PO Box 6042, St Lucia, Queensland 4067 Australia

uqp.com.au
uqp@uqp.uq.edu.au

Cover design by Design by Committee
Cover illustration by Josh Durham
Typeset in 12/16 pt Bembo Std Regular by Post Pre-press Group, Brisbane
Printed in Australia by McPherson's Printing Group, Melbourne

The University of Queensland Press is
supported by the Queensland Government
through Arts Queensland.

Every effort has been made to contact copyright licensees for
permission to reproduce material. If you believe material for which
you hold rights is reprinted here, please contact the publisher.

A catalogue record for this
book is available from the
National Library of Australia

ISBN 978 0 7022 6020 9 (pbk)
ISBN 978 0 7022 6154 1 (pdf)
ISBN 978 0 7022 6155 8 (epub)
ISBN 978 0 7022 6156 5 (kindle)

For my wife, Katie Kate

'... he is colour blind in the red, green and brown colours ... he is hard to frighten ... he is very methodical ... he does not like sunlight because he is very fair-skinned ... he has the tattoo of St George and the Dragon on his chest, on his back and both legs.' —Witness statement about Vincent O'Dempsey given to the Crime Intelligence Unit, Brisbane 1974

'He takes you in the middle of the night, like an angel, and you're gone for good.' —Witness at Vincent O'Dempsey's committal hearing, Brisbane 2015

VINCENT O'DEMPSEY APPEARED in the glassed-in dock of a Brisbane court, his hair slicked back, his gaze shifting to all quarters of the courtroom. Even in profile, he had a bird-like countenance. His penetrating black eyes and the slight, almost imperceptible movements of his head were like that of a hawk, attuned to the slightest shift in the landscape, or the potential for a trap.

In criminal circles his presence had been felt since the 1960s, and while he had brushed up against the judicial system for various petty offences, he remained an ominous figure at the edge of the firelight. Here was the person other serious criminals described as the most feared man in the Australian underworld. It was rumoured he was a cold-blooded killer the likes of which this country had never seen – the man with his own private graveyard that, as Warwick locals quipped over the years, was so full that the bodies had to be buried upright to save space. Now, here he was in the full light of day, like some bogeyman in a dark children's fairytale, or an ancient myth, come to life and captured in the bowl of the court dock. The legendary Vincent O'Dempsey – pugilist, bird breeder, alpaca farmer, bushman and munitions expert out of Warwick, Queensland.

In certain circles he was nicknamed Swami the Magician, because he made people disappear. Others called him the Angel of Death who came for you at night, or Silent Death. When he was imprisoned in his late-twenties for break, enter and steal, and possession of an unlicensed firearm, word filtered through Boggo Road Gaol that O'Dempsey already had at least one murder notched on his belt.

For the next fifty-odd years he would intermittently do time for various drug and weapons offences, and all the while the myth grew around him. In the press and even in State Parliament the speculation persisted that various cases of people missing and presumed murdered were the work of this one man. Yet, O'Dempsey always denied the allegations of murder levelled against him, and despite being suspected of multiple murders on the recommendation of a coroner in 1980, the case never made it to court. For decades, even his own criminal associates wondered: How did he get away with it?

It wasn't until more than half a century after his supposed first kill that police would unearth a criminal accomplice who was prepared to testify against O'Dempsey in court.

Finally, time had caught up with the Night Dragon.

Day of Reckoning

It was the first day of winter – 1 June 2017 – and by 9.45 a.m. in the Queen Elizabeth II Courts of Law building on George Street in Brisbane's CBD, the public gallery was almost full. For more than a month a core group of spectators – detectives, civilians, legal observers, the media – had been gathering in the watery morning light outside Court 7 with its view north to the city's old convict windmill on the Wickham Terrace ridge. They had gotten to know each other during the course of the murder trial of Vincent O'Dempsey, 78. They had come by train and by car and by foot. There were nods and banter.

As the weeks progressed, the appearance of an unknown face in the crowd would prompt observation and questions. 'Do you know who that is?' 'Are they with O'Dempsey's side?' These spectators had become bound by the mechanics of the trial, with its many obvious and hidden parts, its occasional levity, and enduring horror.

On 16 January 1974, a woman called Barbara McCulkin and her two daughters, Vicki, 13, and Leanne, 11, had disappeared from their modest rental home at 6 Dorchester Street, Highgate Hill, in South Brisbane. They were never seen again.

The old Queenslander in Dorchester Street has changed little in the past four decades. Perched on a steep, narrow block, its stumps short at the front and tall at the back, the standard timber and tin

3

worker's cottage was like many that proliferated the city's working-class inner suburbs a century ago.

But on 16 January, 43 years earlier, life stopped at this address. At the time of her presumed murder, Barbara was married to local petty thief and low-level gangster Robert William 'Billy' McCulkin. A heavy drinker and perennial layabout, he had left the family home for another woman in late 1973 but stayed in touch with Barbara and the kids.

The vanishing of the McCulkins came less than a year after a string of arson attacks in Brisbane's notorious Fortitude Valley precinct. One of those fires, at the Whiskey Au Go Go nightclub on 8 March 1973, had killed 15 innocent people in what was then considered Australia's biggest mass murder.

Two men – John Andrew Stuart and James Richard Finch – were swiftly arrested and convicted of the crime. But Barbara, who worked in a snack shop in the city and did her best to provide for her children, knew some powerful truths about the fires. Her house in Dorchester Street had become a veritable clubhouse for McCulkin's criminal associates, including Vincent O'Dempsey and a local gang who would later become known as the Clockwork Orange Gang. In the months before and after the Whiskey Au Go Go tragedy, Barbara had picked up enough information in that small house, with its VJ timber walls, to put away not only many of Billy's friends but McCulkin himself.

When Barbara and the girls vanished, rumours immediately circulated that O'Dempsey, a vicious career criminal along with his sidekick, Garry Reginald 'Shorty' Dubois, had done away with the McCulkins because of what Barbara knew about the Whiskey. Now, more than four decades later, both O'Dempsey and Dubois had been found guilty of multiple charges against the McCulkins, including murder, rape and deprivation of liberty. They were tried separately, but on 1 June 2017, the day of reckoning, they were to be sentenced for their crimes by trial judge, the Honourable Justice Peter Applegarth.

Relatives of O'Dempsey and Dubois, as was their custom during their respective trials, sat in the gallery seats directly behind the extended glassed-in dock to the left of the court behind the bar tables. One of Barbara McCulkin's brothers, Graham Ogden, with his wife and children, also took their regular seats at the rear of the court.

At precisely 9.55 a.m. Dubois was escorted to the dock by correctional officers via a side door. During both his committal hearing and trial, Dubois showed in his gait and demeanour a total indifference to the gravity of proceedings. Small of frame, head shaved, dressed in khaki trousers and a floral shirt that appeared too big for him, Dubois walked to the dock like a truculent child, his feet dragging slightly, his lined face a rubbery, blank palette. Dubois sat at the far end of the dock and placed his right arm along the bench seat like he was going for a Sunday drive in one of his beloved Studebakers.

'So, that's Shorty,' someone said from the crowd in the packed courtroom.

Thirty seconds later O'Dempsey entered the court. Of average height with dark, oily hair, he sat at the other end of the dock to Dubois and fiddled with the courtroom hearing apparatus. For the duration of his trial, and on this day, he was dressed in a dark suit with a white shirt and tie, and slip-on black loafers. He wore his suit like a farmer going to a funeral.

In the quiet before the opening of proceedings, and with O'Dempsey's ears sufficiently connected to the court sound system, the word 'psychopath' was muttered from somewhere deep in the gallery. Three correctional officers took their seats at both ends of the dock. Justice Applegarth entered the courtroom at 10.10 a.m., having been delayed by another case.

'It's reasonably late,' Applegarth said. 'Let's get on with it.'

5

Tony Glynn, QC, O'Dempsey's legal counsel, in his horsehair and black robe, stood. 'My client now wishes to say something,' Glynn said.

'If someone wants to express remorse, I'll hear it,' Applegarth replied. Applegarth had proven himself to be supremely patient and of even temperament during the two lengthy trials that had contained their fair share of frustrating legal argument, given the high-profile nature of this, one of Queensland's oldest cold cases. He had dealt with interruptions from the gallery, witnesses who didn't want to be on the stand, elderly witnesses who were hard of hearing and carried other infirmities, along with the usual potholes a complex trial generates. And now, moments before his sentencing remarks, the convicted murderer, who had continued a reign of terror for most of his life, decided he wanted to address the court. 'What does he want to say?' Applegarth asked.

Glynn said a handwritten note had been provided to O'Dempsey's solicitor, Terry O'Gorman, earlier that morning.

His Worship, not convinced he should give O'Dempsey an audience if he didn't know what he was about to say, was provided with the note. He asked Crown Prosecutor David Meredith his opinion on this highly unusual development, then concluded that O'Dempsey's note was completely unconvincing as a 'protest of innocence'.

He went on to say: '… my view is that anyone who hears this will treat it with the merit it deserves, coming from someone who has been convicted of three murders … I'll allow him to make this little speech.'

Applegarth leaned back in his chair. It was 10.21 a.m.

O'Dempsey stood. 'I'm here before you today wrongly committed, on false testimony,' he said in a weak voice, referring to the evidence of three chief witnesses. '[The] false evidence given by these three … was secured by [Detectives] Virginia Gray and

Mick Dowie … [I] never had the slightest reason to harm the three McCulkins in any way, nor [did] my co-accused.'

The public gallery was tense. In some quarters, incredulous.

O'Dempsey argued that the issue of the nightclub fires in early 1973, in particular the arson attack on the Torino nightclub and restaurant, followed less than two weeks later by the Whiskey Au Go Go atrocity, had ignited in his trial a 'prejudicial smokescreen'. He was adamant he had no knowledge of both fires, despite the fact that a former criminal associate had told Dubois's trial that both O'Dempsey and Barbara's husband, Billy McCulkin, had organised the Torino's fire and that members of the Clockwork Orange Gang had carried it out for the princely sum of $500.

O'Dempsey concluded his speech with a sputter, tangling his words, something at odds with the constant assertion of those who knew him that he had an IQ off the scale. (During his questioning in the 1980 coronial inquest into the murders of Barbara McCulkin and her daughters, O'Dempsey famously answered all 47 questions put to him with 'No comment', including when he was asked his name.)

O'Dempsey resumed his seat but before Justice Applegarth proceeded with the sentencing he took O'Dempsey to task on his unexpected speech to the court, especially in relation to his declaration of non-involvement in the Whiskey Au Go Go mass murder.

After outlining O'Dempsey's lengthy criminal history, and then hearing an emotional and moving victim impact statement from Graham Ogden, brother of Barbara McCulkin (read by his son, Brian), Justice Applegarth described O'Dempsey's assertion of a prejudicial smokescreen as 'interesting'. He said a portion of prejudicial evidence he had earlier excluded from O'Dempsey's trial was a conversation that was overheard between the father of chief witness Warren McDonald and O'Dempsey on a boat trip sometime in the 1990s.

In light of O'Dempsey's challenge, Justice Applegarth told the court the nature of that conversation. According to the evidence, O'Dempsey was told by McDonald's father that convicted Whiskey Au Go Go 'fire bomber' James Finch was coming back to Australia to implicate O'Dempsey in the Whiskey atrocity.

O'Dempsey allegedly replied: 'If he comes back I'm screwed, so he'll have to be knocked [killed].'

Justice Applegarth said that despite O'Dempsey denying any involvement in the Whiskey, 'there's evidence in that form' that he was involved in the crime. The judge said he was revealing this because 'things should be said in the interest of completeness'. He later said that when O'Dempsey asserted he had nothing to do with the fire, the public needed to know there was evidence 'that he was involved'.

With that on the record, Applegarth began his formal sentencing remarks. 'Vincent O'Dempsey, you are to be sentenced on one count of deprivation of liberty and three counts of murder,' Applegarth commenced.

'Garry Reginald Dubois, you are to be sentenced on one count of deprivation of liberty, one count of manslaughter, two counts of rape and two counts of murder. The offences were committed late on the night of 16 January 1974. Your victims were Mrs Barbara McCulkin, aged 34, and her daughters, Vicki, aged 13, and Leanne, aged 11 ...'

In every city in the world there are cold case crimes that, if they're allowed to remain unresolved for long enough, haunt the landscape. It's as if these silent victims are saying – we are not at rest, don't forget us.

Brisbane has had its fair share of these cold ghosts. Cases that became burrs in the fabric of the community. There is a sense that we have somehow failed the victims and their families, by not tying things off. These tragedies scar our history and refuse to heal.

The disappearance of snack shop attendant Barbara McCulkin and her two young daughters was another suppuration in Queensland's criminal history. A lot has been written about the McCulkin case over the years. And with years come rumours on top of rumours. Barbara and her daughters were most certainly dead.

So where were the bodies?

Buried in a lift shaft of a high-rise office block in the centre of the Brisbane CBD, some said. In a dam wall outside the city, said others. The steady mistral of whispers and conjecture had continued right up to the guilty verdicts in 2017 against O'Dempsey and Dubois.

But this was a crime that had very deep roots and was many generations in the making. It was a story of violent family history and of migration, of working the soil, of cruelty and pain. It included troubled youths in reform schools emerging as hardened criminals who would come together to wreak havoc on their community; rape and slashed throats and victims pleading for their lives; gangsters and hitmen. It included police and political corruption and a conspiracy that remained hidden for more than four decades, which allowed a maniac who could have walked straight out of a medieval tale about dragons and a knight laying waste to thousands of innocent lives, to kill at will. All in the shadow of God.

Clans

The history of the O'Dempsey family may have stretched back to the bloody Anglo-Norman invasions of Ireland in the late 12th Century, when Dermot O'Dempsey, Chief of Clanmalier, defeated Richard 'Strongbow' de Clare in the 1170s, but as the centuries passed and the clan dissipated in both power and wealth, there was little to suggest that the family, steeped in Catholicism, might produce a modern killer.

In fact, the Queensland branch of the O'Dempseys presented as nothing more than respectable farming types, despite a persistent reputation for rabblerousing and troublemaking when it came to standing up for their rights. By the 20th century, this was an ever-sprawling family dedicated to community service and the church. Several O'Dempseys would, through the decades, take holy orders. And while many O'Dempsey men would prove fierce on the sporting field and in the boxing ring, they would still turn up for Sunday Mass, black eye or not, and observe the diet on the Sabbath with communion bread and holy water.

It wasn't until the arrival of Vincent O'Dempsey on 2 October 1938, that a flaw in the O'Dempsey clan fabric would be exposed. Vincent was an anomaly, so at odds with his parents, his upbringing, his respectable environment, that he could have been spawned from a different family altogether.

Historic photographs would reveal, however, an eerie resemblance between Vince and his great-grandfather, James Patrick. In pictures the two O'Dempsey men share an identical jawline, and deranged eyes, so unsettling they dominate the face.

On 8 August 1855 James Patrick Dempsey, 26, and his new bride, Johanna, 18, boarded the *Sabrina* at Liverpool dock in north-west England to start a bright new future in Australia. As Robyn Manfield wrote in her book, *Chronicles of the O'Dempsey Family from Rathcannon, County Tipperary to Upper Freestone, Queensland 1855–1997*:

> Under the Irish clan system, O'Dempsey was an honoured and respected surname. However, during the sixteenth century, under English Law, the O'Dempseys were proclaimed outlaws, stripped of their property, and exiled from their native territory of Clanmaliere. By 1793, the family was living in Rathcannon … and were called Dempsey.

James Patrick had spent most of his life working on his father's farm in Rathcannon, County Tipperary, but after leaving school had entered the Catholic Seminary and studied to become a priest. When James and his young wife sailed on the *Sabrina*, Johanna was already pregnant with their first child, Patrick. The Dempseys (the 'O' prefix to the family name was returned by James Patrick upon settling in Australia) were two of 276 passengers aboard the *Sabrina*, and news reports would later confirm that the journey to Australia had been a difficult one. The ship arrived in Moreton Bay on Wednesday 28 November. Apart from passengers and crew, the ship was also carrying clocks, iron and vinegar.

The *Empire* wrote: 'Unfortunately those by the *Sabrina* have suffered much by sickness during the passage, ten deaths have occurred (six adults, four children); and as there were three cases of typhus still on board, the vessel has been placed in quarantine.'

British parliamentary papers would later put on record that eight had died – three adult men, three adult women, and two female children under 14 years of age. The ship was released from quarantine in mid-January 1856. In the meantime, James and Johanna's child was born in the Brisbane Immigration Depot. James decided to settle in Warwick, south-west of Brisbane.

After spending some months in Brisbane, the O'Dempseys travelled by steamer up the Bremer River to Ipswich, then by dray to Warwick. The family's odyssey was recorded by Thomas Hall in *The Early History of Warwick District and Pioneers of the Darling Downs*.

> In wet weather the O'Dempseys would have travelled for many weeks over the Great Dividing Range and through Spicers Gap. The track had a reputation for being dangerous and hard to climb ... bridges in the district were still things of the future, and to cross a muddy creek, the bullock driver had to secure

the creek bed with saplings and branches, before the team could pass over.

James O'Dempsey became one of Warwick's first settlers, and he farmed for a while on the Warwick Agricultural Reserve before moving to nearby Upper Freestone. It would become the O'Dempsey family seat. Aside from farming, he would also work policing the region from Ipswich to Stanthorpe. The separation of Queensland from New South Wales did not occur until 1859, but a special *Police Act 1855* allowed police, magistrates and justices power to appoint special constables. (The Queensland Police Force, as a singular unit, did not operate until 1863.)

By 1869 James was working hard on the farm in Upper Freestone that abutted a spur of the Great Dividing Range. As Manfield wrote: 'Legend says that J.P. cleared, fenced and cultivated the scrub on the back of the mountain range using simple hand tools like picks, crosscut saws, axes, grubbers, shovels, carpenters and fencing tools. He probably had single-furrow iron mould board plough, a set of wooden harrows, harness and saddles.'

James also agitated long and hard for a school in the Upper Freestone area, primarily for the children of the Irish families in the district. He wrote to Mr R. McDonald of the Queensland Board of Education on 26 July 1874:

Dear Sir,

I beg to inform you that there is at present residing on this Portion of the Reserve 17 children aged from 12 to 5 years and 9 from 5 years downwards. The distance from the nearest school is from 5 to 7 miles. I take this opportunity of writing ... requesting information if there is any aid to be got from the board, and on what terms. Also what description buildings have we to erect? Wishing you a safe passage and speedy return to us.

I remain Dear Sir, Your obedient servant.
J.P. O'Dempsey.

It is assumed that a favourable reply was received as a provisional school for the district was officially opened on 19 October 1874 after a construction period of 18 weeks.

James O'Dempsey, clearly intelligent, also liked to share his farming knowledge with his fellow man and regularly wrote to the *The Queensland Agriculturalist*. He also maintained the family tradition of expert animal husbandry, a talent that would be passed through generations to his great-grandson Vincent O'Dempsey. At the Swan and Freestone Creek Agricultural Show of 1885, James would win a 'special prize' in the poultry section for best 'Turkey Cock and two Hens'.

Vince O'Dempsey's sister, Inagh, would later write of James's attempts to 'fight the authorities on paper' to establish a school for the Irish settlers:

> He was highly educated you see and they couldn't down him.
> I think the word proud could definitely be applied to him. The British authorities used to refer to him as 'that troublesome Irishman'. But he got his school. And a private cemetery for the family. It's not used any more of course – no room – and sits all forlorn in the middle of a farm now owned by someone else. I always used to feel ridiculously proud that we had our own exclusive cemetery.

Interestingly, many of James's sons didn't marry. Inagh added in her vignette on the family history:

> They were rather wild in their youth though, one in particular – with the ladies. There was many a time they say when

he had to jump out a bedroom window to avoid being caught. He was actually shot once by an irate husband. When a woman asked a neighbour later where he'd been hit, she was given the reply: 'Missus, if you'd been shot where Billy O'Dempsey was shot, you wouldn't have been shot at all'.

The O'Dempseys were a close-knit clan, bound by their history, heritage and faith, and the land of the Warwick district. The family crest featured a lion framed by two long swords and was adorned at the top with a clutch of seven battleaxes. They even had their own family prayer:

> O, Almighty Father, in your great wisdom you led James and Johanna O'Dempsey from Ireland to these shores in 1855.
>
> Through their faith in You and their labours, they prospered and were the forebears of many succeeding generations. Please grant them, and those descendants who have gone to join them, Eternal Repose.
>
> We beseech You, in Your great mercy, to extend a Guiding Hand to we, the living descendants of James and Johanna, and future generations, so that we may avoid the evils and temptations of this World to enjoy the reward of Eternal Life in the Kingdom of God.

On 10 May 1870, one of their ten children, Thomas Joseph, was born in the family home on the Upper Freestone farm. Thomas (who was also known as Duffy) loved music and joined a local band. According to Manfield's history, 'it was common knowledge amongst his family that he had constructed his own traditional bush violin.'

In turn, Thomas Joseph would have a son named Thomas. Like the men before him Thomas spent his younger days farming the land in Freestone, close to Glengallan Valley. He would go on to wed Mary McConville at the local St Mary's Catholic Church in Warwick in 1930. After he married, Tom would move his family into town and become a stock and real estate auctioneer. During the Second World War he even opened a café that became famous for its fish and chips.

It was possible, from the new O'Dempsey home in Stewart Avenue, to hear the bells of St Mary's Catholic Church, just around the corner at 163 Palmerin Street. Here was a daily reminder of your faith in God. And the church was virtually a second home for the O'Dempsey family who were well respected in town. Decades later people would still refer to Vince's mother as 'Mrs O'Dempsey'.

'They must have been horrified,' says one family friend of the behaviour of their son Vincent. 'His parents were the loveliest, mildest, sweetest people you'd ever want to meet. And his mother was the sweetest. She never missed a church outing. On a Sunday they'd go to Mass two or three times in a single day.'

Daughter Inagh remembered her father, Tom: '... Dad had the gift of the gab like you wouldn't believe. I loved to hear him talk. Even when he swore it sounded musical. To me, he always smelled like soap, cigarettes and love. [He] carried me everywhere after I ... got polio. Used to wrap me up under his overcoat and dance gently with me out under the stars at night while he sang with his lovely tenor voice all the old Irish ballads.'

Apart from Inagh and Vincent, there were other siblings; Noel, Keith, Ron, Darcy, Marcelene, Valerie, Patricia and Damien. Several of them would go on to have distinguished careers in banking, politics, nursing, teaching and the church. Damien would become a Christian Brother, only to be imprisoned for paedophilia.

As for Vincent, he would dabble in animal husbandry, property, house painting and labouring, but his more primitive interests would exclude a straight life. The quiet and intelligent boy fascinated by books on history and the human mind would soon become obsessed with guns, weapons and explosives, and would turn his back on the

Catholic Church, urinating in the holy water at St Mary's where his parents had married, and claiming the six-pointed hexagram on the Pope's mitre represented 666 – the numbers of the Devil.

An Ancient Knight

On 28 May 1942, when young Vince would have been three and a half years old, the *Warwick Daily News* exposed a long-standing mystery behind the naming of the local streets in town.

The amusing story, appearing on page two, would no doubt have entertained the good folk of Warwick, who could have used some levity. There had been no Warwick Rodeo since Australia had entered the Second World War and their town now featured a brutal military detention barracks that would punish, and in one instance murder, troublesome Diggers.

But on this Thursday morning, an article written by F.S. Burnell was headlined, 'WARWICK'S STREET NAMES. UNEXPECTED LINKS WITH ANCIENT LEGENDS':

> Probably there are few visitors to the charming little city of Warwick (Q.) who have not been puzzled as to who christened it by that name and why ... the country round bears no kind of resemblance to the leafy country [Warwickshire] of Shakespeare's birth, while the position of the town, set as it is in a wide plain, is the exact reverse of its English namesake ... Perhaps some local antiquary may be able to solve the mystery.

Burnell's quaint investigation centred on the meaning, if any, of many of the names of that grid of streets of old central Warwick, south of the squiggly Condamine River, particularly those that ran north–south across the Cunningham Highway. There was

Palmerin Street, Guy Street, Dragon Street, Wantley Street, and others.

'However it may be,' Burnell continued, 'a further link with the original may be seen in the name of Guy Street – an unmistakable reference to the extremely ancient English romance of Guy of Warwick.' Could it be that a myth that started in the 13th century, and continued to amuse, enthral and appal over hundreds of years, was laid over that small thatch of streets in a country town like Warwick, Queensland?

The newspaper said of Guy of Warwick: 'This legendary hero, son of a steward of the Earl of Warwick in the days of King Athelstan, is said to have ended his days as an obscure hermit by way of atonement for a life spent in war-like adventure.'

As the tale goes, Guy was a page in the Earl of Warwick's court when he fell in love with the Earl's daughter, Felice, but given his lowly status it was decided he was not worthy of her hand in marriage. In an attempt to prove himself, the knight-in-waiting proceeded to slay a Dun Cow – a giant, aggressive cow owned by a giant – who was terrorising families.

Guy's heroic gesture, however, was not enough to win him Felice. So, Guy of Warwick travelled to Europe and went on a killing spree, beheading giants and slaying dragons. He competed in tournaments and killed dukes and princes. With three other knights, he journeyed to Byzantium where they supposedly destroyed three Turkish ships and laid waste to 50,000 Turks. According to one version of the legend, 'Danes and Saracens, as well as dragons, giants and other monsters alike succumbed to his devouring sword ...'

At one point, Guy of Warwick saved the life of a lion that was being attacked by a dragon. When he returned to England, having proved his worth, he married Felice and was crowned the Earl of Warwick. Yet, cursed by the thoughts of his murderous past, Guy went on a pilgrimage to the Holy Land, ultimately returning home to live as a hermit in a cave. It was only on the brink of death that he sent his wedding ring back to his wife, Felice, who rushed to his side. There are varying versions of the myth that say Felice buried him in his cave, and in others she was so grief-stricken she threw herself into the river below the cave and drowned.

Ten years before the *Warwick Daily News* story on Warwick street names, in 1932, the same newspaper published a similar article about the origin of the town's thoroughfares. A local resident told the paper:

> The wide mile-long streets of Warwick can boast such names as Wantley, Guy, Dragon, and Palmerin. They owe their origin to the legend of old Warwick, which tells how Guy, a Knight of the Palmerins, fought and slew the dragon of Wantley.

Palmerin. Guy. Dragon. Wantley. At the time of the second article, in the thoroughfare directly parallel to Palmerin Street – Stewart Avenue – young Vincent O'Dempsey was growing up in a large, sprawling Queenslander with generous yards and large iron gates out the back. As a boy he would become obsessed with the ancient myth of Guy of Warwick, a story that crossed centuries, about an impossibly brave knight who slaughtered for love – the killer who shed blood across England and continental Europe – lionised in poetry, song and art.

As an old man, O'Dempsey would regale friends and criminal associates with the story of Guy of Warwick. In time, a description of O'Dempsey was given to police by a witness who claimed he had a large tattoo of 'St George and the Dragon on his chest, on his back and both legs'. But the eyewitness had his history confused. The illustration inked into Vincent O'Dempsey's skin was more likely to be Guy of Warwick, slaying the great Dragon of Wantley, the dragon that used to eat children.

A Troubled Child

A famous story about O'Dempsey as a schoolboy still floats about Warwick. Attending St Joseph's Christian Brothers College he was at first seen as a quiet boy who never looked for trouble. As the rumour goes, he cut a hole in one of his trouser pockets so he could tug at his penis in class without detection. One day, one of the Christian Brothers did notice, and insisted on knowing what was in O'Dempsey's pocket.

'What have you got in your pocket?' the teacher demanded, shoving his hand into it, only to find O'Dempsey's genitals.

One fellow student claimed that whenever O'Dempsey was caned by the Christian Brothers, he never flinched or said a word, and was often seen smiling at the punishment that was meted out to him. 'He was a bit of a rebel at school,' says his older brother, Darcy O'Dempsey.

In the late 1940s, when O'Dempsey would have been nine or ten years old, one local said that, under the cover of night, young Vincent and some of his mates would scale the roofs of homes and buildings around Warwick and 'remove the lead nails off the rooves and sell the lead'. O'Dempsey also reportedly used to stick a finger in a pencil sharpener and turn it, oblivious to the pain.

As a teenager O'Dempsey would go on to earn a name for himself in the boxing ring. Training out of the Warwick Athletics Club and the old wooden and tin-roofed gym at the western end of Albert Street, he won numerous regional bouts.

One friend at the time recalls: 'He had about ten fights. He knew how to let them go. He was fit and strong. One of his trainers told me that the harder they'd go in training, the better O'Dempsey liked it.'

Many of the O'Dempsey boys had spent time in the boxing ring, however Darcy O'Dempsey says of his younger brother Vincent: 'He wasn't a boxer, he was a fighter.'

Vincent was also a keen footballer and in 1954, as a 15-year-old, he played for the Warwick Eastern Suburbs junior side. The *Warwick Daily News* was enthusiastic about the newly formed club.

> Stars of the programme will be the junior minor sides. Since the commencement of this junior football these sides have stolen the show each Sunday, and their keenness, together with the practical use given to the skilful coaching they have received, they have provided spectators with the thrill of keen, clean football.

Three O'Dempsey brothers, including Vince, were part of the team. One local said O'Dempsey bet on himself to create havoc on the field. 'He'd back himself to score tries and hurt people,' he said. 'He loved the hard tackles.'

Like his great-grandfather James, Vincent's other interests included breeding hard-feather bantam chickens. At Warwick's 87th annual show in 1954, he won second prize in the black Pekin bantam category, and first place in the hen or pullet section. A year or two later, however, Vincent developed some even more concerning behavioural irregularities. According to a police officer who would later investigate O'Dempsey, Vincent would bag stray cats around town and knife them to death 'through the bag'. By his late-teens, O'Dempsey presented as a peculiar, dichotomous, multifaceted and complex character. A fastidious breeder of prize-winning poultry. A boxer. A big thinker who was fond of quoting the Bible. And a young man who had developed a liking for sudden and extreme violence.

As a member of such a law-abiding, God-fearing family, he had also become obsessed with the police and authority figures. One friend says: 'For some reason he got it into his head that the coppers were scared of the dark. He called them squiggly tails.'

Friends and relatives say it was the cruelty of the Christian Brothers towards O'Dempsey at school that tipped the balance in his personality. 'He was like two people in one body,' says one of O'Dempsey's relatives. 'The brothers turned him bad. They were always flogging him. He was intelligent at school. He didn't have to go to school he was that smart. When he was 14, 15 years old, the teachers were bashing him. It turned him nasty.'

Like many Warwick teenagers, O'Dempsey used to occasionally hang out in the ruins of the old Glengallan Homestead a short drive out of town. The kids used to party, drink, keep warm by lighting fires in the old fireplaces and scribble their names on the ruined walls. It was the perfect place for a bit of late-night mischief. The nearest farmhouse was the Diggles dairy down on Diggles Road, across Glengallan Creek and far enough away from the homestead not to be a problem. 'Everyone went out there and put their names all over the walls,' one of O'Dempsey's friends says. 'You'd go out there to drink piss. It was a big, spooky building. The Sparksman farm was not far away across the paddock.'

Another regular visitor to Glengallan says: 'That's definitely right. Vince and his mates used to go out there.'

In April 1954, when O'Dempsey was 15 years old, the local newspaper reported that a 'gang' of schoolboys had been questioned over stolen property. The *Warwick Daily News* said that a group of boys – aged 11 to 16 – had been quizzed over the thefts. 'On Wednesday and Thursday, the boys – mainly from two schools – were taken to the police station, and rigorous questioning revealed an amazing story of their activities,' the paper said. The 16 boys involved represented several gangs, who were not amalgamated in their operations but worked more in competition with each other. It was believed that several of the boys played a lone hand or operated in pairs. As the newspaper reported:

> It is understood that the lads concerned readily admitted their part in various thefts, the breaking and entering of shops, hotels,

warehouses and private dwellings and a school from where a souvenir pistol was taken.

Articles already recovered by police include four rifles, gelignite, detonator caps, knives, watches, a box of bullets, cigarettes, cigarette lighters, razors, propelling pencils, keys and money.

Some of the boys confessed that three of the rifles had been buried in the middle of a paddock behind the Warwick Base Hospital. They said the guns had been concealed in that way so that other gangs could not get hold of them. They had all been stolen from a shop in Palmerin Street and the loss had not been reported to police.

It was the same in regard to a number of other articles recovered by the police. This included five large sticks of gelignite – sufficient, according to the police, to blow up any large building in the city. This gelignite and a tin of detonators had been hidden underneath the home of one of the boys. With these deadly explosives, some of the lads had apparently intended to manufacture 'home-made bombs' but for what purpose is still not quite clear.

The report said the recovery of the explosives had probably averted a certain tragedy. The police added that they would soon be visiting a cave situated '15 miles from Warwick where several of the boys allegedly admitted they had cached a quantity of stolen property'.

(According to locals and relatives, O'Dempsey was a regular visitor to what was referred to as 'Captain Starlight's cave', a hiding place for the notorious 19th century bushranger. The cave is about ten kilometres out of Warwick in the district of Massie.)

The report also said:

Most of the boys made a clean breast of their part in the thefts. They are all from good homes with a happy environment, and Senior Sergeant A.M. Cooper said yesterday that their parents or guardians had been very cooperative with the police in cleaning up the thefts.

It is not known yet whether the boys will appear before the Children's Court, but it is certain that the lesson already learnt by them – that crime does not pay – will serve as a deterrent to any future 'gang' activities.

None of the boys was named in any of the local newspaper reports about the incident. There were also no subsequent reports about delinquent 'gang' members and thieves appearing before any court. It appears the matter was concluded with harsh warnings from school authorities and the police.

As for O'Dempsey, it was precisely around this time that his father, Tom, took him to be assessed at a Toowoomba psychiatric hospital. There, he was medically diagnosed as 'a psychopath with schizoid tendencies'.

Had the 'gang' incident compelled O'Dempsey's moral and righteous parents to seek help for their troubled boy? And was he the one who had stashed gelignite under the family home in Stewart Avenue?

Bodgie

By the late 1950s, O'Dempsey was a full-blown bodgie. (The male bodgies and female widgies were teenage 'louts' that formed gangs in post-war Australia. They were predominantly from working-class families and expressed their defiance of authority in their dress and mannerism.) O'Dempsey was seen around town wearing tight, leopard-skin patterned pants. He had a couple of tough mates he hung out with. 'Vince's headquarters in those days was the old billiard hall in Grafton Street,' one friend says.

The long, rectangular hall had an awning out over the footpath. Inside, it had a high metal-pressed ceiling. In the 1940s it was known as Jim Mutch's Billiard Saloon and it occasionally hosted tournament events. As the *Warwick Daily News* reported in May 1946:

> Mutch's Saloon is one of the billiard rooms in Queensland equipped with neon lights, and it has every other facility for the comfort and convenience of patrons. The three tables have recently been re-covered and new sets of balls are now in play. Electric heaters are at present being installed for the winter months. Under such conditions the pleasurable pastime of billiards and snooker is sure to boom.

The saloon was not far from the statue of former Queensland premier and member for Warwick, Thomas Joseph Byrnes, in the centre of Palmerin Street. Burns, at just 37, dropped dead in office after only five months as the State's leader. Great things had been expected of him.

Not so for O'Dempsey, there in the dark of the billiard hall, looking out onto the world and planning his next move. As one acquaintance remembers of those days: 'Vince'd have his hair slicked back at the sides, you know, a bit like Elvis but not as tidy. He didn't like the law for some reason. He was a wild lad around town when he was younger. He used to hang out at the billiard hall and the Langham Hotel and you didn't go to those places if you knew he was going to be there.'

When shooting the breeze at the billiard hall years later, Vince was asked about the best way to get 'girls'. One local allegedly heard O'Dempsey say that procurement was easy, you just 'walk up behind them with a rag soaked in chloroform and hold it over their nose, then you can do what you like with them'.

As an acquaintance recalls: 'Vince O'Dempsey was always where the trouble was, or wherever there was trouble he was there. Whether he caused it or not I don't know. But you'd never know when you'd come across him.'

The friend said the billiard hall in Grafton Street was Vince's main lair. 'There were not a lot of women there. The blokes would just play pool and talk crap. There was no alcohol. But it was dark. And it was sleazy. You wouldn't want to go in there.'

As for Vince, he shared little of his life with his family. 'He wouldn't talk to anybody about anything,' says Darcy O'Dempsey. 'You never asked him any questions on anything. He was too smart for anyone to get any leverage on him. Basically, he didn't trust anybody.'

In 1956, just two years after the shocking 'gangs of Warwick' incident stunned the small Darling Downs town, Vince O'Dempsey earned his first conviction. He was charged with stealing and placed on a 12-month good behaviour bond. This was followed in 1958 with a charge of being present 'unlawfully on enclosed area'. He was fined two pounds.

His boxing skills, too, were used for a different purpose as he moved through his teens. Locals recalled O'Dempsey 'and his gang' turning up to local dances and terrorising patrons. 'One night he walked straight up to the guy on the door, punched him in the face and broke his nose,' one local said. 'They just walked straight into the dance and caused trouble for everyone.'

In March 1959, aged 20, Vince was charged with using threatening language. Just two months later he was picked up again for something that would echo into his future. On 13 May, O'Dempsey was charged with 'aggravated assault of a sexual nature on a female child'. He was convicted, fined 25 pounds and placed on a six-month good behaviour bond. One O'Dempsey family friend says that despite these early infractions with the law, Vincent's mother stuck by her son.

'His mum never missed a court case,' the friend says. 'When she died they found scrapbooks with every newspaper clipping published about him. They were loyal to him. And Vince was good to his mother.'

It was around this time, too, that the young O'Dempsey took a 'job' that would introduce him to the basic skills for a criminal career. At school O'Dempsey had met a boy called Brian Sparksman, whose father Jacob 'Dick' Sparksman ran a farm out near the Glengallan Homestead. The Sparksmans were a well-respected family with deep roots in both the Warwick district and the nearby township of Allora. Dick Sparksman, however, also had a sideline as an SP bookie. In the late 1950s and into the 1960s, he employed O'Dempsey as his 'debt collector'.

'[Dick] Sparksman definitely was an SP bookie,' says one O'Dempsey family friend. 'He was a heavy. He had a few airs and graces about him and thought he was better than most ... Nowadays people get into financial strife with drugs, back then it was gambling. If you owed money and Vince O'Dempsey came calling, you paid. I think Vince did a bit of pencilling for him at one stage. Vince would have known who did and didn't pay all over town.'

One source says O'Dempsey went to collect one day from a punter who had no cash. So Vince supervised as the man loaded his own household furniture onto the back of a truck.

In later years locals say a Sparksman cheque to one of the pubs in town bounced. Given the SP bookie had for years been prising money out of district punters, the cheque was mounted on a wall in the bar and remained there for years for all to see. Small towns have their own system of justice, too.

Retired detective Alan Marshall and his partner at the time, Trevor Menary, spent time in the late 1970s investigating O'Dempsey's teenage years in Warwick. They discovered that on 6 June 1959 O'Dempsey's violence escalated. 'He got charged with assaulting an off-duty sergeant,' recalls Marshall. In fact, O'Dempsey had thrashed the police officer to within an inch of his life and was charged with stealing with actual violence in company, and with assault occasioning bodily harm.

The Criminal Court was told that O'Dempsey, 20, and a friend, Desmond John Locke, 19, both labourers, were loitering near the corner of Grafton Street and Acacia Avenue when the incident occurred. Sergeant Francis Joseph Toohill, 40, was off duty when he saw the two men standing near a bicycle that had fallen over. Toohill asked them what they were up to and was told: 'Keep your ———— nose out of our business.'

The police officer was continuing down the street when he heard footsteps behind him, then suffered a blow to the back of his head and fell to his knees. He was robbed of two pounds. Toohill would go on to tell the Criminal Court that he 'still suffered the effects of having been kicked and punched' by the two youths.

According to one source who knew O'Dempsey, it was a brutal beating. 'When police arrived at O'Dempsey's home, there was still blood and hair on his boots.'

On 13 August 1959, O'Dempsey was convicted on two charges – stealing with actual violence in company, and assault occasioning bodily harm. He was sentenced to five and three years' hard labour in prison on the consecutive charges, to be served concurrently. An appeal against his convictions was dismissed in late 1959. He would serve at least two and a half years in prison before being eligible for parole.

Marshall says: 'He [O'Dempsey] had been in and out of institutions and things around that time, and that's when he was diagnosed as a paranoid schizophrenic ...'

One relative had witnessed the incident with the off-duty

police officer. 'I was there, I saw it. Vince was just sitting there and this copper came up to him and gave him a good clip around the earhole. He could handle himself. He gave that bloke a terrible flogging.'

Darcy O'Dempsey concurs that Vince was struck first by the police officer, then retaliated: 'With the police ... it stemmed from anybody who tried to stand over him. He wouldn't cop anyone standing over him in any way, shape or form.'

Despite being represented in court by pre-eminent barrister Dan Casey, O'Dempsey and Locke were found guilty. Chief Crown Prosecutor R.F. Carter told the court that both youths were considered 'standover men' and each had prior convictions.

According to an associate of O'Dempsey's, when he was released from gaol a few years later, police in Warwick 'would walk on the other side of the street from him' when they saw him in town.

The Chermside Gang

In the knockabout suburb of Chermside in Brisbane's inner-north, replete as it was with box-like post-war housing commission homes, another group of friends, bound by adversity and tough times, were also forming attachments that would lead them into criminal careers. As children, they'd all met in and around the local neighbourhood. Garry 'Shorty' Dubois lived with his family in Unmack Street. Tommy Hamilton lived four houses up. Keith Meredith lived not far from Unmack Street. Peter Hall grew up in nearby Kedron.

Despite its deeply conservative bent, even Queensland was not immune to what was happening in the outside world in the 1960s, especially when it came to political and cultural influences. Historian Raymond Evans wrote in his essay '"Real Gone Town": Popular Music and Youth Culture in 1960s Brisbane', that there was a specific moment when Brisbane caught up with the planet and joined the times.

> In my estimation, 'the Sixties' began in Brisbane – as they arguably did in many other parts of the world – on the bright, warm, late-spring morning of Saturday, 23 November 1963 ... For I witnessed something in that moment I had never seen before in Brisbane, nor have ever again. There were people – lone pedestrians – standing distractedly along the footpath, individually lost to their surroundings and openly weeping in the street. The stark headline on the newspapers they held explained it all: KENNEDY MURDERED.

Evans conjectured that the Kennedy assassination also 'begat' the juggernaut that was the pop group The Beatles.

> What began as compensatory and escapist gradually became galvanic and consciousness-altering. Soon, as Bob Dylan later observed, 'There was music in the cafés at night/ And revolution in the air'. But, in Brisbane, in particular, music played in only some cafés and revolution in only certain minds.

Garry's brother, Paul, remembered those times when the friends first met. 'Garry and I would hang out with Peter, Keith and Tom Hamilton often and we were known as the Chermside gang,' he would later tell police. 'We would ride motorbikes and horses and hang out at the local milk bar. I became pretty close with Tom Hamilton and always got on well with him.'

In the beginning, there were some innocent shenanigans. Peter Hall had left high school early to take up a carpentry apprenticeship but still had time for fun with his mates. 'As a teenager I was doing stuff like drinking driving [sic] and blowing up letterboxes using crackers, just nuisance stuff really,' he would tell police decades after the event.

At one point, Hall and Hamilton bought a hearse, an old 1947 Buick, and they would drive around on Sundays 'just being a pair of idiots'. Hall said: 'We had planned to do it up and use it as a kind of mobile party vehicle. We were drinking a fair bit, we were using pot and tried a bit of LSD. Tom and I used to pass ourselves off as brothers ... we both had reddish hair and were similar height and size.'

In the following years the friends would share a house together, and their paths would cross with another Brisbane youth, William 'Billy' Stokes, an intelligent roustabout who also hailed from the same fertile breeding ground as the gang of future criminals. Stokes would later go on to write a series of articles describing members of the gang and their exploits. Giving each of them a nickname, Stokes called Tommy Hamilton 'Clockwork Orange' because he liked to dress up like a character from the 1971 dystopian crime film with the same name. Stokes wrote:

> My first introduction to Clockwork Orange himself had been at a party ... and through conversation we learnt that we had lived just three streets away from each other for many years as school kids ... but we'd never met before ... for the next three or four years we saw each other on a few occasions ... on friendly terms, although we were never close.

Stokes would later say all the gang 'liked to dress flamboyantly, and follow the trend of the Clockwork Orange theme, including bowler hats and fashionable walking canes'. Stokes identified Hamilton as the 'leading character' of the gang. 'As a youth, well before the LSD scene, he [Hamilton] was attracted by the bizarre and the unusual,' Stokes wrote. 'He was in fact once caught by Brisbane police in the act of driving stolen property away from a break and enter offence by using an ambulance.'

Stokes recalled the first time Hamilton introduced him to his gang of friends. Stokes described Garry 'Shorty' Dubois as having 'long straight neat hair with a small and solid build, a Genghis Khan-moustache and casual easy-going nature'. He noted Peter Hall had 'the same height and build as Clockwork Orange. Both have red hair (when not dyed) and on occasions pass themselves off as brothers.'

In Stokes's articles, Keith Meredith was called 'Jimmy'. 'He cooked the evening meals for everyone. They said it was because Jimmy was the best cook and Jimmy agreed. (He was named after rock star Jimmy Hendrix because both sported impressive afros.)

'The Pelican' was Stokes's code name for Garry Dubois's 16-year-old girlfriend, Jan Stubbs. She was described as having 'medium length blonde hair, very pretty, innocent looks, quietly spoken'. Jan wasn't the only girl on the scene. Wherever the gang hung out, girls were in plentiful supply. Particularly schoolgirls.

As Stokes reported:

> The following of school girls that they had at the Chermside residence was a thing that had to be seen to be believed. Most of these young girls were introduced to them by Shorty's girlfriend. The school girls called every day … usually after school, but on occasion would spend the entire day with them.

He claimed that the school girls often slept with the boys from the gang and 'many were introduced to smoking marijuana'.

Stokes himself was not immune to adversity. Before meeting the gang he had been in and out of trouble, and done two tours of duty in the Westbrook Farm Home for Boys in Toowoomba. The Westbrook Reformatory for Boys was opened in 1900 on the former Westbrook pastoral run, 10 kilometres south-west of Toowoomba. In 1919 it changed its name to the Farm Home for Boys, a place where troubled children and teenagers could be morally realigned through hard work and routine. At Westbrook, Stokes would meet his own fair share of deviants, and one boy in particular, John Andrew Stuart, who would go on to become one of Australia's most dangerous and unpredictable criminals.

Knife Boy

By the time he was a teenager, John Andrew Stuart had already developed a reputation on the streets of Brisbane as a a violent thug with a hair-trigger temper. Born on 15 September 1940, Stuart was the fifth child to an aggressive father, David James Cochrane Stuart, and mother, Edna Ruby Stuart. Having left school at 13, it was only a matter of time before he brought himself to the attention of police for his violent outbursts. In the summer of 1956 Stuart was in a hamburger shop in Brisbane's Fortitude Valley when he committed a crime that would define the rest of his life.

The Argus briefly reported:

> Police today charged a 15-year-old boy with attempting to kill following a stabbing in the Valley last night. Another Youth, Kenneth Wallace Steen, 19, is dangerously ill in Brisbane Hospital with stab wounds in his stomach and wrist.

During the investigation, police found the weapon, a three-bladed pocketknife, hidden in Stuart's flat. The court ordered his mother to guarantee her son's good behaviour until he turned 18. (By this stage she was raising her children alone, having separated from her violent husband.) Stuart was warned if he didn't keep his nose clean he'd be sent to the Westbrook Farm Home for Boys.

It only took three short months for Stuart to find himself back in trouble for stealing a car. As promised, he was sent to Westbrook for two years and two months. It was an experience that left a lasting impression on him, as it did many other inmates.

The superintendent in charge of Westbrook during the 1950s was the feared sadist Roy Golledge. While the institution's virtue was praised both in the press and State Parliament for decades, it was in reality a place of horror and brutality. Rather than preparing troubled boys as model citizens, it created generations of criminals who would go on to wreak their havoc in adulthood.

Mark Greenhalgh was a contemporary of Stuart's at Westbrook. He wrote of his experiences in a submission to a Senate committee in 2008: 'Most of the warders used sadistic methods to control and punish us, but the worst of them all was the Superintendent, Mr Roy Golledge. This man seemed to take great pleasure in humiliating us publicly, flogging us with his heavy leather belt while we knelt naked at his feet. You could receive anything up to 60 lashes and you always ended up bleeding profusely. Sometimes boys lost consciousness. They were the lucky ones.'

At the Farm Stuart befriended a host of boys who would later join him in his adult criminal career. One of those friends was Billy Stokes, who would also serve two terms at Westbrook. He also crossed paths with the young Tommy 'Clockwork Orange' Hamilton from Chermside. By all accounts, Westbrook was primary school to Boggo Road's secondary school. At Westbrook, the boys were introduced to the horrors of incarceration that would prepare them for adult prison.

Another young inmate, who had been incarcerated at Westbrook as an 'uncontrollable child', remembers Stuart and Stokes on the farm. 'Just looking into his [Stuart's] eyes was like staring at chunks of ice,' he recalls. 'His eyes were dead. There was no reflection. I used to shudder when I had to look at him ... There was a large water tank outside in the yard and it was a lovely shady spot during the summer time,' he says. 'Stuart took that on as his domain, along with four or five other blokes. No one went near there unless you wanted trouble.

'Stuart's mother used to come up every couple of months in a Ford Single Spinner. She brought a girl for Stuart. There was a little park across the road from the complex and they'd meet out there.'

As for Stokes, he was a pretty tough cookie. 'I saw him get the strap once and he wouldn't say a word. If you howled, Golledge would stop. He and Stuart were tough. They could take it. Stuart got some awful floggings from Golledge, but it didn't seem to bother him.'

The inmate also steered clear of the rampant sexual abuse in Westbrook. 'The food was virtually inedible but you knew that if you gave the boys who worked in the kitchen some sexual favours, they'd slip you a proper feed,' he says. 'I know for a fact that Stuart had some boyfriends, or "girlfriends", or whatever you'd like to call them, at Westbrook.'

The inmate recalls another boy who Stuart befriended during that time. John Bell would later go on to become a bouncer at many of the popular entertainment venues around town. 'Bell was a fitness fanatic,' the inmate recalls. 'He was forever doing push-ups and jumps.'

Bell's daughter, Kathy, says after her father was released from Westbrook he joined a motorcycle gang. 'My dad was the leader of the group. It was called The Tarantulas,' she says. 'And they all had motorbikes and they all used to go down to the park and beat up the poofters and all that sort of stuff. John Stuart was in the gang but Mum always said that he was like bipolar, even back then. He'd go in and out of gaol, he'd get into trouble, and she was the one that first said to him, "Just tell them you're crazy and they'll let you go, or they'll put you in the nut house for a little while and then you'll get out." And so, that's what he did. Every time he'd get into trouble he'd just say he was crazy and then they'd let him out again.'

Stuart and Bell were both out of the institution by the spring of 1958. Back on the streets of Brisbane, the competition was on to prove who could be the toughest bodgie in town. However, unlike Stuart, the young Bell understood the importance of a proper job.

'He was an apprentice butcher,' Kathy Bell recalls. 'He wanted extra money because he had the two children. And so, that's when he first went to go to work for John Hannay in West End. They'd all hang around at the Crystal Palace [theatre] at Windsor. And John Hannay had a few clubs, or he was affiliated with clubs back then …'

She recalls that everyone in that milieu was doing dodgy deals. 'Right up until I got married my dad would go down to the Wharfies Club every Friday where they would sell stuff for, you know, ridiculous amounts of money, you know, cheap stuff,' she says. 'We'd always get our Christmas presents from there and stuff that was stolen from Myers or wherever else, and Johnny Morris used to run the club down at the Wharfies Club … they were all best friends, all of them … Johnny Hannay and Johnny Stuart.'

According to Plunkett, Stuart's informal clubhouse, of sorts, was the Hub milk bar across the road from the Dawn Theatre on Gympie Road, Chermside. It was at the Hub that Stuart would mingle with the Clockwork Orange Gang. And it was through associations with this gang that Stuart would later meet the formidable criminal Vincent O'Dempsey.

A Disappearance

By early 1964 O'Dempsey, now in his mid-twenties, was finally out of gaol for assaulting Sergeant Francis Toohill. He immediately took a job working on the construction of the Leslie Dam in Warwick.

There was work to be had there for fit young men, and word got around as far away as Brisbane that if you needed to earn a quick quid, the Leslie Dam site was the place to be.

One criminal, who would later become an associate of O'Dempsey, drifted up to Warwick with some mates and headed to the dam site 'for a change of scene'. But when he saw the workers' dongers and experienced 'the bloody flies all over your face all the time', he swiftly high-tailed it back to Brisbane.

As for O'Dempsey, securing a legitimate job straight after incarceration would fit a pattern he'd use time and again in the future. Invariably, a brief sojourn as a 'square head' would then see him slide back into the underworld and darker pastimes.

At the Leslie Dam, O'Dempsey befriended a co-worker named Raymond Vincent 'Tommy' Allen. The 22-year-old Allen then assisted O'Dempsey in the burglarly and arson of the Pigott & Co. jewellery store in Warwick. They also stole the store safe.

Retired detective Alan Marshall remembered clearly the Tommy Allen investigation. 'We dug deeper with Allen and we found out that O'Dempsey used to drive Tommy back to Fortitude Valley in Brisbane where Tommy saw his mother, and used to spend the weekend there,' Marshall said.

In 1964, investigating officers made a breakthrough on the Pigott & Co. case when they stopped one of O'Dempsey's associates driving his distinctive cream and cherry 1957 Holden. Marshall said: 'The police came along and got this German fellow who was driving the car and they matched up the paintwork from the safe that was stolen out of the jeweller's, and it matched the paint in the back of the car.

'Then they found other things like a hacksaw blade … with a hacksaw blade, they're nicely painted, and when you use them the paint comes off. And the amount of paint that was missing was from the leading edge of the hacksaw blade, just happened to be the distance going backwards and forwards through the bars at the back of Pigott's. So they had a fairly substantial case.'

The German decided to leave town and drove O'Dempsey's car to Sydney. 'He left the car at number one wharf and pissed off overseas,' said Marshall. Before the German left he called O'Dempsey and told him where he'd left the car. So Vince and Tommy Allen hitchhiked by truck down to Sydney to pick it up. As Marshall recalled: 'While they were searching through the car little Tommy Allen finds a watch and O'Dempsey grabs hold of the watch and says, "Give me that. That come out of the Pigott's jewellery robbery." So they jump in the car … they couldn't find the keys to it [but] they finished up getting the car started and drove back to Warwick.'

The dust settled but it wasn't long before Tommy Allen was brought in by police on suspicion of sexually assaulting a young woman.

'And he spilt the beans,' recalled Marshall. 'He agreed to give evidence against O'Dempsey. Allen said, "Look, I've just been down to Sydney with O'Dempsey. And I found this watch. And he's posted it back to himself in an [empty] pack of Kool cigarettes".'

'Back in those days the Post Office actually worked on the Saturday. The police came around to O'Dempsey's place after the delivery of the mail to catch O'Dempsey with the stolen watch. And then of course he came back to the police station and during the formal questioning all that O'Dempsey would say [is]: "You're the detective … that's for you to fucking well find out."'

After O'Dempsey was charged over the robbery, local police actually secured Tommy Allen a job with the railways, but his tenure didn't last long. 'The police got him that job and he went out to a little place called Karara,' one investigating detective remembers.

Karara was a little one-horse town on the south-western railway line, 208 kilometres west-south-west of Brisbane and not far from Warwick. It boasted a tiny wooden station and a station master's house replete with a corrugated-iron water tank. The population of the town was in the low hundreds. 'Tommy was working there and he was a bit of a lairy sort of bloke,' the detective says. 'He had leopard-skin trousers. So you can imagine, leopard-skin trousers … they stood out like the proverbial.'

Tommy Allen's mother, Ena Clarke, lived in Baxter Street, Fortitude Valley, and her son would often drive from the Darling Downs to see her. A few weeks before her son and O'Dempsey were due to appear in court on the theft charges, Tommy was with his mother when three men in a black car drove up to her house and threatened Tommy. She thought one of them might have been Vince O'Dempsey, but she couldn't be sure.

The three men got out of the car and picked on Allen, but his mother told them to be fair and fight him one at a time if they had to. Her son was young, strong and a trained boxer. Ena held a broomstick across the doorway in order to let them in one at a time.

The first person through was knocked out by Tommy. The second swung at Tommy, missed, and struck Ena's husband. He was out cold. The third, who Ena Clarke thought was O'Dempsey, hopped into the black car and drove off. Tom chased the car and managed to grab the steering wheel through the open driver's window before falling onto the road. The driver then did a U-turn and tried to run Tommy down, missing him by a metre. The car drove off.

A few weeks later, when O'Dempsey appeared before the court on robbery charges, his mate Tommy Allen was nowhere to be seen. It didn't take long for Vince to work out that Tommy had ratted on him.

Marshall says: 'O'Dempsey went into court on the Monday. O'Dempsey's parents were held in high repute there. And the next thing O'Dempsey's out on bail and young Tommy and Vince are driving around in the car. They go up the main street there near the Post Office and O'Dempsey said to someone, "Oh, I'm just taking young Tommy to Sydney". Young Tommy's never been seen since.'

Without Tommy's evidence, the case against O'Dempsey collapsed.

Marshall recalls: 'When we checked with the railways there was five pound, ten pence and tuppence uncollected from his wages. That was the last he was ever heard of. That money was never collected and was still held by the railways.'

A missing person report was completed on Raymond Vincent 'Tommy' Allen. And that was the end of that.

'Now, Vincent O'Dempsey was the last one seen with Tommy Allen,' Marshall says. 'O'Dempsey was told about Tommy Allen spilling the beans on him, he was fully cognisant of the fact that Tommy had done that, because the police had actually told him during the interview. That was the rock that Tommy Allen perished on.'

The vanishing of Allen was the beginning of a lifelong phenomenon surrounding O'Dempsey – anyone who threatened his liberty simply disappeared without trace.

The Sydney Mob

After his release from prison, in the heady days of the early 1960s, and with Tommy Allen no longer a threat to his freedom, Vincent O'Dempsey made frequent visits to Sydney, where he established some powerful and lasting friendships that reached deep into the underworld. One of those friendships was with the old-time mobster Frederick Charles 'Paddles' Anderson. (Anderson supposedly earned his nickname due to possessing a large pair of feet.)

Anderson was deeply embedded in the Sydney and Melbourne underworlds by the 1930s, and his early criminal activity occurred in that twilight zone between the violent golden era of the razor gangs and the likes of Frank Green and Tilly Devine in the 1920s and 30s, and the advent of the modern gangster from the late 1940s through to the 1960s.

Born on 7 February 1915, Anderson attended Fort Street High School in Petersham in Sydney's inner-south-west. (Other alumni included the crime boss Abe 'Mr Sin' Saffron, as well as Governor-General John Kerr, actor Michael Pate, and future New South Wales premier 'Nifty' Neville Wran.)

When Paddles Anderson began a life of crime, men were wearing heavy suits and hats. By the time it ended, with his death in the mid-1980s, it was called organised crime, replete with professional hitmen. Anderson gained his notoriety in June 1940 when he was charged with murdering John Charles Abrahams in Collingwood, in a crime described by the then Crown Prosecutor as one that more 'befitted a city like Chicago than Melbourne'. During his trial Anderson famously alibied himself, by inviting a taxi driver to join him for a meal at the time of the alleged murder. He told the court he and the taxi driver had steak and eggs. When Anderson was found not guilty, he thanked the jury.

One of Anderson's great talents was to cultivate contacts and friendships in high places. And he knew the importance of getting corrupt coppers onside. Anderson was smart enough to attach himself to one of Sydney's most ruthless detectives, Ray 'Gunner' Kelly, which kept him out of serious strife for the rest of his underworld career.

As Michael Duffy and Nick Hordern reported in their book, *Sydney Noir: The Golden Years*: 'The picture of the power structure of organised crime in Sydney ... omits Frederick "Paddles" Anderson who ... was older than most of the other leading gangsters [in the 1960s].

'Some observers, including reporter Bob Bottom and crook Karl

Bonnette, have suggested Anderson was the most powerful criminal in Sydney for many years, possibly from the 1950s right through to the 1970s.'

'Not much happened unless it went through Fred ... Fred was the man; he was the smartest of all of them,' Bonnette, a former associate, reportedly said after Anderson's death. 'You could go and get advice off him about anything. He had connections everywhere: judges, politicians; he was accepted in a lot of different circles and he had a bit of class. I'd often go to his house for dinner and that's where I first met Lenny McPherson.'

By the time Paddles Anderson became aware of the talents of Vince O'Dempsey in the mid-1960s, he was, at 50, the reputed titular head of the Sydney crime scene. Anderson, as was his habit, sought out and established connections with other hardened criminals. 'Vince used to work for a bloke called Paddles Anderson,' says one of O'Dempsey's former associates. 'Now mate, a lot of people talk about Lenny McPherson and George Freeman and all that. But Paddles Anderson was the godfather. He made black people turn white. He had that much power and that much money.'

The associate says Anderson was a big fan of hard men. 'Paddles loved people tough, you know? He loved tough people – people who could fight, people who could handle themselves and people that keep their mouth shut,' he says. 'And you always need someone to do your dirty work for you.'

Others who knew O'Dempsey in this period said he always found work in Sydney as a 'gunman'.

It was true that in the world of corrupt police and criminals in the 1960s, Queensland and New South Wales had some curious, almost frightening, parallels, with each state boasting notorious characters who eerily mirrored one another. As Duffy and Hordern point out, the criminal circle in Kings Cross was small, 'both socially and geographically ... there was a close connection between the Sydney and Brisbane underworld, far more so than between Sydney and Melbourne, with criminals and police moving seamlessly between the two cities.'

The New South Wales police had a host of bad apples but none more so than Gunner Kelly. Inspector Kelly, arguably Sydney's best-known detective of his era, famously said once: 'I've shot brumbies. I've chased steers. But there's nothing to touch the thrill of a manhunt.'

At his peak during the 1960s, the mere mention of Kelly's name would strike fear into the criminal milieu; he had a huge array of criminal informants and would later use them for his corrupt practices. According to author David Hickie in his book, *The Prince and the Premier*, 'He [Kelly] became the best-known crime investigator in New South Wales, who always seemed to turn up at the right place at the right time. His success was based on the extensive "espionage" service he built up over several decades, a grapevine notorious for its sordid nature. The many criminal phiz-gigs [informants] who worked for him usually did so in fear of the consequences if they refused.' One of his leading informants was Frederick 'Paddles' Anderson.

New South Wales detective Frederick Claude 'Froggy' Krahe, like Kelly, also had an enormous number of contacts in the underworld, and lived off his reputation as a hard and feared man. He would end up having an affair with brothel madam Shirley Brifman from Queensland. And through Brifman, Krahe developed a relationship with Glen Hallahan and Tony Murphy. It was the hard-nosed, Brisbane-based Murphy that most resembled Krahe, given they were similar in age, cultivated a dangerous, hardman image, and shared Brifman as a lover.

Then there were the gunmen Stewart John Regan and Vincent O'Dempsey. The boy from Upper Freestone in the Darling Downs soon developed a reputation in Sydney as a reliable 'gun for hire'.

He was organised and meticulous and a man who understood that 'business was business'. Years later, when O'Dempsey reminisced about his youthful exploits at the end of a weapon in the 1960s and 70s, he described his work as 'just business'.

Friends of O'Dempsey during this period described his special 'shooter's outfit' – a raincoat and beanie – that he'd wear to avoid any gunshot residue. They said he would burn everything after a job, including all clothes and shoes, and that he preferred to travel or move around under cover of darkness.

O'Dempsey was also intimately acquainted with his surroundings at all times. He planned things down to the letter, drew up maps and took notes on potential hazards. He was permanently alert to being followed.

As one colleague observed: 'He wasn't a loose cannon that would sit there and then he'd fly off the handle or anything like that ... he was Cool Hand Luke all the time. Everything went into that brain of his ... he'd digest it and then nut it all out and then he'd say, "Right, this is what we've got to do."'

The colleague also said O'Dempsey was always prepared in the event that he might get caught. He had several 'hidey-holes' where he stashed guns, money and drugs off major highways and roads between Warwick and Sydney. 'He said never bury anything where they're going to widen the road, and always bury it in a container that's tight, so white ants can't get into it and water can't damage it,' the colleague said. 'He told me one time when he got in the nick he was stuffed, but he knew he had 20 grand of his heroin money snookered away somewhere. He said, "Money's your best friend when you're inside and when you get out of the clink – money's your best friend."'

Still, in many respects, while O'Dempsey and Regan may not have been like brothers, their upbringing, methods and predilections were part of the same broader family. In some instances, they bore some striking similarities. In the 1960s Regan, at just 17, was working as a fist for hire for various brothels, and living off the earnings of prostitutes, just like O'Dempsey. Regan was about seven years younger than O'Dempsey, but both had been born and raised in country towns; Regan in the historic gold mining town of Young, in the New South Wales central west, about 370 kilometres from Sydney.

Regan was the only son of Arthur and Clare Regan. Regan would call his mother 'The Colonel'. He was raised a Catholic, as was O'Dempsey. Regan wanted to join the Army as a young man but was precluded courtesy of flat feet. O'Dempsey was enlisted briefly in the Army before he was discharged following allegations of sexual assault against another recruit. Both men were extremely conscious of their health. Regan didn't drink alcohol, he preferred orange juice. O'Dempsey rarely drank and was a committed vegetarian.

Both men would leave prison and begin their careers as bouncers, Regan at strip joints and clubs, and O'Dempsey at Brisbane's mock auctions and at brothels. Regan would eventually run a large number of prostitutes; O'Dempsey would later follow him down that path.

The two men also had similar nicknames. Regan was 'Nano' or 'The Magician', because he made people disappear. O'Dempsey would be dubbed 'Silent Death' and later 'Swami' for the very same reason.

It is unclear how the men met, though in the early 1960s Regan was in control of several brothels and had ambitions to take over the prostitution scene in Kings Cross, and O'Dempsey was living off the earnings of a prostitute in the same sleazy suburb. Both men also shared a passion for property and real estate. Close friends of O'Dempsey would confirm that he and Regan would later become 'business partners' in a property in Vince's home town of Warwick. But that was in the future.

Billy and Barbara

By the mid-1960s, O'Dempsey had established a reputation for violence in Sydney and had already done time for the serious assault of a police officer in Warwick. Rumour that he'd 'vanished' Tommy Allen followed in his wake. Coupled with the fact that he was a ballistics expert and not averse to carrying weapons at all times, including pistols and knives, the word in both criminal and police communities along the east coast of Australia was that O'Dempsey was a man to be reckoned with. He would later be called one of the last of the old-time gangsters.

As O'Dempsey was making his presence felt up and down the coast between Brisbane and Sydney, a young mother, Barbara May McCulkin, was living a life on the move with her husband, Robert William 'Billy' McCulkin. McCulkin was in the Navy Reserve and had been posted around various bases before briefly settling in Nowra on the New South Wales south coast.

Barbara, who had grown up in the country town of Maryborough, Queensland, was not only coming to terms with motherhood in a strange town but had started wondering about the man she'd married. The reality of her marriage was falling short of the dreams she'd had as a girl. Since living with Billy, she had learned in no uncertain terms that he liked a drink, could be violent, and that he mixed in unsavoury company.

When little Barbara May was growing up in the sugar cane and timber town north of Brisbane she would drive her three brothers mad with her incessant tap dancing. The only daughter of James Gardiner and May Alice Ogden, she and brothers Neville, Barry and Graham lived in an old Queenslander in Pallas Street. 'She was a popular girl,' brother Graham remembers. 'She was likeable, and most times she had a happy demeanour. There were no problems. I don't think she even smoked.'

For the Ogdens, money was always tight. An additional worry was an ill mother. May Ogden had contracted tuberculosis and was often ill with chest problems. 'Mum spent a lot of time in hospital,' Graham said.

Barbara, who was not academically inclined, left school and got a job working at Kings Café in Queen Street, not far from the Mary River. In her late teens, Barbara fell pregnant. She wanted to keep the child but her father disallowed it. The baby, Jocelyn, was subsequently adopted out. Even so, Graham Ogden said his sister was bright and bubbly, with a 'wicked sense of humour'.

At some point, working at Kings Café, Barbara met Billy McCulkin from Brisbane. Just over five foot six inches tall, with brown wavy hair and green eyes, McCulkin had always been a roustabout. His nose had been broken so many times in fights that a detective would later call it 'Billy's east-west nose'.

In his Record of Service with the Navy's Strategic Reserve, McCulkin listed his profession as 'storeman and packer'. Billy joined eight days after he turned 18 in March 1957. He saw service at several naval bases – HMAS Tobruk, Sydney and Penguin – in the late 1950s. Coincidentally, in the winter of 1959, a fellow Queenslander – Noel O'Dempsey, brother to Vincent O'Dempsey, from Stewart's Avenue, Warwick – also served briefly at Penguin, in the suburb of Balmoral on Middle Head in Sydney Harbour.

In June 1960 McCulkin went on to marry Barbara, who was already four months' pregnant with their first child, Vicki Maree, born in Sydney on 9 November. Billy took two weeks' leave for the occasion. Their second daughter, Barbara Leanne (known as Leanne), was born two years later on 26 June, when Billy was based at the HMAS Albatross, the RAN's air base near Nowra south of Sydney. By the end of that year, Billy parted ways with the Navy and began kicking around Sydney. In 1966, he temporarily separated from Barbara. It was during this period, in the mid-1960s, that O'Dempsey and McCulkin began a friendship on the streets of Kings Cross.

They were a curious pair, McCulkin and O'Dempsey. McCulkin was short, stocky and drank too much. O'Dempsey, however, imbibed very little and was extremely conscious of his diet. McCulkin was a hanger-on. As one associate observed: 'Billy McCulkin was just hanging onto other people's coat-tails, trying to be a part of the group.'

Former detective Alan Marshall got to know McCulkin well through various investigations during the 1970s. 'Yes, he's a very complex personality ... and his biggest problem was the alcohol. Like he was the most ugly-looking man you'd ever come across. [His nose] had been flattened across his face so many times. He actually did a bit of work for a couple of solicitors at one time to try and collect some unpaid fees. He knocked on the door this one time and this bloke said, "What do you want?" Billy said, "I want the money for the solicitor's fees." The bloke just went *bang*, and knocked Billy out. When Billy went and saw the solicitor he said, "I don't want any more to do with this, I'm out of here." Because Billy wasn't very big, he was only about five foot five inches.'

It was an extraordinary time in Sydney's Kings Cross, with brothels and illegal gambling rampant. O'Dempsey was living off the earnings of a prostitute who worked out of the infamous Rex Hotel. There was also no shortage of Queenslanders in Sin City in the early stages of their criminal careers, who would have undoubtedly crossed paths with O'Dempsey on the small intersection of streets that made up the notorious inner-city suburb.

As O'Dempsey and McCulkin began forging a friendship, former Atherton girl Shirley Brifman was also setting herself up around the corner as one of the city's most notorious brothel madams. Brifman also kept a room at the Rex, where she would entertain corrupt Detective Glen Hallahan when he was in town – which he frequently was. Brifman was also close to leading Brisbane detective

Tony Murphy, and when she wasn't back in Brisbane on business where they could catch up, they corresponded by letter.

Brisbane detectives, Glen Hallahan, Tony Murphy and Terry Lewis (who would later become Police Commissioner) would also collaborate with their New South Wales counterparts and regularly visit the big smoke. In the early 1960s the detectives, known as the Rat Pack, had consolidated 'The Joke' with Licensing Branch officer Jack 'The Bagman' Herbert. The Joke was an elaborate system of graft and protection payments that Queensland police collected off the back of illegal gambling, SP bookmakers and brothels. Over time, it was a network that infiltrated all corners of the state and yielded hundreds of thousands of dollars for the police involved.

Another woman, Norma Beniston, also known as Simone Vogel, was similarly making a name for herself around Kings Cross during that time. As a prostitute starting out, she would rack up 170 convictions before finally moving up to the Sunshine State and establishing herself as a leading brothel madam. Vogel would be instrumental in setting up the new generation 'massage parlour' industry in Brisbane. Although she may not have known it yet, her path was also destined to cross with O'Dempsey and participants in The Joke, with disastrous consequences.

At some point in 1966, McCulkin returned to Brisbane and caught up with his mate O'Dempsey. McCulkin would seek work only when he had to, and when he did earn money, he drank it away at the Lands Office Hotel in Brisbane, along with his criminal mates. A plan was soon hatched for O'Dempsey and McCulkin to rob a safe from the Waltons department store in Fortitude Valley. Both were 'ratted out' by a police informant to the notorious detective Glen Hallahan. It was rumoured that local tattooist William 'Billy' Garnett Phillips was the 'dog' who gave them up.

O'Dempsey was charged with break, enter and steal, possession of an explosive substance without lawful excuse, and unlawful possession of an unlicensed firearm. He was sentenced to five years in prison.

Curiously, McCulkin was held on remand for a month and then released. Had McCulkin been the beneficiary of some police favour? Or had the court been lenient given his relatively clean criminal record? Either way, it must have rankled O'Dempsey that he copped the full brunt of the offences, while his co-accused skipped free.

Billy Phillips, known as the King of the Brisbane bodgies, was not the only one doing favours for police. Hallahan had also recruited the talents of former Westbrook inmates, young John Andrew Stuart and the future Clockwork Orange Gang member Tommy Hamilton. Both would go on to crack safes and commit robberies on the command of Hallahan, and the Rat Packer would split the proceeds with his stable of thieves. It was all part of The Joke.

One friend of Hamilton says: 'Tom was doing business with Hallahan in the 1960s. He'd do jobs for him and if Tom was picked up the charges would be dropped. It was mainly to do with stolen goods. [Detective] Tony Murphy was there in the mix too. Tommy was a good crook. He used to get messages to and from Hallahan through the Nundah police, not far from where we all grew up. That's how he got the word through about jobs and stuff. They were all kicking back money to the corrupt cops.'

At some point the distinguished detectives Murphy and Hallahan had crossed the line in terms of their use of criminal informants. Instead of gleaning information from them to solve crimes, the detectives were now using those informants as tools to commit crimes on their behalf. Tommy Hamilton, John Andrew Stuart and Billy Phillips were on Hallahan's team. McCulkin, fortuitously for him, was attached to the honest officer Basil 'The Hound' Hicks, while Vince O'Dempsey, the most prized and the most dangerous informant of all, had a future beckoning with Tony Murphy.

Invariably, in their early years, this loose constellation of young criminals would orbit around Phillips and his tattoo parlours. Criminal Billy Stokes says: 'When he [Phillips] opened a tattoo shop opposite the South Brisbane train station in 1961 it was a regular meeting place for lots of the boys. The shop had a small bed behind a partition and anyone who picked up a willing girl could take her there for a root. Once, showing that he was also interested in cops and robbers games, Phillips flashed a revolver around the shop.'

When McCulkin was released on remand in late 1966, he returned to his wife Barbara and their children, Vicki and Leanne, and they rented various properties in Brisbane. Barbara worked to support the family. There was always very little money. Barbara was so desperate to keep the family afloat that she had a workmate open a separate bank account to secure part of her wages and keep them out of Billy's hands. She also made sure her wider family was not aware of her problems at home.

'Barbara not only kept a clean and tidy house and held down a part-time job in a café, she provided a stable home life for her family with the resources she had,' her brother Graham said. 'Barbara was completely discreet with us when it came to her husband, Billy McCulkin. While we knew him to be a sometimes difficult and moody man, who had been violent towards her, she never criticised him or discussed anything about their marital problems in our presence.

'But I never liked the bastard.'

Boggo Road

Brisbane's notorious Boggo Road Gaol, not far from the South Brisbane cemetery in the suburb of Dutton Park, was no place for the faint-hearted in the 1960s. It was a perpetual carousel of young inmates who would, within a decade, develop the city's cabal of hardened criminals in concert with corrupt police. The repercussions of their actions in the violent, tumultuous decade that followed would reverberate into the 21st century.

'It was a finishing school for the boys who went to Westbrook [Farm Home for Boys],' says one former inmate of Boggo Road. 'By the time you got out of there you had absolutely no respect for authority. When you see what happens in there and the shit that goes on, it's almost hard to believe.'

On any given month in Boggo Road Gaol in the 1960s, you could acquaint yourself with the likes of John Andrew Stuart, Garry Dubois and older inmates like Arthur Ernest 'Slim' Halliday and Gunther Bahnemann. Many would form serious friendships on the inside and become criminal associates on the outside.

One former inmate, incarcerated at 17 for the unlawful use of a motor vehicle, went inside in 1964 on a 12-month sentence. 'I went to work in the kitchen,' the former inmate recalls. 'There was another guy, he was the head cook and he was a nice guy, he was … a lot older than me, and he said if you're going over to the stores – from Two Gaol, that's where the store was, you had to go through this tunnel. He told me to watch the screw in charge of the kitchen. He said, "Never get on the back of a barrow."'

The 'barrows' were metal boxes containing prisoners' meals that were delivered by the prison kitchen hands, usually boys, from One Gaol. 'The head cook told me that when you're going through and he stands and opens the gate and you walk through the carrier, he said the screw tries to stop you and play with your dick,' the inmate recalls. 'I said, "You're fucking kidding."'

'He said "No," he said, "I'm fucking telling you." So after that I came back and he said, "How was the tunnel?" He used to call it The Tunnel of Love.

'I said, "You were right about that screw."'

James Finch was another inmate who would go on to earn lifetime notoriety for his future role in the Whiskey Au Go Go inferno. Like John Andrew Stuart, his co-accused of that crime, Finch had endured a troubled childhood at the hands of a brutal father. Born in the UK, as a boy he was sent to a Dr Barnardo's children's home in Barkingside, Essex. His father was abusive towards the family and when he was seven, his mother, unable to cope, dropped her son off at the home promising to pick him up the following week. She never returned. When Finch first arrived at Barkingside, an official report concluded that conversations he had heard at home 'persisted in colouring the boy's mind with lurid horror stories'. It added: 'At this stage, the boy's mind reflects fantasies of murder, burning, shooting and destruction.' Two years later, young Finch was sent to Australia and saw out his youth at Barnardo's Mowbray Park Farm Training School in the town of Picton, 80 kilometres south-west of Sydney.

Finch's Mowbray Park Farm report said he was a 'tough little boy who resents any show of affection or sympathy'. Even so, within three years he was declared 'free of problems' and left school at 15. A year after leaving Mowbray Park Farm, Finch was charged with damaging a railway sign with 'rifle fire'. Then, in February 1962 he was sentenced to eight months' detention for breaking, entering and stealing, and car theft. After numerous counts of reoffending he wound up in gaol.

'He wouldn't fucking back down to a soul on earth,' says an inmate who knew Finch in Boggo Road. 'Finch wasn't a bully, not then.'

As for John Andrew Stuart: 'He was in a special cell with a wire door and he was under escort the whole time and I don't know what he was doing or how long, I can't remember. But he was always a smart-arse and he was handcuffed to double escort [two guards] once and there was a real bad screw. One afternoon there was no sewerage in the cells or anything and he [Stuart] used to have a plastic bucket, and here's this bad screw, I can't think of his name. He's standing there with piss and shit all over him. Stuart had got him to the door somehow.'

Even as a man in his early twenties, Stuart had a formidable, and growing, reputation among his fellow criminals. 'He wouldn't cop any shit,' the inmate says. 'I suppose you'd have to be a bit mad.'

In fact, not long out of Westbrook, Stuart had already established a pattern of behaviour that would define the rest of his life. It was well known that he never went out in public without a weapon. He favoured a knife, which he would strap to his ankle. Over the coming decade, he would repeatedly commit crimes – initially break and enters, to support his heroin habit, but he would later graduate to rape, assault and in one instance attempted murder – and end up in prison. While inside he would be transferred to and from psychiatric hospitals, which he regularly absconded from, earning himself a reputation as an escape artist.

In June 1962 Stuart sawed his way out of the notorious psychiatric ward, Ward 16, at Brisbane Hospital with a table knife. 'Within eight minutes of his escape, every available police car and policeman was called into the manhunt,' a local newspaper reported. Stuart had stolen the private vehicle of a policeman from the hospital grounds and would don the police tunic and cap he found inside the vehicle, to aid his escape.

However, Stuart's freedom was short-lived. The next day he was spotted by a detective in the stalls of the Regent Theatre in busy Queen Street in the Brisbane CBD, after an anonymous tip-off. One of the pictures screening that morning was *The Threat*, an American film noir starring Michael O'Shea and Virginia Grey. (Incredibly, the plot was not unlike the situation Stuart found himself in on that Saturday morning. The film centres on murderer and lunatic, Arnold 'Red' Kluger, who escapes from prison and wants to exact revenge on the people who put him inside.)

Outside the theatre in Brisbane, three detectives rushed to the Regent and just as the 11.30 a.m. interval started, Detective Fred Humphries, on entering the theatre, recognised Stuart. He was eating an ice cream. 'I went over to him and asked him to accompany me to the foyer of the theatre,' Humphries told the press. 'As we were walking up the aisle, with Stuart ahead of me, he turned and punched me on the chin throwing me off balance. Stuart ran and I chased him. While he was running he put his hand in his hip-pocket as if reaching for a gun. When we got into the foyer I fired warning shots ... Stuart leaped down a flight of stairs and slipped on the marble floor.'

In the end five shots were fired, the bullets having 'ricocheted round the hall and lodged in the ceiling and walls'.

Stuart was ultimately locked up again. The Sunday *Truth* reported: 'Doctors said his psychiatric examination showed he had a high intelligence and was familiar with many standard textbooks on psychiatry. They said he could simulate ... symptoms ... particularly those of schizophrenia.'

As punishment for his misdemeanours in Boggo Road, Stuart was often consigned to the Black Hole. 'It was literally like a dungeon, an actual black hole,' says one prison guard who worked there at the time. 'You'd walk down these stairs into this dungeon, and the only light in there came through those little breather slits between the bricks, like you have in the walls of houses. It was really barbaric.'

In 1964 Stuart would once again be released from gaol, but it didn't take long before he found himself back in trouble. On 31 December 1965, just as Vincent O'Dempsey was about to see in his first New Year in Boggo Road, Stuart was arrested and charged in Sydney with a suite of offences that would guarantee him a long stretch of time off the streets. These included the attempted murder of the hitman Stewart John Regan and the malicious wounding of Giuseppe Cappa on 20 December, in Sydney. During the attack in the suburb of Paddington, Stuart had been in company with James Finch.

Finch would ultimately be charged and imprisoned for the Regan shooting, though criminal associates say that Stuart fired the pistol and Finch took the rap for him. Billy Stokes would later write about this extraordinary 'Wild West-style' shoot-out in the streets of inner-Sydney between the madman Stuart, his close mate James Finch, and Regan, Sydney's number one hitman and serial killer.

'Both [Finch and Regan] were armed at the time and the way the story's told it was just a case of Finch being faster on the draw,' wrote Stokes. 'They had been arguing over bail for a friend of theirs, Danny Landini [who had also befriended Stuart in Brisbane's Boggo Road Gaol in the early 1960s]. He had been arrested, with Regan and others, on a charge of rape.'

While Regan and the others had been granted bail, Landini had been left in gaol. Finch believed that Regan, who had plenty of money, should have bailed out Landini. Regan refused.

Regan took a bullet in the shoulder but refused to testify against Finch. It didn't matter. Finch was found guilty of shooting Regan and imprisoned.

On New Year's Eve, 1965, Stuart was also charged with feloniously wounding Robert Lawrence 'Jacky' Steele with intent to murder on 26 November, also in Sydney. A rape charge was also laid against Stuart and his co-accused, the red-headed gunman and fellow Brisbanite, Raymond 'Ducky' O'Connor.

Stuart ended up pleading guilty to maliciously wounding Steele, although he would continue to profess his innocence for the rest of his life. He was sentenced to five years' gaol, but another three years were added in early 1967 when he was found guilty of attacking a detective in Long Bay Correctional Complex.

Corrupt New South Wales detective and now convicted murderer, Roger Rogerson, remembers the incident that saw Stuart's sentence increased. 'I'll tell you how mad he was,' Rogerson recalls. 'This is my recollection ... He was locked up at Long Bay. He made an allegation that he'd been bashed or flogged by arresting detectives.

'Two guys from headquarters went out to investigate his complaint, Carl Arkins and his sidekick. They were with Internal Affairs ... they'd telephoned the gaol before they went out. They had special interview rooms where police could interview prisoners. They met in this room and Stuart jumped up, king hit Arkins and smashed his jaw. Then he went to court. Charged with grievous bodily harm.'

In a career spent mixing with some of the heaviest criminals Australia has ever produced, Rogerson says there were only three that were worse psychopaths than John Andrew Stuart. 'That's Christopher Dale Flannery, Stewart John Regan and Raymond "Ducky" O'Connor [another of Stuart's childhood friends],' says Rogerson.

At Stuart's sentencing for the Steele offence he indicated to police that he would be returning to Queensland when he finally got out of prison. It was an ominous sounding bell that should have been heard all the way from Sydney.

As for Vince O'Dempsey, he was now a seasoned inmate. But the tedium of prison didn't stop him planning for the future. He had one big ambition that he shared with a fellow prisoner.

'He had an idea that he might blow up police headquarters in Brisbane,' the prisoner says. 'Vince said he'd checked it out and that you can go down into the undercover car park where there's no ... this is in the 1960s, no security, no gates. He said there's a certain number of rubbish bins and waste bins, and you could pop the explosives in there, and away you go.'

Vince and Shorty

Boggo Road was also where the lifelong friendship and criminal working relationship between Vince O'Dempsey and Garry 'Shorty' Dubois began. O'Dempsey, back in prison for the second time after stealing a safe with Billy McCulkin, was just 28.

'They were very close in there,' says another inmate at the time. 'Vince used to come and get Shorty and pull him aside and tell him things. He confided things in Shorty. Shorty was serving a sentence for rape. It was a big sentence for a rape by yourself. And Vince was a heavy. You heard the talk. He was this, he was that. He seemed to have a hold on Shorty.'

One of Dubois's close friends, who visited him a few times in Boggo Road, says Shorty's eight-year sentence for rape was excessive. 'I know for a fact he was set up on that,' the friend insists. 'It wasn't rape. They picked up a bunch of girls in Chermside and went out partying and had sex with them. And when they were dropping them off, the younger brother of one of the girls has seen them getting out of the cars and went and told the mother. It escalated from there and to save themselves the girls said they were raped.

'The youngest one there was the one who professed all along that it wasn't rape, that it was all consensual. The ones charged with having sex with her, they were only charged with carnal knowledge. Two other girls who had sex still claimed rape for a while, and two of the blokes who were with them were sent to gaol, the same as Shorty.

'Months down the track these two young ones who had cried rape, changed their story and went to a solicitor, the other two [blokes] were pardoned and released ... the only one who went down for rape was Shorty.

'His mother lost her house paying money, she hired a private investigator, she did everything she could to try and get a retrial for him but they would never allow it to happen. I attended a couple of court sessions. The police had groomed her [the girl] really well. She had pigtails and no make-up, she looked like a schoolgirl again. Her testimony was spot on to get him arrested. He got eight years.'

The friend says Dubois was changed by his long stretch in Boggo Road. 'I think it soured him a fair bit, and that's when he fell under the spell of Vince O'Dempsey in there,' he says. 'I suppose being locked in there with him is a different thing, but when I met him [Vince] on the outside there was no entrancement. There was mistrust. He scared the fucking living daylights out of you when you looked into his black eyes. You knew he was a preacher. Slowly, over a period of time, stories emerged about him that consolidated the strange feeling I had about him.'

One inmate remembers another thing about Shorty Dubois. 'He seemed to be predisposed to Charlie Manson [the American cult leader and mass murderer],' he recalls. 'I thought he was half-joking, but he was serious ... Shorty even looked like him. A short man. The moustache. The heavy rock scene. Drugs. LSD.'

Manson had made headlines around the world when his Family cult committed a string of shocking murders in the United States in July and August of 1969. One of the victims of the cult was Sharon Tate, the pregnant actress and wife of film director Roman Polanski. Tate had pleaded for her life before being stabbed to death. The inside of the murder house, in Benedict Canyon, north of Beverly Hills in Los Angeles, was awash with blood.

While Shorty may have been baying with excitement over Manson's murderous antics, O'Dempsey, to all who observed him in gaol during those years, was the model prisoner. In fact, he used his lag time to further educate himself. 'He was always doing these courses,' one fellow inmate says. 'Poultry farming. Animal husbandry. Agriculture. He could speak about anything at all, on any topic. He was quiet. Reserved. But once he got to know you he'd be just like a normal person. But there was something there, I felt.'

The inmate says O'Dempsey was sometimes reflective about his childhood in Warwick. 'He said all his brothers and sisters fought, the usual stuff,' he says. 'He talked about the Christian Brothers and all that shit.' O'Dempsey would later reveal to a criminal associate that he hated Catholics, despite his own mother's devotion.

O'Dempsey also shared some information about his brief stint in the Australian Army, after the disappearance of Tommy Allen in 1964 and before his arrest for the safe robbery in 1966. O'Dempsey said he had been undergoing training at the Holsworthy Barracks outside Sydney when he was given a dishonourable discharge. 'He told me there'd be no short-haired poofters in the Army,' the inmate recalls. 'Then he said when you had a shower down there at the Army base it got all steamy, and he just grabbed a soldier in the next cubicle. He said he raped him. He admitted that to the boys and everyone laughed. O'Dempsey thought that was funny.'

There was one thing, however, that set O'Dempsey apart from the crowd in Boggo Road. 'He had an air of complete confidence about him,' one inmate recalls. 'He didn't give a fuck about anyone or anything. Whether that was because he already had a couple of notches on his belt at that stage, I don't know.'

Another former inmate recalled arriving in prison and spotting O'Dempsey and McCulkin together, after they were arrested for cracking the Waltons safe. 'I hadn't heard about O'Dempsey at that point, he was in the remand yard when we were there … him and Billy McCulkin,' he says. As for O'Dempsey, 'I thought I wouldn't like to fuck with you. It was his demeanour and the way he spoke and that, he was pretty confident and he had a neck like a bull as a young bloke. The rumours would come out that he'd put someone underground, you know. You hear that about a lot of people, but then something about this one I believed.'

He said you had to switch on and learn how to survive from day one in Boggo Road. The ex-prisoner said even in that gruel of hardened men, Vince O'Dempsey stood out. 'I don't think he drank tea or coffee,' he remembered. 'I think he used to exercise. I wasn't in the same yard as him but I'd speak to him … when we used to get into [the same] yards you could play cards … he was a mad card player and he used to get the fucking shits if he lost, too.'

The ex-con also befriended Garry 'Shorty' Dubois. 'He was good, you know, I never seen the other side of him at all,' he said. 'He was pretty quiet, he used to be very, very fit and I was in the same yard as him, like in the last year or something, or whatever it was, and he was alright.'

The inmate said in the 1960s it was an 'offence' to exercise, but the prisoners had ways of keeping fit. 'Oh, you'd do chin-ups on your bloody shed awning, push-ups, sits-ups with a bolt around the stool … all that sort of stuff,' he said. 'You couldn't run or anything. O'Dempsey had been a boxer, yeah. They'd say he was good; very, very hard. I don't think he'd been beaten.'

The prison screws gave O'Dempsey a nickname – Silent Death. 'That's what we called him – Silent Death,' one prison guard recalls. 'He rarely spoke to anybody inside. He kept to himself. He was a loner. When he looked at you with those steel eyes, your hair stood on end. He looked at you and you just about pissed yourself. You wouldn't think that anyone could look that evil.

'You just got the feeling that you could die at any moment with O'Dempsey. He'd stick you with a knife. He'd shoot you and wouldn't bat an eyelid. For years after I used to have a recurring nightmare that my car broke down in the bush and I was out there alone. Then suddenly Vince O'Dempsey came out of the bush.

'He was a very, very ruthless man. He was the most evil man that I ever encountered in prison in more than 30 years on the job. No question.'

The Gift

In gaol, while O'Dempsey largely preferred his own company, it did not mean he was deaf and blind to the currents that rippled through the Boggo Road community: the gossip, the mischief, the scams, the illicit drugs, and news beyond the gaol walls where criminals continued, day and night, to turn a quid.

Right or wrong, O'Dempsey had heard that tattooist Billy Phillips had ratted him out over the Waltons safe job. There was a logical assumption, too, that McCulkin may have also sold him down the river, given the way he had evaded any serious gaol time for the job. He may have been sitting in prison but O'Dempsey was well connected on the outside. As a feared criminal, he could still have an impact and get things done.

Phillips lived in a rundown Queenslander on a steep ridge at 29 Earl Street, Petrie Terrace. It was a convenient location for the corrupt Detective Hallahan, who lived less than a hundred metres away in St James Street, and liked to call on his neighbour for information on a regular basis; sometimes Billy sent a girl over to Hallahan's flat, other times the detective dropped by Earl Street to smoke marijuana. It was all just part of an ordinary day for Phillips, who lived with his de facto wife, Tracey, three little children and any number of friends and associates who happened to drift by.

By the late-1960s the imposing, bearded Phillips had started mixing with 'some very heavy characters'. He had a lengthy criminal record, primarily for assault, and was struggling financially. As a way of bolstering his tattoo business, which operated out of the Earl Street house, he was dabbling in the sale of illegal firearms. By the age of 26, Phillips had gained a reputation for being able to procure handguns and shotguns and was the first port of call for interstate criminals looking for a weapon.

At 8.50 a.m. on Monday 9 October 1967, postman Jonus Mickus, in his Postmaster General–issue shirt and wide-brimmed hat, lugged his post bag up Earl Street, dropping off the mail. He delivered a small package to the Phillips home and continued on his route. Ten minutes later, working Belgrave Street, parallel to Earl Street, Mickus heard a tremendous blast issue from Number 29.

Vaulting the Phillips's back fence, Mickus rushed through a rear door to the house where he found Phillips's wife, Tracey, 23, screaming and writhing on the bedroom floor. Billy Phillips was unconscious beside her, and their five-month-old son, Scott, was knocked out on the bed and bleeding from facial wounds. Bomb shrapnel was embedded in the victims' bodies. The two other Phillips children were wandering about the house, dazed.

In a rare and disturbing event for Brisbane, the Phillips's had been sent a letter bomb. Addressed to Phillips and clearly intended for him, Tracey had innocently opened the parcel, the size of an alarm clock and wrapped in brown paper. The impact blew off her left hand and mangled her right, and her upper torso and face were mutilated.

Police later learned the bomb contained a nine-volt battery detonation system and gelignite. It was housed in a small, Asian-style trinket box made of magnolia and birchwood. Did the assassination attempt stem from underworld knowledge that Phillips had been working as a police informant?

Surgeons were unable to save Tracey Phillips's right hand and she was also blinded. Her face was disfigured and it was discovered she was pregnant and lost the baby. Phillips and his son recovered.

Neighbour and friend Glen Hallahan quickly set about interviewing some known criminals to try and establish who may have sent the bomb. As part of his investigation he contacted brothel madam Shirley Brifman in Sydney. Brifman would later recall talking to Hallahan in an interview with police: 'Tracey Phillips copped the bomb. Glen told me that Billy stood at the door and said to Tracey, "Don't open that, it will be a bomb" ... Being a sticky beak she did open it.'

At the time of the bomb, O'Dempsey was sitting in Boggo Road on his safe-cracking and weapons charges. He had been locked up for more than a year and was due for release in late 1970. He was with some of his fellow inmates when news of the bombing came over the radio. O'Dempsey immediately turned to some of the inmates and confided to them that the bomb had been delivered in a jewellery box. This information was not yet available to the public.

Years later, criminal Billy Stokes would write in his waterside workers magazine, *Port News*:

> The Loner [O'Dempsey] is well known to police. He is considered a very violent man capable of violent acts, and is, in fact, the man who claims to be the instigator of the parcel bomb that was posted to a Brisbane tattooist, William Phillips, several years ago. The fact that this parcel bomb was opened by Phillips' de-facto wife, who subsequently suffered the blast with her children, is only a pointer to how callous some violent men can be.
>
> Although The Loner was serving a term of imprisonment when the parcel bomb was posted, he liked to make it well known that it was on his instructions that the bomb was posted to Phillips because of a personal dispute between them.

Decades later, one of O'Dempsey's lovers would tell the police, and a court hearing, about Vince and the Phillips bomb. When police suggested she confess to what she knew about O'Dempsey and his past, she said in a record of interview: 'You can't protect me. Billy Phillips's wife's hands got blown off. Vince was in gaol and Vince was responsible for it from Boggo Road Prison.'

The police asked: 'What's your source of that information?'

O'Dempsey's former lover said: 'Vince. Vince told me he did it. That he was responsible. That he didn't mean for it to happen to her. He told me the whole background version of the story.'

Billy Stokes later said: 'In gaol during the 1960s, Vince O'Dempsey told me that he thought Phillips had informed on him to police, and because of this suspicion when Phillips was posted that parcel-bomb, some thought O'Dempsey may have arranged it.'

Another criminal associate says O'Dempsey was fascinated by explosives and was an expert on the subject. He says O'Dempsey used these skills in his 'safe-cracking days' in the 1960s. 'He promised me, like, he'd teach me about explosives,' the associate says. 'So I got these electric dets ... detonators ... and had two of them in a plastic bag, in a sandwich bag in me pocket. And he said to me, he said, "The first lesson, never carry two dets in a plastic bag in your pocket together. One spark, you're fucked. It'll blow your chest clean off."

'I said, "You're fucking joking, I thought you'd have to have a spark to set them off?"

'And he asked me: "Would you risk it?"

'I thought, fucking little bit too dangerous for me, fucking explosives. But they used to blow safes and that, see? When they'd knock a safe off they'd blow the door out.'

The associate had also heard a lot of talk over the years about the bomb sent to Phillips's place. 'But to my understanding ... he [Vince] didn't do it, right?' the associate says. 'Billy Phillips was seen with O'Dempsey after the bombing ... Vince tried to quieten it all down, you know, to make it look like it wasn't him. But see, he gave the order. There's no two ways about that, and Billy's sheila got her fucking hand blown off, didn't she?

'There you go.'

Not long before Vince O'Dempsey was released from gaol, he told a friend in gaol that he had a visitor appear in his cell. He said the devil had come and sat on the end of his bed. O'Dempsey said the devil spoke to him but the language was indecipherable.

The friend replied: 'I thought he might have told you to keep up the good work.'

A Black Day for Society

Vince O'Dempsey was released from Boggo Road Gaol in Brisbane's Dutton Park – just a couple of kilometres south-west of Highgate Hill – in December 1970. Before he was set free, he had some minor altercations with some of the Boggo screws who were harassing him as he waited, in his suit, to be let out.

Another prisoner was also due to be released at the same time. The second O'Dempsey got out, according to the other prisoner, he remarked that it was is 'a black day for society'. That's exactly what he said. Boggo Road … that's what furnished O'Dempsey. He came out a brand new shining fucking monster.'

O'Dempsey immediately went to stay with Billy McCulkin at his newly rented property in Dorchester Street. McCulkin would later tell police that O'Dempsey was there for about six weeks and was a model house guest. He used to go to bed early and he kept to himself.

His recent stint in gaol had certainly been his most prolonged time away from his home town and after his release O'Dempsey split his time between Brisbane and Warwick. By 15 February 1971, he had returned to Warwick and commenced work at a poultry farm in Dragon Street, across the railway line, just west of town. The farm was owned and run by a highly respected family in Warwick. 'Vince was just a factory worker in the abattoir,' says one former co-worker at the farm. 'He was dealing with knives and things like that. On any given day we were processing anywhere between 1500 and 3000 chickens. Vince was a good worker. He'd kill about 400 to 600 per day.'

During 'smoko', the workers would gather around the table in the smoko room and trade stories. 'He was an extremely interesting man to talk to,' the co-worker recalls. 'He could tell you anything you wanted to know about Appaloosa horses. He used to talk about his time in Boggo Road. He'd say you can get anything you like in prison, from tobacco to drugs. Blackmarket stuff.

'He used to insist he never, ever did any of it himself, the drugs and stuff. But he was the instigator, the organiser of the blackmarket stuff. Vince'd be in there in the smoko room eating his cake and chatting away. He was a very smart man, very cluey. But he had terrible eyes. Scary blue eyes. They were chilling.'

The co-worker recalls O'Dempsey expressing his hatred for the police. They were all 'pigs' to him. One day the co-worker said O'Dempsey approached the poultry farm workers during another break. 'Vince said to me that he never, ever killed anybody, he always got someone else to do it. He said that to a group of us. He said he'd never been found guilty of any murder, and that there were always ways around it. I really believed that man the day he said that.'

After two months at the poultry farm, O'Dempsey simply didn't turn up for work one day, and never returned. The farm's employment records show that the date O'Dempsey formally ceased employment was 23 April 1971.

His tenure may have been fleeting, but he left a lasting impression on his fellow workers. 'You often wondered what made him tick,' one said. 'We'd just sit there and listen to his stories and hear the things he had in his brain and just be amazed. You'd ask yourself – is he human? It was like he stepped out of a fairytale. Out of a book. We were naive I suppose. But we were left to wonder – did that really happen?'

While most of O'Dempsey's family still lived in Warwick, including his ageing parents, he also maintained a few old friendships. A creature of habit, at 32 years old O'Dempsey was fit from prison. He returned to his old rugby team, the Collegians, for a weekly hit-out.

To some of Warwick's young men at the time, he was already a legend. He'd bashed a copper almost to death. He'd done two stints in prison. He may have killed a man. When he was in town, playing pool, or going from one pub to another in Palmerin Street, the young toughs followed him like he was 'the Pied Piper'.

But O'Dempsey had plans, and fresh out of gaol he couldn't get traction without money. It didn't take long to realise that there was more money to be made in Brisbane. It was Billy McCulkin who got him a job at Queensland criminal identity Paul Meade's 'mock auction' shop in Queen Street.

Mock auctions were a scam that stemmed back to the Victorian era, where criminal associates of those running the auctions would act as fellow customers purchasing superior goods at bargain prices. The auctioneer would then win the trust of gullible buyers and sell them inferior or faulty goods at inflated prices. McCulkin would later tell police he worked 'wrapping things' with O'Dempsey at Meade's auctions. O'Dempsey, in fact, acted as both security guard and spruiker, enticing pedestrians to come into the auctions.

'You had to buy a box at the door to get in,' says one former visitor to the mock auctions. 'The condition of getting through the door was to buy a box. One day these two guys came in and they didn't have a box and O'Dempsey, being the pedantic bastard that he is, noticed this. He said they can't be in here. He thought they were jacks [police].

'He went over to them and he pointed out a sign on the wall which was one of those signs that says, you know, the management reserve the right to refuse entry to anybody. They told him to piss off so he read it to them again and asked them if they understood it. They told him it didn't apply to them because they were coppers. He said, "Who the fuck do they think they are?" When he got worked up his face was very stern. The eyes, they'd penetrate your skull. He told them to get out and said he'd remove them if they didn't. They left.'

O'Dempsey also enjoyed a good practical joke. A former associate recalls a day at the mock auctions when a lady tried to return a clock that didn't work. 'Vince said, "No worries Madam I'll fix it up for you." So ... they had this rat trap and they caught this dead rat. They threw it in the box and wrapped it back up and said, "There you go Madam. She's all fixed."

'He used to get on the [front] door and ... spruik out, "Come one, come all." Oh God, he was a funny one ... we did have some good times, you know?'

O'Dempsey would also make frequent trips to Sydney. It was there he met his future de facto wife, the prostitute Dianne Pritchard. Pritchard had somehow gotten herself involved in a sensational murder in Sydney in late 1968, when O'Dempsey was serving time in Boggo Road in Brisbane.

A woman, Miriam Mordo, 49, had been killed by a bomb placed in her car in Five Dock in the city's inner-west. Four men were charged, including Kingsley Harris, 26, of no fixed address. Harris allegedly told police he had been offered $2500 to frighten Mrs Mordo because she had made one of his co-accused, Paolo Falcone, 54, a baker in Five Dock, a 'slave' by giving him the 'evil eye'.

Dianne Margaret Pritchard, 18, of Victoria Street, Kings Cross, was charged with being an accessory after the fact, having harboured, maintained and assisted Harris following the murder. She was pregnant when she was charged. She was found guilty and sentenced to four years' imprisonment.

One of O'Dempsey and Pritchard's friends says they would have most certainly met in Sydney in the early 1970s. 'She was a prostitute in Sydney at the time and everyone in that community knew each other,' he says. 'She must have been introduced to him by his mate Stewart John Regan. She never had a brain to bless her with.'

Pritchard was also terrible 'on the drink'. Friend Carolyn Scully, sister to Tommy Hamilton, says: 'Well, she had a hard life. She got on the grog. She was shocking. She could be pretty aggressive if she was drinking. You couldn't say she was a good mother or anything, but she liked to be happy. She liked to go out. Liked to enjoy herself.'

Regan, like O'Dempsey, was deemed a psychopath by criminals and police alike. He would soon establish a small business empire in south-east Queensland, buying and selling land and renovating and flipping properties. Regan was particularly partial to the Noosa region and at one point would go on to make a property investment with O'Dempsey and businessman Paul Meade. But Regan's main source of income, his bread and butter, was on the mean streets of Sydney.

One newspaper report outlined Regan's credentials as a brothel keeper and hard man in the Cross: '… the surly criminal maintained a Harem like some Eastern sultan,' it wrote of him. 'Police knew that Regan's exploitation of Kings Cross prostitutes had been the basis of his fortune and believed that he kept his five key girls disciplined by knuckle and boot techniques. These five girls … earned up to $7000 a week between them, of which Regan took more than $5200 … the girls said he brought them flowers and gifts to the Kings Cross flats he provided for each of them.'

Mirroring Regan, O'Dempsey would soon become Brisbane's own vice hard man, and control the trade for corrupt police.

When O'Dempsey was in Brisbane, he would occasionally drink with McCulkin and others at the Lands Office Hotel, a hive of local and interstate criminals and corrupt police. They were known as the 'Lands Office Mob'.

O'Dempsey eventually secured his own flat in Harcourt Street, New Farm, but he still stayed in touch with McCulkin, dropping into Dorchester Street to offer racing tips.

McCulkin later offered a description of O'Dempsey as a man who took 'short quick steps like a woman'; that he held one arm in front of himself with his arm bent at right angles when talking; that he kept fit and did not smoke; that he had an intense interest in guns, particularly sawn-off shotguns; that he was in the Army and topped the class in ballistics; that he was colour blind; that he was hard to frighten, methodical, and tight with money; that he didn't like the sunlight because he was fair-skinned and burnt easily; and that he had a tattoo of St George and the Dragon on his chest, on his back and both legs.

O'Dempsey shared one trait with McCulkin. Both had tattoos of mice on their penises. It was why McCulkin was referred to as 'The Mouse'.

When he was back in Brisbane, O'Dempsey also stayed in touch with the young criminal and convicted rapist, Garry Reginald 'Shorty' Dubois, whom he'd met in Boggo Road. Dubois, in turn, would regroup with his old neighbourhood gang, including Tommy 'Clockwork Orange' Hamilton, Peter Hall and Keith Meredith.

Peter Hall later confirmed to police that by the 1970s the gang had graduated to a virtual full-time break and enter crew. 'We would usually drive around beforehand and check places and things out,' Hall recalled. 'We would go for small things, hairdressers and things, then if there was a bigger job that needed more men we would arrange to meet up at a time and place during the night and do the jobs together. We had a few contacts we used to get rid of the gear. It was just how we lived. We also had people we knew that would give us shopping lists and we would go and do shoplifts to get the items and sell them to the consumers at good prices.'

And where there was crime, there were corrupt police. Peter Hall remembered that the gang had a tidy arrangement with local coppers. 'There were some coppers we spoke to back then,' he later told police in a statement. 'Money would change hands, like a couple of hundred, and charges would be broken down … we never got off scot-free. 'They [the police] were from Nundah station, and when we first met they were nasty to us, so over time we got to know them. Sometimes they just got to keep the stuff they took off us. It didn't hurt to ask, sometimes if we got caught we would see if they could help. I can't remember their names but they busted me and Tom [Hamilton] at a house at Wavell Heights one time and after that we had a bit to do with them.'

Hall also recalled that Vince and Shorty were friends. 'They had been to prison together early on when Shorty was in his late teens. I noticed Vince seemed to have a hold over Shorty, and what Vince said Shorty would agree to. Vince was a bit older than us and was a solo kind of bloke, we knew him but he was not part of our crew.

'I knew he was someone who carried a handgun at various times and he was generally considered as a dangerous man that was not to be messed with.'

As for Vince, he was trying to turn a buck anywhere he could. One day in Queen Street, an acquaintance of O'Dempsey's from Warwick was in Brisbane on business and bumped into him. 'I remember that day,' the friend recalls. 'We'd stepped up onto the footpath and this voice says, "Hello, mate!" It was Vince. He was wearing a white suit and he sort of stepped out of an alcove. He asked me if I'd like to buy a watch. It was not long after he left the poultry farm. I said we didn't have time to talk. He was very polite.

'But we wanted to get away from there.'

Under Observation

Police Commissioner Ray Whitrod had only been in the top job since 1970 but in a very short time he and his methods had generated an enormous volume of enmity among the rank and file. He wanted his officers educated. He wanted more women in the force. And he wanted to rout out corrupt officers, especially the mythical Rat Pack he had been warned about before taking the top job – Terry Lewis, Tony Murphy and Glen Hallahan.

To weed out the bad apples, Whitrod established a special investigating group of men he trusted implicitly, and who were not afraid to bring down their fellow officers. His Police Minister, Max Hodges, gave Whitrod his full backing on this elite force. Among Whitrod's trusted officers were Detective Sergeant Basil 'The Hound' Hicks, Detective Senior Sergeant Jim Voigt, Detective Inspector Norm Gulbransen, Don Becker, Senior Constable Gregory Early and others who would come in and out of the fold.

By 21 September 1971, the newly formed Crime Intelligence Unit (CIU) was in full operation, working not in headquarters in the city, but out of a group of rooms at the police college in Laurel Avenue, Chelmer, west of the CBD. Their mission was to obtain information about any systems of graft and corruption to prevent the growth of potential 'crime rings' or 'crime bosses' using standover men and other means to achieve their ends. The CIU would also look at preventing Queensland police officers being leveraged by criminals and their networks.

From the outset, Whitrod declared that his CIU would initially focus on some 'target' criminals. One such target was the Clockwork Orange Gang. An officer familiar with the case at the time said: 'As early as 1971–72 the CIU started working with the Feds on the Clockwork Orange Gang and their links to the Painters and Dockers Union. The CIU brought in the help of the Federal Narcotics squad, the Commonwealth Police ... and Customs.

'The opinion was that the Clockwork Orange Gang was a group of heavy criminals and they were starting to get a little bit too big for their boots.' He said the gang was easily the biggest and most dominating criminal gang in Brisbane in the 1970s. 'With these guys you can see over time a natural evolution,' he said. 'They start out as kids at places like Westbrook. They begin with a bit of break and entering, some shoplifting, and they work out ways to make more money as time goes by.

'Invariably there are police in there working with them, and those police take on some of these criminals as informants. Sometimes the informant will commit a crime, and the police will let them get away with these things, turn a blind eye, as long as they give the cops information on other crimes. At the same time, informants are trained in their own system as well. And over time police will give back information to the informant, so it all swings around together as the police, the crims and their relationship with each other evolves.'

The CIU was prescient in keeping the Clockwork Orange Gang under surveillance. Detective Basil 'The Hound' Hicks had a couple of informants, including John Andrew Stuart, whom he'd known since he was a teenager in the late 1950s when Stuart was first sent to Westbrook. Billy McCulkin was also an occasional informant to Hicks, who would record all of their conversations and compile intelligence on the movements of various suspected criminals. At times McCulkin would talk about Vincent O'Dempsey.

'At one point he [Billy] was S.P. betting from the Lands Office [Hotel] and O'Dempsey may have been involved,' Hicks later said. 'But he [Billy] went on quite a bit about ... talking about him, what he's capable of doing. He talked about he'd heard he'd murdered people.'

The CIU noticed that over time the Clockwork Orange Gang's criminal enterprise seemed to be evolving. Less than 18 months after the unit's formation, the gang, or fractured elements of the gang, would elevate their criminality that would ultimately end in murder.

As the police source said: 'Think about the sort of informant you might want to cultivate if you were a police officer. For people like Detective Tony Murphy, your aim was to get the best criminals as your informants. If you got that, you were the best police officer.

'And just think if you had criminal Vince O'Dempsey as your informant. He could go anywhere, talk to anyone, and get any answer. That's the ultimate informant.'

For years, Tony Murphy had been one of former Queensland police commissioner Frank Bischof's favoured 'boys', his prize detective. When Bischof retired in 1969, former ASIO man, head of the Commonwealth police and an 'outsider' to Queensland, honest Ray Whitrod, was given the job.

Within two years Whitrod had identified the so-called Rat Pack and had gone about dismantling it. Hallahan resigned, and Murphy was charged with perjury stemming out of evidence he gave before the National Hotel royal commission in late 1963. While Murphy's case never got through the courts courtesy of the suspicious 'suicide' of the main witness against him, the prostitute Shirley Brifman, he developed a pathological hatred of Whitrod and was intent on destroying the commissioner.

Murphy himself was tough, relentless and no stranger to violence. He commanded and received his men's loyalty. In return, he was unwaveringly loyal to his friends, and brutal towards his perceived enemies. These were qualities he shared with O'Dempsey, and it seemed inevitable that they would cross paths.

As one associate observed: 'At one point Vince was a strong arm for the vice trade, right? Like if the molls were playing up or anyone stepped out of line he'd fucking ... [you] couldn't go and stand on the street corner and say, "Righto, well I'm going to get the molls there and just open up business."

'If he [Vince] found out he'd come around and fucking pull the guts out of me. That'd be it, you wouldn't survive. You had to get his permission.

'If the bikies turned up and said, "Right, we're fucking going to open a brothel here and I'm going to put some molls in" they had to go through Vince. They weren't allowed to just go and set up then. Vince would fucking bomb them.

'Was he a middle man for corrupt police? That's something I don't know. Everybody was corrupt back then, so I don't know. Like, if you're asking for a copper's name, the only copper I know is Murphy. They had problems, they go to Murphy, Murphy will fix their problem.'

A Menace Returns

Convicted felon John Andrew Stuart was finally due for release from Sydney's Long Bay Correctional Complex on 25 July 1972. Sydney police warned their Queensland colleagues that Stuart was heading back home once he was discharged. They said he planned to hold a press conference of some description.

There were many who were wary of his homecoming.

Police in Brisbane issued a special crime circular to all officers warning them of Stuart as a 'very active criminal' who should be 'treated with extreme caution'.

In what may or may not have been an extraordinary coincidence, just as Stuart arrived home in Brisbane, two of the country's most significant and feared gangsters paid a visit to the Whiskey Au Go Go nightclub in Fortitude Valley. They were none other than Sydney crime figures Lenny McPherson and Paddles Anderson.

The Whiskey Au Go Go, commonly called the Whiskey, had been purchased by 30-year-old professional company director, Brian Little. Little and his brother had invested in the club on the advice of entertainment guru John Hannay. Hannay was a well-known booking agent for musicians, and managed bands for nightclubs all over town through his company Prestige Artists.

Over the years Hannay had also dabbled in the restaurant game. In the mid-1960s he opened The Cave coffee lounge in Elizabeth Street and then The Pearl Restaurant across the road. According to author Geoff Plunkett in *The Whiskey Au Go Go Massacre*, The New Zealand-born Brian Little had been booking entertainers through Hannay's business since December 1971. They named the club after the world famous Whiskey Au Go Go in West Hollywood.

> The club was an instant hit with its clientele ... the Littles were netting $1500 per week. In June 1972, another club, the Sound Machine Discotéque at 74 Elizabeth Street, folded. Following the instant success of the Whiskey, the Littles, with Hannay's encouragement, took over the failed nightclub. Renaming it Chequers Nightclub, they aimed for the high-end market ... the club opened in mid-August to great fanfare, with the lavish opening attended by Brisbane's VIP set.

The Brisbane Whiskey, however, was a far cry from the West Hollywood venue. Even the Sydney club, which had been trading successfully under the same name in William Street, had go-go dancers. Brisbane did not. From the outset, though, the Brisbane Whiskey did attract all sorts of criminals and ladies of the night. According to a police statement by Whiskey bouncer John Bell, it was Brian Aherne, owner of the notorious Lands Office Hotel in the city, who brought Sydney's two big crime gangsters to visit the Whiskey.

'[Brian] introduced me to two men, one named Lenny McPherson from Sydney, and the other Paddles Anderson, a more frailer type of man,' Bell said. 'They were very respectable at all stages.'

Why would two of Sydney's biggest heavies be paying the Whiskey a casual visit at precisely the time Stuart had returned to Brisbane?

Of no fixed address, Stuart had spent his first few months out of gaol staying with family and friends in Brisbane. He was regularly stopping by 6 Dorchester Street, Highgate Hill, to catch up with his mate Billy McCulkin. In the spring of 1972 Stuart was also proving a disturbing element on the club scene in Brisbane, and especially at the Whiskey Au Go Go. Hyperactive, a drug addict and a perennial troublemaker, he was constantly on the lookout for a job to pull or cash to scam. If that involved violence, then so be it.

During the next few months Stuart made repeated attempts to engage the owners of the Whiskey in conversation and made a number of threats. First he demanded money from the Little brothers, and then offered his services for protection against the Sydney gangs who he claimed were intending to take over the Brisbane clubs.

According to Plunkett, Stuart attempted to stand over Hannay for $2000, believing Hannay owed this amount to an entertainer who sang at the Lands Office Hotel. Records viewed by Plunkett suggest that Stuart and McCulkin also tried to intimidate Hannay outside Chequers Nightclub, and left a number of threatening messages for the Little brothers, which suggested Hannay would get 'seven bullets in the heart'.

Stuart was also telling Detective Hicks of the CIU that he had been contacted by Sydney gangster Lenny 'Mr Big' McPherson, who wanted to meet him at the Iluka Resort building in Surfers Paradise on the Gold Coast. Stuart said it appeared McPherson wanted to talk about a racket extorting nightclubs in Brisbane, and he needed Stuart's help.

True or false, these allegations to Hicks were the birth of an alibi for a despicable crime that would be months in the making.

The Prisoner of Dorchester Street

What dreams did Barbara McCulkin have, this young mother from a small country town, as she sat in her rundown rented Queenslander with its view of a petrol station in inner-Brisbane? Had she envisaged this – the worker's cottage with the slumped fence and cracked window out front, the abusive and philandering husband, the convicted criminals breezing in and out of the house – when as a child she performed a sketch in a Sunday School concert called 'A Wedding in Fairy Land'?

By late 1972, Barbara had been married to Billy for almost 12 years, and life with him and their two children – Vicki, 12, and Leanne, 10 – in the house at 6 Dorchester Street, Highgate Hill, was far from fairy land.

How could she have seen this, coming from a good country family, having grown up in a sprawling Queenslander not far from the Mary River in Maryborough, 255 kilometres north of Brisbane? Here she sat, already feeling old and neglected, at her sewing machine, making her own and her daughters' clothes while her husband was in town, drinking heavily with workmates and criminal associates.

The only star in Barbara McCulkin's firmament as the year drew to a close was the bulb of her sewing machine. Then 33, Barbara was a good mother with an uncertain future. Billy had rarely seen full-time work since his time in the Royal Australian Navy in the late 1950s and into the 1960s, and money was always tight. They had no car (Billy McCulkin professed that he couldn't drive), so Barbara and the children's social life was restricted to public transport and the kindness of friends with a vehicle.

Since 1971 she had worked at the Milky Way snack bar in the Brisbane CBD. Her employer, Joseph Toth, would later describe her as 'an excellent worker, a reliable worker, very nice'. At the Milky Way, Barbara struck up a good friendship with her co-worker Ellen Gilbert. It was in Gilbert she confided about her deteriorating relationship with her husband.

'Mrs McCulkin informed me that her marital relationship was not normal and that her husband came and went at will from their place of residence,' Gilbert would later reflect. '[Barbara] informed me that her husband had beaten her and that she had not been able to attend work as a result of the beating received from him.'

On one occasion he bruised her arm and broke all the crockery in the kitchen. That night she took her daughters and stayed with Mrs Gilbert. Joseph Toth would later confirm that Barbara often came to work showing signs of injury, inflicted by Billy. Toth said sometimes Billy would telephone the café and say: 'Barbara needed a good biffing so she can't come into work today.'

McCulkin, drunk, would often boast about his sexual conquests to his wife. Barbara knew that he had fathered a child with some 'Russian' woman. He had also slept with one of Barbara's close friends. That time she unsuccessfully tried to kill herself with an overdose of sleeping pills.

Billy McCulkin would later say about that period in his life: 'Why does anyone leave their wife? Because they're incompatible or far fields are green, or something.'

By early 1973, McCulkin and Stuart were hanging out almost daily at Dorchester Street. Stuart was telling stories to local tabloid reporter Brian 'The Eagle' Bolton about how Sydney gangsters were set to instigate a comprehensive extortion racket over Brisbane nightclubs. If the clubs didn't comply, they'd be torched. Bolton sensed a good story, and began quoting Stuart in inflammatory articles about the Sydney crime push.

Then a small incident occurred in the Brisbane suburb of Fortitude Valley that on the surface seemed to bear out Stuart's wild allegations.

Lucy Kirkov, assistant to Whiskey manager John Hannay, was hearing rumours about her boss and could barely keep up with his business ventures. She'd been working for him since she was a teenager, when he first opened The Cave coffee lounge in the city in the mid-1960s, and although she knew he was gay, he had a peculiar emotional hold on her.

As well as managing clubs for the Little brothers, Hannay was also running his own establishments. In late 1972, he asked Kirkov to help set up a bar and restaurant called Alice's in Brunswick Street, just around the corner from the Whiskey Au Go Go. At the time she was uncertain about Alice's, its purpose and its intended clientele. 'It had like a bar, where you can make coffee and things like that, and maybe two tables and chairs. I did meet a guy that Hannay brought along with him one day, and he said, "Oh, meet so and so. He's a gangster from down south." It was a guy called [Lenny] McPherson.'

Kirkov says Hannay owed money all over Brisbane, to clubs, musicians, suppliers, and his reputation had hit rock bottom. 'Hannay never paid his bands, see? He used to have all these bands play, and he'd say, "Go and see Lucy … and she'll pay you." But I had no authority. I didn't even have a cheque book, so I couldn't do that. So they all come to see me for money, and I couldn't pay them … there was nothing I could do. I used to have to take money to a post box, and I forget what, who that was for, but it was always, "Can you drop this in the mail?" or "Can you drop that there?" No questions asked, I'd do it.'

It had been a similar experience when she was managing The Pearl Restaurant. She recalls, 'He didn't have a liquor licence and he used to say to me, "Don't serve any grog tonight, there's going to be trouble." And I couldn't understand why. Because you know, like, why would there be trouble? But obviously the Licensing Branch coppers or … somebody's told him that [there might be a raid] because I used to think, you know, how does he know all these things?'

Alice's operated for a short time and instantly garnered a reputation as a meeting place for men in search of underage boys. Kirkov soon realised it was the replacement venue to The Cave, which in the 1960s became the local hangout for teenagers below the legal drinking age to meet. When Kirkov had first started working at The Cave she noticed that the regular clientele included young effeminate teenage boys, and groups of even younger boys, aged around 13 years. She said Hannay would often befriend the kids, and because he didn't like the way they dressed, he used to buy them clothes.

'One day I sat with them and I said, "How come you guys are here every afternoon?" and they said they went to therapy, and I said, "What kind of therapy?" They said, "Well, we're going for therapy because we don't know whether we're gay or not." I told them I thought they'd know if they were or not. They said, "No, because we like women's company, but we like men's company better."'

Kirkov recalls: 'There used to be a team of three police who used to come in for morning tea, lunch; another lot for afternoon tea and dinner, and all that sort of stuff. It was always [Tony] Murphy, [Glen] Hallahan, and there was another guy but I don't know what happened to him.'

A friend of Hannay's at the time confirms the police presence at The Cave. Police Commissioner Frank Bischof had recently set up his Juvenile Aid Bureau and put Tony Murphy in charge. 'John was probably most involved with Glen Hallahan,' he says. 'As for Bischof, we used to call him "Bischof the boy killer". The word was he shot a paperboy in Melbourne Street, South Brisbane. At that hotel, the Terminus.'

Years later, when asked if it was true that Bischof was a regular visitor to The Cave, Hannay replied, 'Yes, Bischof.' When asked if he knew Tony Murphy, Hannay nodded. It was nothing new. In his line of business over the decades, he knew virtually everybody in the city when it came to restaurants, nightclubs and entertainers, let alone police and politicians.

According to author Geoff Plunkett, around the time that Kirkov was helping Hannay to manage Alice's, Hannay was sacked by the Little brothers. John Bell took over the Whiskey's management. By this stage the Littles's clubs were in debt and accountants had been appointed to liquidate both the Whiskey and Chequers.

Then, less than two months later on 16 January 1973, Alice's went up in flames, supposedly taking the financial records of the Whiskey Au Go Go with it.

Police suspected an insurance scam but nobody was charged with any offences in relation to the fire. Criminal Billy Stokes says: 'When Hannay moved into the Whiskey Au Go Go he had the liquor licence, he was the only one authorised to write a cheque, he did all the hiring and firing of everyone there, but his official role was as the bookkeeper, and sort of like a manager ... he said he kept all the Whiskey records at Alice's restaurant ... there was a fire in Alice's and the records were lost. Now after those records are lost this is when everyone learned the Whiskey was broke and owed a squillion.'

And what of the Whiskey records? Had Hannay arranged the torching of Alice's not only for insurance, but to incinerate incriminating evidence in the Whiskey's ledgers showing that large amounts of money had mysteriously gone missing?

One close friend of Hannay's at the time said: 'I don't think John kept any financial books for the Whiskey. At the end of the year, if you had to pay tax, you'd do the records up then.

'John didn't keep records.'

Torino's

Brisbane was suddenly a city of fires.

In January 1973 two arson attempts were also made on Chequers Nightclub in the city, the other salubrious venue owned by brothers Ken and Brian Little. The fires were only small and because the damage was minor, the Littles didn't report them to police.

Meanwhile, journalist Brian Bolton was continuing to receive information from John Andrew Stuart about the Sydney protection racket that he threatened would soon be overtaking the nightclub scene in south-east Queensland. According to records witnessed by author Geoff Plunkett, just four weeks after the fires at Chequers and Alice's, on 20 February 1973, Bolton made a call to Police Minister Max Hodges to pass on some important information.

'I suppose you've been told of the bombing threat on the Whiskey Au Go Go?' Bolton asked Hodges.

'No, what's that all about?'

'I've told [Police Comissioner] Mr Whitrod and Inspector [Don] Becker of several yarns I've had with John Andrew Stuart, you know of him?'

'Yes.'

'And he says that an extortion racket is soon to blow up in the nightclubs in Brisbane and the Gold Coast,' Bolton continued. 'He says the men behind it are going to blow up an empty club, first as a warning, and if none of the owners takes any notice they're going to blow up the Whiskey Au Go Go because it's the easiest one to get at, while it's full of people.'

'No, I haven't heard anything about it,' the Police Minister said. 'Next time I'm talking to Ray [Whitrod] I must ask him what he knows.'

Then, something happened that suggested Stuart's prophecy was coming true. Five days later, at around 9.25 p.m. on 25 February 1973, a quiet Sunday evening in Fortitude Valley was shattered by a massive explosion in Torino's restaurant and nightclub at 671 Ann Street, not far from the precincts main bars and clubs.

Decades later, Clockwork Orange Gang member Peter Hall confessed to the crime. He said he and the gang had been seconded by Vincent O'Dempsey and Billy McCulkin to bomb Torino's. 'We were paid to set the place alight, and we were told it was arranged by the owners of the club,' Hall said in a police witness statement in the murder trial of Garry 'Shorty' Dubois in late 2016. 'The deal was organised by Vince O'Dempsey through Shorty. We were told that it was an insurance job, and we were paid $500, which was split four ways.'

Peter Hall recalled setting the Torino's fire. 'I remember this night we did a drive-by, there were no lights on inside, so we parked the car and walked in, we forced the side or back door and took in big containers of petrol,' he later told police. 'It was pretty dark and I didn't know the place, there was an upstairs area and I went up there. No one was there ... we had been told no one would be on the premises, but we checked. We had two big plastic containers which contained fuel. We spread it all around in there, just downstairs, made a petrol trail to just outside the door we had forced and set it alight. I think it was Tom [Hamilton] who lit the match.'

Hall said they almost blew the Torino's shopfront onto themselves, such was the power of the explosion. 'As we were leaving the front windows blew out,' he recalled. 'We thought the fire would just follow the trail, we didn't realise the fumes would cause an explosion of sorts. We didn't really know what we were doing and we almost blew ourselves up. No one was hurt but we gave ourselves a fright.

'I recall we were driving the green Studebaker, it was parked a block or so away and we ran back to the car. We watched the fire for a bit from a distance.'

Brisbane woke to the news that the Torino Restaurant and Nightclub – run by brothers Frank and Tony Ponticello – had been 'bombed'.

Police suspected a bomb, given the extent of the damage, yet detectives were puzzled. The blast seemed disproportionate to the space being targeted. It appeared the perpetrators may have used a combination of gelignite, petrol and the building's gas main. The Ponticello brothers told police they knew nobody who had a grudge against them.

'That was our first and only big job,' Hall admitted. 'This was a big deal for us, up until that point we were just break and enter people, but it was good money and we got quite a buzz or an adrenalin hit out of it.'

At the time, Tommy Hamilton and Peter Hall also confessed to Tommy's sister, Carolyn Scully, about their involvement in the Torino's fire. 'It was Billy McCulkin that organised all of that,' she recalls. 'That's what he told me. Vince wasn't even here [in Brisbane]. Peter told me, then Tommy told me. And then he [Tommy] said about the money. He was supposed to get $500 and then $500 afterwards and he [McCulkin] didn't give him the other $500. He just cheated them out of it.

'And I said, "You've done what you've done for what? And you could have been killed. What a fool. What a stupid thing to do." They wanted the money, that's all. Within a week and a half the police investigated it and said it was a gas leak. So it's over and done with. Finished. No one knew.'

Over in Dorchester Street, Barbara McCulkin had for some weeks been picking up information about the impending 'fires' through the rogue's gallery of criminals visiting her husband, Billy. The house was full of chatter about the arson jobs and Stuart's claims that Sydney bigshots were behind the string of fires. Even Vicki and Leanne were piecing together snippets of information they heard in conversations in the house in those early months of the year.

According to sources, Vicki was sharing stories about the fires with one of the children of Billy Phillips. By this stage, the Phillips's family was living directly behind the McCulkins, and shared a gate on the back fence, an escape route of sorts, when needed, between the two families.

Barbara continued to work at the Milky Way café despite the mayhem around her, and cryptically said to her workmate Ellen Gilbert about the Torino's bombing: 'I'll tell you something funny about that one day.'

What did Barbara have to tell that was so humorous? Could it have been that she knew who was behind the Torino's arson, her husband included, and that the fools had nearly gotten themselves killed blowing up the joint?

For journalist Brian 'The Eagle' Bolton, the blaze at Torino's confirmed that a wave of terror was about to hit the city. It was vindication of the scare stories he'd been running for weeks. Bolton wrote:

> The bombing of a Valley nightclub last Sunday was just the first shot in a massive extortion racket by Sydney criminals demanding protection money from clubs between Brisbane and the border. One Sydney crime lord and another ranking crime

boss are plotting to milk at least $10,000 a week from dozens of clubs and class restaurants.

When *Sunday Sun* put the result of its investigations to the Police Commissioner Mr Whitrod, he said: 'Police are working on this line of inquiry.'

Bolton wrote that criminals were set to demand 'a huge slice of the takings using the protection racket threat as well as a choking split of fees paid to entertainers they will insist be employed by nightspot operators'. The story continued:

The demands, it was decided, would be made after the first warning – the bombing a few weeks later of an empty Brisbane nightclub. If the nightspot operators did not heed the follow-up ransom demands, expected in the next couple of months, the bombing weapon would be used with no warning.

It was all wild and heady stuff from Bolton. John Andrew Stuart had told him this was coming, and it had. But the problem with the story, and Bolton's theories of a southern takeover, was that you had to trust and believe John Andrew Stuart, a notorious liar. Despite all of his warnings, Stuart was nowhere near Ann Street on the night of the Torino fire. In fact, in what would amount to a fortunate coincidence, he was languishing in the city watchhouse, having been arrested earlier that evening for being in possession of a concealable firearm.

What Bolton and the police didn't know was that the perpetrators of Torino's were not from the Sydney badlands. They were local boys, who, after the job, had gone home to their rented place in Brisbane's inner-north and drank the bottles of liquor they'd stolen from the now incinerated restaurant and bar. They were also unaware at this stage, that Stuart's close friend, James Richard

Finch, had just arrived back in Brisbane from the United Kingdom and that together the two would become embroiled in the plot of one of Australia's worst mass murders.

One associate says he visited the home of some members of the Clockwork Orange Gang the morning after the Torino's bombing. 'I had met O'Dempsey in Boggo Road [in the 1960s],' he says. 'I didn't meet Dubois until after the end of 1972. I met McCulkin around town, [and] at the auction shops they had in the heart of town.

'The Clockwork Orange Gang, they rented a nice house. They had two Studebakers. Shorty Dubois's girlfriend was still going to school, and she'd bring her schoolgirl mates back to the house. On the Monday morning I was on my way to work in town and I popped in to say hi. Hamilton admitted to torching Torino's. Hamilton, Dubois, Hall and Meredith, they all told me that. They were all laughing.

'They said O'Dempsey and McCulkin got them to do that.'

A Warning

Just days after the bombing of Torino's on 27 February, a Brisbane Commonwealth Police officer, Sergeant Bill Humphris, reported in to Detective Sergeant Jim Voigt from Whitrod's Crime Intelligence Unit (CIU) with some interesting details he was receiving from an informant.

Humphris reported that Stuart had told his informant that the 'B … brothers' intended on bombing the Whiskey Au Go Go nightclub on Petrie Terrace, 'by placing a bomb on the ground floor of the building while patrons were being entertained on the floor above'. Apparently they had told Stuart he could earn as much as $5000 per week if he would approach nightclub owners on behalf of a Sydney syndicate. Stuart allegedly told the informant they would first have to bomb a couple of clubs to show the owners they meant business.

Humphris's information, however, was not immediately passed up the chain to Whitrod. Why? Given Voigt's reputation for honesty and diligence, had the information indeed been passed on to the commissioner's office but blocked before Whitrod could see it?

Detective Basil Hicks of the CIU also had a number of conversations around this time in which Stuart insisted that there was going to be another fire. On 28 February Stuart visited Hicks at his office and told him that four fellows from Sydney were asking him to make contacts around the clubs, so they could 'come up and bomb one and collect money from the others'. At one point Stuart was close to tears. He told Hicks: 'You don't understand. They told me what they were going to do ... and they'll expect me to do my part. I want someone to [go] round the clubs with me while I tell them I won't have any part in it.'

The problem was, each time Stuart told his story, the details changed. According to author Geoff Plunkett, Hicks wrote notes on his recorded conversations with Stuart:

> I don't believe his story about the people from Sydney ... It is possible he is just making the whole thing up to get more attention from Brian Bolton ... Also he wants to make it known that if anything happens he is not responsible.

According to police records seen by Plunkett, Jim Voigt also made notes on the intelligence coming in from the Commonwealth Police in relation to the Torino's incident.

> We believe the recent fires have been for insurance purposes ... We know that Stuart has been standing over club owners in Brisbane. However, we of the Crime Intelligence Unit

are of the opinion that threats by Stuart and recent publicity is only a front for owners of various places to burn them down for insurance reasons, and we are almost certain that was the case with the burning of Hannay's nightclub.

It seemed extraordinary that at this point in history, in the days before the Whiskey tragedy occurred, various nightclub owners and managers across Brisbane, assorted local gangsters and nightclub crooners and band managers, a journalist, and members of the Queensland State police force and of the Australian Commonwealth Police were aware that a nightclub was going to be variously firebombed or, incredibly, hit with hand grenades, and that it was likely to be the Whiskey Au Go Go, and that it would probably take place around Wednesday 7 March. But the warnings weren't heeded.

Indeed, in the days leading up to the Whiskey tragedy, rumours were also filtering through to political circles. On the first day back from Christmas break, there was some curious and strangely prescient debate happening in State Parliament. During Question Without Notice, Russell Hinze – not yet a Cabinet Minister – addressed his own Minister for Works and Housing (whose responsibility also included the police), Max Hodges.

In parliament, Hinze asked Hodges if he had seen a statement in the previous Sunday's *Sunday Sun* about a group of southern criminals who appeared to be coming to the Brisbane and Gold Coast areas and standing over restaurant proprietors. Hinze asked: 'Is he prepared to assure the House that ample police protection is available both on the Gold Coast and in Brisbane to stamp out any Mafia-type hoodlums who may try to enter this State?'

Hodges replied: 'This matter is under control by the Police Department. I can give the honourable member that assurance.'

It was a loaded question from Hinze, directed at one of

the government's own Cabinet Ministers and by proxy Police Commissioner Whitrod. Why would Hinze direct a Question Without Notice to a member of his own government? Had he been swallowing journalist Brian Bolton's fantastical reports of a Sydney crime gang takeover of Brisbane nightclubs, or did he know something that nobody else did? Or was Hinze joining the growing band of those opposed to Ray Whitrod's commissionership of the Queensland police. The dissenters, with detective Tony Murphy at the forefront, had been railing against Whitrod even before he was formally sworn in as commissioner in 1970.

Whitrod's attempt to modernise the force through education, the admission of more women and the introduction of a system of promotion based on merit and not seniority, had more than pricked at the rank and file. There was open sedition. And the rancour had finally caught the attention of Premier Joh Bjelke-Petersen.

Whitrod had survived several votes of no confidence in his leadership from the powerful police union, and had stood firm against the threats and childish practical jokes. But there was a sense in the first months of 1973 that anything was possible when it came to destabilising his power.

It appeared Whitrod was under siege from both the government and the Opposition. All that was needed to underline his incompetency and unsuitability for the job was a major, perhaps shocking, public catastrophe. As it transpired, that would serendipitously occur in less than 48 hours.

Prelude to a Tragedy

On the evening of 7 March 1973, Lucy Kirkov, former manager of a number of clubs and restaurants owned by impresario John Hannay, was having drinks in the Whiskey Au Go Go nightclub. Among the city's surfeit of nightclubs and drinking spots, the Whiskey had quickly earned a seedy reputation. Petty gangsters and corrupt police came and went. Working girls were rumoured to be operating out of the long, rectangular first-floor club.

Kirkov occasionally worked at the Whiskey, and knew the new manager, John Bell, and the Little brothers. The likeable Bell was a well-known figure in the local club scene, in part for his imposing size, and his attractive, genial, fun-loving personality. He had taken over from John Hannay when Hannay was sacked in November the year before.

Bell's daughter, Kathy, recalled the days her father worked at the Whiskey nightclub. 'If I wanted to see him I always went into the Whiskey,' said Kathy, who was about 13 years old in early 1974. 'I'd meet him there, and I met, you know, all those sort of famous actors who used to sing in there. But yeah, I'd always come down to the Whiskey because they all did their business during the daytime and then he would sleep of an afternoon, and then go back to the club.'

She said she remembered her father talking about how there was talk at the time of criminals wanting to extort clubs and restaurants throughout Brisbane. 'Well, he did say that they were trying to take over,' she recalled. 'But Brisbane was such a small country town back in those days. And he used to say to me all the time, "I don't know what they want", you know.

'But I know my dad really loved [Premier] Joh Bjelke-Petersen because they could do whatever they wanted, they never had to worry about the law. You know, it really was a paradise up here [in Queensland]. Basically, you know, they said there was no casinos up here and there was no poker machines up here. But just about everything else went on. I think that John Stuart left down there [Sydney], thought he could take over [up here] because he knew people, and everyone went, "Nah, you're nobody, really."'

Kathy said corrupt police were always in and out of the Whiskey. Bell had a good relationship with some of them. So much so that Bell telephoned and warned them that something was going to 'go down' on the night of the fire.

'Dad said that they always had to pay somebody,' she recalled. 'And, you know, I remember him saying about Russ Hinze always coming and getting money. They always had bags of money. They always had police in there … I don't know who they were. But there were always corrupt police in the Whiskey or down at the Wharfies Club. It didn't matter where you went, there was always corruption. Dad always said the police were corrupt and he loved it, he thought it was great, you know, they made so much money because the police were so corrupt and they would come to the club.

'The police did know about the Whiskey Au Go Go that night, you know, because my dad had rung them and told them that Stuart would be in that night and they were told that something was going to go down. They were like, "No, no, nothing's going to happen." But it did happen, of course.'

Lucy Kirkov enjoyed drinking at the Whiskey, particularly the special 'staff nights' where off-duty staff would get together for a dance. On the evening of Wednesday 7 March, the night of the fatal fire, she was at the Whiskey when two men – both strangers to Kirkov – appeared at the reception desk. It was just after midnight.

'I was at the Whiskey that night to see somebody or do something and I saw James Finch and John Andrew Stuart at the front door,' she recalls. 'They didn't come in and sit down, they were just at the front door. I was about to leave and James Finch asked me if I wanted a lift home. They ended up leaving and I said to Belly [John Bell], who are they? And he told me that was Stuart and Finch.'

Criminal Robert John Griffith, an associate of Stuart and Finch, and erstwhile informant to Detective Tony Murphy, also happened to be driving through the Valley in the hours before the fatal fire.

Griffith said in a statement that he had become aware from talk on the street that something was going to happen at the Whiskey Au Go Go.

'As I drove past I saw Vincent O'Dempsey standing in the shadows to the right of the entrance to the [Whiskey] nightclub,' he said. 'I recognised O'Dempsey immediately.'

Inferno

Just as Bell had predicted in his unheeded warning to police, there were about 30 to 50 people at the Whiskey as midnight ticked over to 8 March. A young local band called Trinity was keeping the small crowd entertained while they waited for the main act, The Delltones, to arrive and do their show.

Trinity member Bevan Childs said it was the opportunity of a lifetime to play with The Delltones. 'Oh yeah, they were pros, you know?' He recalls: 'I don't know how many sets [we did], I don't know what time The Delltones left. I mean they probably would have had two gigs in town that night, probably an early one and a later one. Yeah, probably later than ten or something like that. So they would have been well gone by midnight I'm guessing.

'After our set, you know, after playing with The Delltones, we just sat down and had a drink.'

★

Just a few blocks away, nightclub performer and impressionist, Lyndon Brown, had finished his last set for the night at the seedy Flamingos club and planned to head up to the Whiskey to meet friends for a nightcap. Flamingos, in Little Street just off Wickham Street, was a joint frequented by the Lands Office crowd – tattooist Billy Phillips, Stuart, Finch, even Vince O'Dempsey – and fights among patrons were not uncommon.

The seasoned and popular Brown knew everyone in the scene, from Hannay to the Little brothers to John Bell. In the months leading up to 8 March, he'd also heard some disturbing news on the grapevine. 'We knew that one of the clubs was going to get hit, and I was a bit worried about Flamingos, there was only the stairs and front door and you had to go down into the dressing room. You got dressed under the stairs in a little room down there.

'We used to talk about it quite often. There'd been a bit of a power struggle happening in the Valley at that point for quite some time, with the Sydney mob. I used to try and keep out of it. I had my own job to do.'

But Brown did discuss the troubles with Flamingos owner Abe Yassar and bouncer Alf Quick. 'I knew Alf at Flamingos,' recalls Brown. 'He was on the level. He was just a doorman, that's all. You met everyone through Abe. I met a lot of the crooked cops through them. They came in for a drink and he'd just feed them and talk to them.

'Billy Phillips and Finch and all them, they'd come in virtually every night, into Flamingos. They'd sit down and have drinks ... That's why I knew we weren't going to be hit.

'Abe was the first one to tell me that a club was going to go up. Prior to that, all that trouble going on with the Bellinos and the rest of them, the Wickham Hotel, that's where it started ... The Wickham had been one of the main points for trouble, and a lot of people were a bit scared about going in there. A lot of the rough nuts down there were giving everyone a hard time. I'd heard there was a bit of protection money being put on people to look after them so they wouldn't get hurt around the place.'

Brown said several familiar faces were at Flamingos the night the Whiskey went up. 'There were a few of them in there that night,' he says. 'I'd been down to the pub on the corner ... [but] I just raced back to Abe's to do the show at around midnight. I did the show and they were sitting in there at their normal table … I didn't think anything of it.

'I had to go down to the Whiskey directly after my show to meet up with a couple of friends who were supposedly in there. I was going to have a catch-up and a drink. I finished the show, had a beer with Abe, jumped in the car and went down to the Whiskey.'

At close to 2 a.m Stuart would make a fuss about the time and even asked Quick to use the phone to call and establish the exact time. He was adamant that he be placed in Flamingos. It was imperative he had an iron-clad alibi at that hour, given he knew what was about to happen.

Brown, in the meantime, had hopped in his car and was making the short drive to the Whiskey.

It was just after 2 a.m.

★

It might have been the early hours of a Thursday morning, but there were plenty of people out and about in Fortitude Valley, and within a short proximity of the Whiskey Au Go Go. Kath Potter was just around the corner from the entrance to the club. She was in the public phone box on St Pauls Terrace trying to find her boyfriend, whom she'd arranged to meet at the Whiskey.

Kath had a hunch he might be at Chequers, so she phoned the club, only to be told that he was at the Whiskey. Frustrated, she tried to get further clues as to where he might be. 'All I can tell anyone is that, yes, I was at Whiskey Au Go Go on the night in question with my girlfriend Elizabeth,' she recalled. 'We went there at the request of my boyfriend at the time to meet him and have a couple of drinks and then go home as it was a week night and I had work the next day. Liz and I had a couple of drinks, looked for Bob [but] couldn't find him, so the pair of us went down to the phone booth that was outside the club and over the road from the Shamrock. [We] made a phone call to Chequers up in the city to see if he was there and coming down. I was told Bob had left for the evening.'

Michael Kevin Dee, a truck driver and motor mechanic of Toowong, had been drinking inside the Whiskey with Ernest Peters and his son Desmond, two friends from the country who'd been in Brisbane buying a horse at the yearling sales. It had been a heavy drinking session, and by 2 a.m. Dee had had enough.

'Oh, I'd had a fair bit to drink,' Dee would later tell the inquest. 'I'd had a fair session with these blokes. We'd been to the races prior in the day.'

Dee emerged into Amelia Street.

At that moment, Constable David John McSherry, of Brisbane's Mobile Patrols unit, and his partner, Constable Kaye Suhr, decided to drive past the Whiskey Au Go Go and turned into Amelia Street. They were travelling in police vehicle 525.

'We came along St Pauls Terrace from the Brookes Street end from memory, and I swung right,' McSherry recalled. 'That's when I spotted that fellow getting into an iridescent blue … Holden Premiere … Anyway, he was having trouble getting his keys either out of his pocket or into his lock. No central locking in those days, you know. So I think I just remarked to Kaye, we might just swing around the block and follow him. So we went down Amelia Street and came around the block.'

The suspected drink driver was Michael Dee.

Meanwhile, Kath Potter was still in the phone box when her friend Liz noticed something unusual. A black car had cruised into Amelia Street and stopped in front of the Whiskey Au Go Go. Liz tugged at her friend, trying to get her off the phone.

'While we were in the phone booth, this big long black car pulled up, three men in black got out, pulled a petrol drum from the back of the car out of the car and started to roll it towards the bottom of the stairs of the club,' Kath recalls. 'Liz saw it better than I did and remarked about it being very strange and I was watching while speaking on the phone. The next minute the three men shoved some material in the opening of the drum, moved it closer to the entrance and lit it.

'By this time I had hung up the phone and we were both just standing there gawking, and of course the next minute there were flames, a bang and all hell broke loose. I grabbed Liz and said, "Come on, let's get out of here."'

Arthur Parkinson, slaughterman, was a light sleeper and had arisen in his flat at 56 Amelia Street, just a hundred metres from the club. He was 'two-thirds' asleep when he heard footsteps running down Amelia Street and a car door opening.

'[The] car door opened and this voice [was] saying, "Let's go. Let's get out of here", or something like that expression,' he told the inquest. 'I couldn't be quite sure on what was said. Then I heard the door slam and the car take off at high speed. Going away from the Whiskey Au Go Go. I heard the screams as the tyres rounded the corner.'

Parkinson could hear breaking glass, and human screams.

Across the road, near the McDonald's pastry shop, James Vernon Stewart, a council street cleaner from Wavell Heights, noticed a 'blue glow' in the foyer of the Whiskey.

'It started to get bigger … it started to burst into flames,' he told the inquest. 'It was starting to get a fairly bright light on it then. I couldn't help noticing because there was something peculiar about that light, you know. I just couldn't make it out … it just busted and burst into flames and put the whole building up in fire. All I know from then on … it was a couple of girls that were screaming out, they want to get out, they want to get out.'

A drunken Michael Dee was still fumbling about his car when he heard breaking glass. 'When I heard the noise I sort of half turned around and tripped on the chain … that is around this garden [at the side of the club],' he told the inquest. 'I looked up and the place was alight.'

Stewart, the council worker, saw a police car making its way down St Pauls Terrace and tried to wave it over. It was constables McSherry and Suhr, having just driven around the block.

They had missed the arsonists by just moments.

'By the time we got back the place was on fire,' McSherry recalled. 'The rest of it was just more frantic than anything else. I called [police radio] to report the situation and requested the fire brigade. And then I got out of the car and tried to gain access to the back of the place but there was a very high steel fence with gates and I think it might have been double gates. And they had the big pointy spikes on top. I'm six foot and it was quite a bit higher than me. And there was no way of getting over it, there were no foot holds, you couldn't climb over it. I suppose it was designed that way.

'I remember running around the front to St Pauls Terrace to see if there was any other access doors other than the main door, which was off Amelia Street ... I just came around from St Pauls Terrace to around the front and John Bell who was the manager, a big fella, he jumped off the awning and ... he bloody near landed on top of me, I nearly shit myself. I knew him but not well. You know just from ... because he was an associate of John Hannay who we knew, and Hannay was a dodgy bastard at the best of times.

'I just said to him, "What's the situation?" He told me ... I don't remember the number of people that he said. I think he might have said, "There's 100 or more people in there, and there's no way out." I went back and frantically called bloody, called up [police radio] because the fire brigade hadn't arrived at this stage ... I don't remember what I said but apparently I dropped the f-bomb in trying to accentuate the urgency of the situation and got into strife for doing it later.'

Inspector Daniel McGrath was on duty at police headquarters, North Quay, when McSherry's call came through. 'At about 2.08 a.m. ... I was in the Operations room at Police Headquarters when a call came from Mobile Patrol 525 advising that there was a fire at the Whiskey Au Go Go ... [Constable McSherry] advised that the Ambulance and Fire Brigade be advised immediately and this was passed on to the duty officers at the Headquarters. [McSherry] advised that the position was serious, the place was in flames.'

Flamingos entertainer Lyndon Brown was in his car on St Pauls Terrace when he saw the Whiskey fire. 'When I got there the place had just gone up,' he recalls. 'I pulled up. I could see smoke as I was coming around the corner. I jumped out of my car and you could hear it actually roaring. I tried to chuck a rubbish bin up to the top window to smash it but I couldn't, there were flames shooting out from all over the place.

'A lot of people in the Whiskey didn't know the windows were there because they had heavy curtains across them. You'd think it was just a wall. I know Johnny Bell was there. I knew him from the days of Sydney way back before he started in Brisbane. He was a bouncer at the Three Swallows down in Sydney.

'My friends, I found out later they'd left at probably ten minutes before the thing happened. The whole front of the building was full of flames.'

It was just after 2.12 a.m.

★

Meanwhile, true horror was unfolding inside the Whiskey Au Go Go. Donna Phillips usually manned the bar at the Whiskey but had been asked to work at the front desk earlier that night. She recalls answering the phone at one point and a gruff voice saying, 'Can I speak with Brian Little?' When she asked to take a message because she couldn't locate her boss, the caller hung up.

She claimed she told Brian Little about the call and not long after he exited the building with a woman, who Phillips assumed was his girlfriend.

'I was right at the exit door,' she recalls. She was looking forward to the end of her shift and had "just taken a glass of water from co-worker, waitress Decima Carroll, when a fireball shot up the front stairs and into the club. 'I ... turned, put the glass back down and then I saw the fire erupt through the front door. It came up the stairs. I didn't hear any ... I have no recollection of ... an explosion. You know, I was since told there was no explosion in that sense. Although the fire certainly burst through the entrance.

'It was just a great ... it was an eruption ... The curtains caught fire behind the top bar and a barman started to run away. His shirt was on fire and he ran around along the front windows ... he turned the corner of the bar along St Pauls Terrace side and then fell over. And I watched him on his knees for a few seconds and I wondered what he was doing. I don't know whether he was trying to steady himself or whether ... he was on his knees for a couple of seconds and then he fell to the floor.'

Phillips saw Johnny Bell and his mates having a drink at a table not far from the bar near the entrance. She remembered him jumping up and running in her direction towards the back of the club. 'Then two men in suits have run over and slid the sliding door [open] and turned to me ... I was frozen on the spot ... if those two fellows or anybody else had not run for it, you know, I would have been a goner ... the lights had started to go out in a wave from the back bar. Then the smoke was starting to billow ...

'As we ran down the steps, I'm not 100 per cent sure but I think the lights started to go out. And I remember having to climb over something. I'm sure one of the fellows said to me, "Better be careful". I was a scuba diver back then, very athletic and a bit of a rock hopper. I said to myself, "It's alright, you can do this, I'm alright." I have no memory of slipping. I don't know whether there was grease on the floor inside the door or not. However, I planted my feet, I was fine.

'We've run from the door to the gate, the six foot-tall security gate. We've looked back because we could hear glass … being broken. I did hear later, or read later that somebody had smashed the artist's room with a chair. Smashed the window with a chair to get out.

'Nevertheless, we heard the smashing of the glass, people screaming and one of the fellows that's climbed the gate first with the help of the second fellow, the second one's helped me over … Then I walked across the road and all I remember there is that I sat down on the footpath … [someone] put a blanket around me and asked me if I was okay.'

Bevan Childs, the saxophonist for the band Trinity, was sitting with other band members at a table near the stage, having a drink together between sets. Their instruments were resting in stands on the stage. He was drinking beer, others were having spirits. 'Then everything just went black,' Childs says.

When he'd first arrived at the club earlier that evening he noted the dressing room on the right-hand side of the stage. In the dressing room he'd had a look around and seen … 'a long table, and above that was a long window, a rectangular window and you couldn't see out of it, it was so high up. So I jumped up on the table and looked out just to see what was out there. And the roof of the building next door was only about a metre below that window. So when it happened I thought bang, I know what to do.'

Childs didn't panic. He dashed for the dressing room. 'I guess for me it was just a flight thing, you know?' he says. 'It was just like – bang. I went straight there … I said [to the others], follow me …'

He and fellow bandmate Graham Rennex smashed the high window out with their shoes and managed to clamber to safety.

Another Trinity member, Ray Roberts, simply picked up his guitar case and rammed one of the windows on the St Pauls Terrace side of the building. 'Ray was probably the only one who got injured,' Childs remembers. 'As far as I know there's only two ways to get out of the building. The way Donna [Phillips] went out and the way we went out. But Ray, he found a third way, he picked up his guitar, put it … he just went through the window, boom, and got cuts on his head.

'When we got out there on the roof, I think there was a fire escape from that into a back lane. And then there was the three of us I think, Dave [Neden], Graham and I standing in front of that pub in St Pauls Terrace and I thought, oh shit, I should go back and get me saxes, this is stupid, you know? Obviously just, you know, and that's why [fellow bandmate] Darcy [Day] died, he tried to get his saxes.

'We were just watching the flames and … all the services and fire trucks we were standing around waiting. And of course it took a while for us to realise that people are dead inside, you know? I thought, Darcy would have got out, I thought, well, everybody would have got out.

'Suddenly the penny dropped. Yes.'

At a long table in front of the stage and dance floor, young police officer Hunter Nicol was enjoying a drink with three friends. One of the men, Bill Nolan, had befriended Nicol when they worked together at the Canungra military jungle training centre in the Gold Coast hinterland. Nolan was in the 10th Independent Rifle Company. Nicol had been a military police officer.

Earlier that evening, Nicol had gone over to the Witton Barracks at Indooroopilly to meet up with Nolan for a few drinks in the mess. It was there he met Les Palethorpe for the first time. Les was down from Townsville army base where he was a lance corporal with the regimental police. 'I only met Les that night,' Nicol recalls. 'He was a hell of a nice bloke. We thought we'd go into town. We knew that the Lands Office Hotel had Laurel Lea on that night (Lea was a popular Australian singer at the time who regularly featured on the music television shows *Bandstand* and *Six O'Clock Rock*). She was pretty big, so we thought we'd go and see her. Unfortunately the place was packed out and we couldn't get in. It was full.

'The Delltones were playing at the Whiskey Au Go Go. Let's go down there. So I jumped in my car and we were driving down. I had a Hillman Hunter Royal sedan.'

Incredibly, Nicol and his two friends spotted Palethorpe's mother (who lived in Brisbane) walking down Adelaide Street as they headed to the club. 'From memory we were driving along and Les said, "There's my mother." He'd only come down from Townsville that day, so we stopped and he jumped out and we're all talking to her for a while, she's all pleased to see him not knowing what was going to happen that night,' says Nicol.

Nicol, from Ayr in Far North Queensland, and from a family with generations of police officers, was physically fit and had trained with both the State and Federal military police. Later in the evening, his attention was captured by a man near the front entrance to the club. 'I can remember looking over to the left,' he says. 'I saw who I believed to be a male person, somebody in authority there. A manager, duty manager, owner, it was obvious by his dress, demeanour, everything else, he was the boss there. He was in charge. He was standing not too far away talking to a woman.'

Nicol, who was happily sipping a bourbon and Coke, suddenly heard an almighty roar. 'The next minute I hear this whoosh, and felt a hell of a heat hit me, a whoosh and a roar, flames and thick heavy smoke came roaring in. Someone yelled out, "Fire!"'

'Everyone started to scatter. It was that quick. The smoke. In less than a minute we were all overcome. We were all fit in those days. I had a hanky with me. I poured my drink over the hanky. It was wet. I put it over my mouth and that and went down low. That's what I'd been trained to do. You couldn't breathe, it was that quick. I thought I saw an exit sign. I heard the roar. I thought somebody must have activated a fire hose but it wasn't, it must have been the flames. I headed over to where I thought the exit sign was.

'Somehow I got totally disorientated. A girl was standing on the dance floor screaming, "We're going to die, we're going to die!" I've grabbed her and dragged her with me. I've ended up in the kitchen area. There were little windows. I saw people getting into it. I wasn't sure if it was a window. I could see something; it turned out it was the night sky. At that stage I was really stuffed. I totally and utterly 100 per cent believed I was going to die.'

Years later, John Bell would tell his daughter, Kathy Hancock, about the tragedy of that night. 'He basically said everyone was screaming,' Kathy says. 'They couldn't get the back door open. He was trying to get people out. It was horrific.'

When bar attendant Donna Phillips made it outside she was in a state of shock. 'I walked across the road. I sat down on the footpath. We've sat there while all the emergency services have arrived. Sometime later, one of the barmen from Chequers arrived ... with Brian Little's brother [Ken] ... from the other club.'

The Chequers Nightclub barman she recognised was Darryl Charles Schlecht. Less than a quarter of an hour earlier, Schlecht had closed up at Chequers and driven his boss Ken Little up Barry Parade to the Whiskey.

'Well, as we came up Barry Parade and we just ... I saw the smoke come out of ... coming out of the St Pauls Terrace side of [the] Whiskey and fire engines and flashing lights and things. I dropped him [Ken] off at Barry Parade, just on the corner of Brunswick Street and then I went and parked the car, and came back.'

Darryl enquired about the welfare of people inside the club, in particular his friend, the barman Peter Marcus. Donna Phillips was still sitting in a daze on the footpath opposite the smouldering club.

'I saw this fellow Darryl,' she remembered. 'And it was Darryl, he was a very close friend of the fellow who was the barman. When I told him I saw him fall, he became hysterical. And somebody said, "You've got to take him to [the] hospital, he's in shock."

'So he and I went to the hospital. He was seen to. One of the nurses said to me, "Are you alright?" And I said, "Yeah, look, I'm fine," doing my best version of, you know, the British stiff upper lip. Then I came back, I guess I came back, I'm still not sure. And then I don't remember anything else after but I'm assuming I walked home. I have a recollection of having a shower and noticing that I had black soot on my skin ... I washed that off, hopped into bed, woke up the next morning and told my husband ... and he said, "You better have the day off then."'

Hunter Nicol managed to get out the window but didn't see anyone come out after him. 'I got onto a bit of a rooftop,' he recalls. 'I've jumped down. The fire escape was shut. I couldn't see if it was locked or not. I ran around behind the building. It had six-foot high fences facing onto St Pauls Terrace. Don't ask me how but I jumped it ... it was pandemonium. It was just so quick. Les would have been dead within a few minutes. It was really hot. I got scorched lungs out of it. I was covered in all this greasy soot. You couldn't see anything. The way it billowed in through the place, I reckon within 30 seconds we were overcome with smoke. It came in like a storm front. Really thick and putrid.

'What killed them was not only carbon monoxide, this stuff on the floor was nylon. Nylon and plastic chairs, they burn and they give off cyanide gas. Not many vicitms actually got burnt.

'It was terrifying. I went through a stage of terror, and then I accepted the fact that I was going to die. There was nothing I could do about it ... Les ended up in the far corner, heading towards the fire. I think people went that way not realising where the exit was. They didn't have a chance. It just roared through that place. Whether it was the air conditioning that assisted it. We didn't have a hope.'

It was around 2.20 a.m.

★

Firefighter Arnold Eggins from Kemp Place Fire Station in Fortitude Valley arrived at the scene about 30 minutes after the first emergency call came in. Two pumps had initially attended but back-up was swiftly called. 'I was involved in carrying one of the fatalities out of the building,' says Eggins. 'It was certainly the most fatalities I'd ever witnessed at one incident.' Firefighters had the blaze under control by 2.21 a.m. When the conditions were deemed safe, authorities – including constables McSherry and Suhr – began removing the bodies. 'Kaye and I carried out one or two bodies,' McSherry says. 'I tagged the bodies. It was one of my tasks. I wrote who found which body and where on the tags. We tried to cover them as best we could. It was a terribly traumatic situation for everyone involved.'

It was not yet 3 a.m.

★

According to author Geoff Plunkett in his book *The Whiskey Au Go Go Massacre*, not long after this detectives from the Criminal Investigation Branch arrived at the scene of the Whiskey tragedy. As he writes:

> At this time Detective Senior Sergeant Robert 'Brian' Hayes (who was in charge of the Homicide Squad and this investigation), Detective Sergeant Ronald Redmond and Detective Sergeant Thomas (Syd) Atkinson (all CIB) arrived at the Whiskey and walked around the smouldering ruins. Their shoes crunched on the debris and caused the still-warm ashes to waft in their wake.

Inspector Les Bardwell, head of the police scientific section, had been alerted about the fire by the Operations Room and at around 3.30 a.m. arrived at the Whiskey. En route, he learned that the death count was mounting. First nine. Then 12. Then 14.

Commissioner of Police, Ray Whitrod, arrived not long after, with one of the force's most senior detectives, Don 'Buck' Buchanan. Buchanan's son, David, heard the story of that moment from his father sometime later. 'My father said, Whitrod nearly fainted as the crime scene was so terrible,' David recalls. 'My father was disturbed by the fire.'

Bardwell took detailed notes of what he saw in the early hours of that tragic morning. 'There was carpet on the floor of the vestibule, steps and also the main area of the nightclub, with the exception of … some wooden parquetry floor obviously there for dancing,' Bardwell would tell the inquest. 'On the ground floor, this in the vestibule, I saw a four gallon and five gallon steel drum, both of these were in the horizontal position with the bung out. One was situated towards the centre of the south-western wall and the second under the staircase. Examination disclosed that one of the drums was empty of fluid but there was a strong odour of petrol emanating from it, whilst the second drum had fluid in it, and it also had a strong odour of petrol …'

He was confident that there were no more than 50 people in the club at the time of the fire. He also concluded that the contents of the two drums at the entrance to the club was super-grade petrol, and the brand probably Amoco.

It was close to 4 a.m.

★

It didn't take long for *Sunday Sun* reporter Brian Bolton to get to his desk that morning and find two notes that John Andrew Stuart had left for him the night before. After making his phone call at Flamingos, as witnessed by bouncer Alf Quick, Stuart had pre-aranged to meet Bolton at his office in the Sun Building in the Valley, just around the corner from Flamingos. He had wanted to go on a tour of the doomed clubs with Bolton and tell them face to face, with the journalist as his witness, that he was not involved. Instead, Bolton fell asleep and didn't make their post-midnight meeting. Bolton later told Humphris: 'Stuart has left me a note here at my desk signed about 10 minutes after the fire started, abusing me for not keeping our appointment.'

Police needed to find Stuart.

It was almost dawn.

Mass Murder

Had the deadly firebombing been a part of John Andrew Stuart's predictions of a Sydney gangster takeover? He had been warning the owners of the club, the Little brothers, that the Whiskey was going to be hit. And he'd been shouting loudly to police and the newspapers that another fire was imminent.

Sydney detective Roger Rogerson says he was flown from Sydney to help in the investigation. He knew John Andrew Stuart as a 'lunatic'.

'Stuart kept saying it was Sydney criminals, the Mr Bigs – Lenny McPherson, George Freeman; he was dropping a lot of names,' said Rogerson. 'And there was a journalist [Brian Bolton] up there writing up stories about Sydney crims taking over the Valley. It was all bullshit he was getting from Stuart. It was a way of setting up an alibi. It was all crap.'

Police immediately carried out a city-wide sweep of Brisbane's known criminals and potential suspects, and brought them in for questioning. According to a police source, Vincent O'Dempsey was one of those brought in that morning and interrogated. Another who was swiftly nabbed was none other than Stuart's good mate Billy McCulkin. He was interrogated for several hours before being released.

By 10 a.m. McCulkin was in the bar of the Treasury Hotel at the corner of George and Elizabeth streets in the CBD where he talked with his friend (and future wife) Estelle Long. McCulkin had known Long for years. She was a long-term lover to bookmaker Paul Meade, who had employed both McCulkin and O'Dempsey in his mock auctions business before it was shut down by authorities.

Long later recalled to police: 'I was living and working at the Treasury Hotel and when I got into the bar at opening time Billy was already there. He looked terrible, kind of panicky and I asked him what was wrong. He told me he'd been picked up by the police about the Whiskey Au Go Go fire. I didn't know what had happened and he told me about the fire and all the people who had died. He said he had been there at the police station all night and that they gave him a hard time. Billy didn't tell me what he told the police but he seemed very worried by this.'

John Andrew Stuart was finally tracked down and brought into headquarters with a solicitor. He was similarly subjected to intense questioning but let go without charge.

The news soon reached the ears of members of the Clockwork Orange Gang, and Tommy Hamilton was also worried. His sister, Carolyn Scully, remembers talking to her brother on the day of the fire: 'Tommy ... came to have a coffee ... he put the cream in the fridge and he said, "I'm just going to go, and I'll be back, I won't be long." He was back in five minutes and he was in shock. He says, "Do you know what's happened?" And I said no because I wasn't watching the TV.

'He said, "A nightclub has been blown up, 15 people are dead. They're going to think the people who blew up Torino's did this too." But at that point in time I didn't know about Torino's. I knew how they came home that night but I didn't think anything of it. Because it wasn't until after that that Peter Hall told me, and it wasn't until after Peter told me that Tommy told me.'

One associate, who was close to the Clockwork Orange Gang, said when he heard the news of the Whiskey, one thing struck him. 'In the back of my mind was Torino's,' he recalls. 'It was very similar. Stuart and Finch. They'd known each other since they were teenagers. Stuart didn't drink but he was always in nightclubs and clubs. Stuart and Finch were very close. Then there was the Clockwork Orange Gang. They were different teams.

'Finch and Stuart. It was never suggested that they did Torino's because Finch was still out of the country and Stuart had been arrested that night when Torino's went up. He was in custody on that Sunday night. I cannot find out who arrested him. It's odds-on that Stuart wanted to alibi himself for that night.'

They Did It

Nothing prepared Barbara McCulkin for the morning of 8 March 1973. If the weary mother of two had been standing on her back landing at Dorchester Terrace just after 2 a.m. that day, and she had looked across the city towards Fortitude Valley, just behind the Story Bridge, she would have seen a smudge of orange fire in the darkness.

By the time Barbara awoke and prepared breakfast for the children and got them ready for school, the bodies had been laid out in a car park beside the club and the process of identifying the victims was underway. When she was to learn the news of the deadly blaze proper, with all the information she'd picked up for the past several weeks at 6 Dorchester Street, she would enter a blind panic. On seeing the early edition newspaper reports on the fire in the corner store just a few doors down from her cottage, Barbara's first response to the tragedy was: 'Oh my God, they did it.'

In its late edition on the day of the fire, the *Telegraph* featured the fire on its front and back pages, as well as comprehensive reports inside. The lead story, written by veteran police reporter Pat Lloyd, was headlined simply: 'AUSTRALIA'S WORST KILLINGS'. He wrote that a special police task force had been set up to orchestrate early morning raids and bring known underworld figures to the Brisbane CIB.

> Their main theory on the bombing is that underworld extortionists are to blame. But, so far, they have been unable to find anyone willing to talk on the issue. Police say there is little doubt today's bombing horror might be linked with the February 25 fire-bomb blast which gutted the Torino Night Club …

On the morning of the fire, John Hannay's former gopher and Whiskey barmaid, Lucy Kirkov, set about organising her day. She lived in New Farm, one of Brisbane's oldest suburbs perched just two kilometres east of the CBD and hugged by the Brisbane River. New Farm bordered Fortitude Valley and its sleaze and vice had leached into New Farm soil. The peninsula suburb was littered with Queenslander workers' cottages and the occasional modern brick block of flats.

On the morning of the Whiskey tragedy, Lucy, unaware of the fire, had set off from home to walk to town. 'It wasn't until I went past there to the hairdressers that I seen it'd gone up,' she says about the Whiskey fire. 'That was the first I was aware of it.'

Kirkov says not long after she left home that morning she saw Hannay on the corner of Merthyr Road and Brunswick Street in his Mustang. 'Now I can't mistake Hannay, I've known him for too long to not be able to recognise him.'

When Lucy later told police she'd identified John Hannay in New Farm on the morning of Thursday 8 March, just hours after the fire, the police told her she was 'bullshitting'. According to official police documents, they believed Hannay had left Brisbane on the morning of Wednesday 7 March and arrived in Rockhampton by car at around 5 p.m., several hours before the fatal fire.

'The coppers said, "For your information" … and I said, "Before you go any further, I suppose he was drinking with coppers up in Rockhampton," and they said, "Yeah that's right."

'He [the police officer] asked me if I knew how long it took to get from Brisbane to Rockhampton, and I said, "Yep, it's eight hours by car, and an hour by plane." But I definitely saw Hannay that day … I swear on the Bible. He was in Brisbane that morning, so he had to have been in town the night the Whiskey went up.'

A Hitman Comes to Town

The blaze at the Whiskey Au Go Go fired off tremors and triggers that initiated overt and covert actions across the country. This inferno, this evil act, touched everything from the highest office in the land to the darkest recesses of the criminal underworld.

Australia had never seen anything like the Whiskey. It was a crime difficult to immediately comprehend for most. But a handful of people instantly digested its meaning, and implications. One of those was Sydney gunman Stewart John Regan, himself a psychopath and serial killer who had terrorised Sydney for almost a decade with his ruthless and schizoid nature.

Regan was an occasional asset as strong arm and enforcer to the major Sydney gangsters of the day, including Paddles Anderson, Lenny

McPherson and George Freeman. But his total unpredictability also made him a liability. Regan was also acquainted with John Andrew Stuart and James Finch. In 1966, after a shootout in the streets of Paddington in inner-Sydney, Finch was charged with maliciously shooting Regan with intent to inflict grievous bodily harm. Finch was sentenced to 14 years in prison but served less than half that.

According to criminal sources, Regan and O'Dempsey were certainly known to each other in the 1960s and 70s, to the point where they'd sometimes do jobs and 'swap identities'.

When the Whiskey blew, Regan was on a plane directly from Sydney, arriving in Brisbane on Thursday 8 March. Why had a known killer like Regan been in such a rush to head into the heat of a crime of the magnitude of the firebombing of the Whiskey Au Go Go? Had he heard of the tragedy on the news? Had he been phoned by somebody in Brisbane? What possible interest could Regan have in the Brisbane fire?

Nevertheless, he had come like a moth to a flame and took no time getting in touch with Queensland police. Detective Pat Glancy was on duty at headquarters on the morning after the fire and took a call from Regan. 'He asked me if he was wanted [for the fire],' Glancy later recalled. 'He wanted to know if he was to be interviewed … He told me he'd come up from Sydney … He said if I interviewed him one-on-one in a neutral location he would do it without a solicitor. But if we wanted to talk to him in police headquarters he'd bring a legal representative.'

Glancy said he met Regan in a Chinese restaurant in Fortitude Valley. Glancy added: 'He was one of the coldest people I've ever met. He didn't drink. He had orange juice. He didn't smoke. He was quiet. Whereas John Andrew Stuart was a loudmouth, he was a bloody idiot.'

In the restaurant, Regan learned that police were looking for Stuart in connection with the Whiskey fire, and the assassin magnanimously offered to help track down his old foe. He even offered to kill Stuart for the police. 'He was either trying to help us or get us off his back,' Glancy said. 'I mentioned Billy Phillips and how he might know where Stuart was.'

Glancy and Regan apparently then drove to Phillips's house and Regan made a beeline down the side of the house to the back door. When Phillips emerged Regan enquired about Stuart's whereabouts. The enraged tattooist said he had nothing to do with the Whiskey.

According to Glancy, Phillips was initially unaware of his visitor's identity. 'I'm John Regan,' the visitor said, and Phillips turned 'white as a ghost'. 'Remember this,' Glancy recalls Regan telling Phillips, 'if you mention to the police that I'm up here, it'll get to me and I'll come back and see you.'

Regan returned to Sydney on the Saturday morning. When he was later told of Finch's and Stuart's arrests, Regan was elated.

The Hasty Inquest

As parliamentarians assembled in the House at the bottom of George Street, just a few hours after the shocking mass murder at the Whiskey, none would have forgotten the Questions Without Notice from the member for the South Coast, Russell Hinze, just days earlier. Now 15 innocent people were dead, and the culprits were on the run.

The Minister for Justice, Bill Knox, stood at 11.27 a.m. to inform parliament, and the people of Queensland, that a coronial inquiry was imminent. 'After a conference that was held this morning, I have to announce that a coronial inquiry into this tragedy will be opened this afternoon under the chairmanship of Mr D. Birch, Stipendiary Magistrate,' Knox said. 'A number of people will be submitting evidence before the inquiry, and I hope that others will come forward too.'

It was, in any other circumstances, extraordinary that an inquest could be instigated into an event that had only occurred nine hours earlier, and with some of the bodies of the victims still unidentified, down in the city morgue. Who, of substance, would be called to give evidence? How could anybody hope to extract a meaningful picture of the firebombing and its aftermath when there was as yet no perspective on an atrocity of such magnitude?

Minister for Housing and Works (and Police), Max Hodges, followed Knox on the floor of parliament. After expressing his deepest sympathies for the relatives and friends of those who lost their lives, he alluded to the ongoing investigation and assured the House that everything that could be done was being done by the police.

Hodges told parliament that since the fire broke out at 2.08 a.m., police had conducted interviews with over 100 people, some with those 'fortunate to have survived the holocaust', along with members of the public. 'In addition, a large force of police officers are currently scouring the city … There has been a virtual purge by Consorting Squad members of underworld personalities and those who live on the fringe of the underworld. No stone is being left unturned in this incident.'

The *Telegraph* reported:

> Complete uproar and chaos broke out in State Parliament today as the Government defeated two attempts by the Opposition to debate the Whiskey Au Go Go murders. For almost half an hour members shouted at each other in the rowdiest scenes in Parliament for many years.
>
> The Government defeated a move by the Opposition Leader, Mr Houston, for the immediate setting up of a Royal Commission

into increased incidents of organised crime extortion and other rackets emerging in Queensland.

The vote was lost 31–42.

Later that day, Stipendiary Magistrate Doug Birch convened the Whiskey Au Go Go inquest in Millaquin House at 30–36 Herschel Street at North Quay. According to legal observers at the time, it might have been an unusual move to hold an inquest within hours of the crime and deaths it was examining, but on the other hand, the Whiskey Au Go Go mass murder was a commensurately unusual event. 'These were special circumstances,' one former magistrate says. 'He couldn't have proceeded to take very much evidence. It was a formality, to open it.'

Birch, a highly respected and well-liked magistrate, wasted no time. 'Well,' he said, 'I will open an inquest into the cause and origin of a fire which occurred on the 8th day of March, 1973, whereby a property known as "Whiskey-Au-Go-Go" Nightclub ... was damaged and whereby the lives of Colin William Folster, William David Nolan, Leslie Gordon Palethorpe, Peter Marcus, David John Westren, Fay Ellen Will, Ernest John Peters, Desmond John Peters, Jennifer Denise Davie, Paul Ferdinand Zoller, Desma Selma Carroll, Carol Ann Green, Darcy Thomas Day, Wendy Leonne Drew, and Brian William Watson, were lost,' Birch told the court.

Soon after, Birch explained the unusual circumstances surrounding the hastily convened hearings. 'Because of the nature of the incident, it has been decided to open the inquest today, and for that reason it has not been possible to advise all those who may be interested,' he said. 'Action has been taken to bring the inquest to the notice of as many persons as possible.'

The first witnesses called were representatives of the Licensing Commission and Fire Brigade and detailed the various work orders that were in place and revealed that there had been 'unauthorised alterations' made to the club, including a reception area and a liquor servery near the back of the club. Leo Terence McQuillan, secretary of the Licensing Commission, confirmed that the work had not obstructed any of the club's exits, and was of a high standard, the club's windows had had their winding mechanisms removed and been riveted so they could not open. McQuillan explained: 'The premises are air-conditioned. These windows were left open and the Commission had received many complaints concerning noise emanating from the entertainment even to the early hours of the morning from these premises.'

The next witness was Vivian William Dowling, Chief Officer of the Metropolitan Fire Brigade, Brisbane. Dowling was asked where he believed the fire started. 'It is my opinion that the main seat of the fire was around the main staircase, that is the staircase nearest to Amelia Street,' he replied. 'That is the entrance. In this particular position the damage was the greatest throughout the building.'

Dowling said he studied the means of travel of the fire because he could not understand why it had spread so quickly. 'The rapid spread of fire within the building was far in excess of any normal spread of fire,' he concluded. 'It is my opinion that because of the closed windows fronting St Pauls Terrace the people inside panicked. They knew or had an idea or had been told where the escape was but the fire resistant door had closed and with the lights having gone out within the building they were groping in the dark and in the smoke-filled area. They missed the door and went into a little alcove by the side and this is where we found three and another group of five.'

Dowling agreed that the fire was suspicious and 'had been assisted by some sort of accelerant'.

On Friday 9 March witnesses at the inquest observed the heartbreaking evidence of the relatives of the dead. One after another, Coroner Birch asked them if they had identified the bodies of their deceased loved ones the day before. It was a parade of pure sorrow.

After 2.30 p.m. on that Friday, with the perpetrators of Australia's worst mass murder still on the run, the inquest called pathologist and deputy director of the State Health Laboratory, Dr Merrick John O'Reilly. He agreed that he had performed post-mortem examinations on a large number of the Whiskey victims. Dr O'Reilly was asked to tell the court what the 'principal cause of death' was.

'In every case the major cause of death was due to inhalation of fumes, the major portion of which was carbon monoxide,' he told the hearing. 'There may have been other products of combustion, but these are being currently investigated by the Government Analyst at the moment. But we do know that the first eight of those had high concentrations of carbon monoxide in their blood.'

He said there was no evidence of injuries that could have been a factor in their deaths. The bodies carried on average 40 per cent to 60 per cent saturation of carbon monoxide. Anything above 40 per cent was considered a lethal dose. Dr O'Reilly said the victims would have been dead within two to three minutes of inhaling the toxic fumes. 'I should perhaps add that consciousness would have been lost before death would have occurred,' he added.

Days and Nights at Headquarters

Constable McSherry, who'd come so close to actually witnessing the torching of the Whiskey when he was on patrol the morning of the fire, returned to CIB headquarters in Makerston Street, North Quay. It had been one of the longest and most traumatic shifts of his young career. But the ordeal was not over yet. He was ordered by his superiors to stay at the CIB indefinitely. 'I was told, "You're going to have to stay here late and just be on tap if we need you."

I had a number of detectives asking me questions, most of which I couldn't answer.

'Syd Atkinson and, I'm sure, Ronnie Redmond were there because I got to know Ronnie pretty well after that. I remember sitting with him in the witness room and Syd Atkinson was in there and he was the fellow I met the most. He was the one that sort of got in my ear quite a bit. But you've got to bear in mind that the hierarchical structure of the police back then was a lot different to what it is now. A fellow with my service was a bit like the kid in the corner – speak when spoken to, you know?'

McSherry says he witnessed many potential suspects brought into headquarters that morning. 'I saw people coming and going in the company of detectives but I didn't know who they were,' he recalls.

From Thursday morning after his shift finished until Sunday, McSherry was literally confined to headquarters as the investigation played out. He was not allowed to return to his wife and their rented flat in Ascot. 'I think from memory I just slept in a bloody chair,' he recalls. 'I was 24 and obviously, you know … the enormity of the situation wasn't lost on me. I was happy to do whatever I had to do to assist in any way.' He says, 'to this day', he has no idea why he was asked not to leave the headquarters precinct.

'I really can't fathom why they kept me there but they did. I saw their comings and goings and I wonder if they were just thinking, if I saw someone that I recognised [from the crime scene] then I might say, "Hang on, I saw that fellow in or out of the club", you know? But that didn't happen, I didn't see anyone coming or going that I recognised. Either from that night or from previously.'

Nevertheless, detectives wanted McSherry there for a reason. He had been the first officer, with Constable Kay Suhr, on the scene, and had literally missed witnessing the torching of the club at the front entrance by a matter of seconds. But why would the likes of Atkinson and Redmond ensure that the young constable not leave their sight? Was he pressed by any senior detectives about what he actually saw that morning at the Whiskey?

'They got me to go through books of photographs, you know, but without ... looking for any particular person ... which made good sense if you think about it. They said to me, "Just keep looking ... just let us know if there is anyone you recognise, either from the event or prior to that."

'I remember leafing through the black and white photographs, you know, watch house photographs, with the blackboard across the chest. And I'm trying to put myself in their shoes and wondering what they possibly expected, given I'd already told them I saw nobody set fire to the place.

'It was lost on me ... I was just sitting in the corner and serving no purpose whatsoever. Whoever made the decision to keep me there, I don't know who it was. Because there was hectic bloody activity, obviously. So that's probably the biggest event that ever happened in Queensland at the time.'

It was days before McSherry was permitted to return home. His partner on patrol that night, Constable Suhr, was not asked to stay at headquarters. McSherry never worked a shift with her again.

Barbara Flees

Less than 48 hours after the fire, Barbara fled Dorchester Street with her children. She took the girls to separate friends and then she went to stay that Saturday night with her friend from the milk bar, Ellen Gilbert.

'... after the burning of the Whiskey Au Go Go night club in the Valley, Mrs McCulkin phoned me and asked me could she come to my place and stay the night with me,' Gilbert would later tell police. 'She ... arrived at my home conveyed there by her husband, Billy

McCulkin, and another person. After she arrived at my home she said she did not want to stay at home as she was very upset. She said something about the police and her house being bugged. I formed the opinion that Mrs McCulkin was very frightened and concerned for the safety of herself and her children and she had deliberately split them up.'

Why had Barbara McCulkin taken such drastic action? Did she have information concerning the culprits behind the firebombing? What had she overheard at 6 Dorchester Street? Whatever it was, it was enough to make her flee her home.

Barbara wasn't the only one worried in the aftermath of the Whiskey. So too were members of the Clockwork Orange Gang. Peter Hall later said at the trial of Garry Dubois that having done the job at Torino's, he and his mates were concerned that police might link them to the Whiskey. 'I recall a few weeks after we did the Torino's the Whiskey Au Go Go fire happened,' Hall would later confess. 'It made us all panic because people were killed and we were concerned that we would be implicated. We were out doing break and enters that night, the four of us in two cars. I was with Keithy [Meredith]. I am sure none of us were involved.

'I am also sure because I would have found out about it. Obviously when we found out about it the next day we realised they might look at the Torino's [fire]. I am aware that it has been suggested that Tom Hamilton was involved in the Whiskey Au Go Go fire but I don't believe that it's true.'

Former Whiskey bouncer John Wayne Ryan, who grew up in the same neighbourhood as most of the Clockwork Orange Gang in the Chermside area, claimed he had been warning all and sundry about a firebombing at the Whiskey but nobody would listen. He knew that Tommy Hamilton and some of the Clockwork Orange boys had torched Torino's less than two weeks earlier, and had learned that the Whiskey was 'going to go off' next.

Ryan knew Billy McCulkin was behind Torino's, and he was concerned about Billy's wife, Barbara, and the girls. 'John Andrew Stuart had been to her home [at Dorchester Street] a few times in the lead up to the bombing,' Ryan said. 'And she said she was present when Billy McCulkin was on the phone making arrangements about the fires, plural. She had information on the Clockwork Orange Gang and its links to some Queensland police.'

In the meantime, little Leanne McCulkin was attending Yeronga State School when her friends found her in tears. One of those friends, Alan Evans, would later tell a court that he asked Leanne what was wrong. 'She was crying her eyes out one day … she was really upset,' Evans said. 'She said … her father had something to do with it [the Whiskey].'

Heads Must Roll

When the true, horrific gravity of the fire's 15 deaths began to sink in, the press and the public were clamouring for someone to be held accountable for the mass murder. The culprit had to be caught, and swiftly. The perpetrator was a maniac, a mad killer, and if he could set fire to a building with dozens of people in it, he was capable of anything. How had the police force allowed this to happen? What was the Queensland police motto? Firmness with Courtesy? Where was the firmness with a criminal, or criminals, permitted to slaughter 15 innocent people?

Behind the scenes police were trying to piece together information from a number of different sources. On Saturday 10 March, John Andrew Stuart had another prolonged phone call with Inspector Basil Hicks, who recorded their conversation. In that conversation, he hinted at a broader conspiracy behind the Whiskey attack.

According to a police report witnessed by author Geoff Plunkett, the following conversation ensued.

> 'Okay now,' a rambling and at times incoherent Stuart told Hicks, 'so all I'm gonna go along with and what I have tried to get the *Mirror* to go along with. Gees they're gonna give it a shocking cook tomorrow. I've seen some of the stories [in the newspapers].'
>
> 'Whose [sic] going to get the cook?' Hicks asked.
>
> 'Not youse. Not youse,' Stuart stressed. 'Not the CIU. It's Whitrod and [Police Minister] Hodges. They're gonna give them a shocking cook. They're out to get them. They wanna bring them undone.'
>
> 'Why Whitrod and Hodges?'
>
> 'It's political, Basil,' Stuart answered. 'It's not just Bolton, it's the [news]paper.'

Lawyer Des Sturgess, in his memoir *The Tangled Web*, would later reflect on the 'politics' behind the Whiskey, as Stuart put it to Hicks. Sturgess was Brisbane's go-to lawyer for large, complicated and controversial legal cases in the 1970s. He had a particular talent for being on-hand in cases that would find themselves in the Supreme Court in George Street, and would go on to represent a veritable roll call of famous, and infamous, Queensland police. He offered counsel to corrupt Rat Pack copper Glen Hallahan, who was charged with corruption by Whitrod's CIU in late 1971, and offered legal advice to corrupt former police commissioner Frank Bischof and Licensing Branch officer Jack 'The Bagman' Herbert.

In his memoir, Sturgess observed that one of the criticisms of the Whitrod era of police enforcement was 'the allegation of incompetence costing 15 lives'. Decades later, the attempt to slot the blame for the Whiskey on Whitrod's incompetence continued to be discussed by retired detectives. Former leading CIB detective A.B.

'Abe' Duncan was one vocal critic. 'If ever there should have been a royal commission or an inquiry into the police force, it should have been over the Whiskey. That should have been top priority. I'll say that to my dying day. It would have revealed that Whitrod and his men slipped out of the job. It was absolute negligence.'

Corrupt former police commissioner Terry Lewis concurs: 'Oh … it was gross negligence on somebody's part. How far up it got, I don't know.'

On the Sunday, Brian Bolton wrote an article that reflected public sentiment about the Whiskey atrocity and echoed the sentiment of Stuart's conversation with Hicks the day before. The front page headline of the *Sunday Sun* was: 'HEADS MUST ROLL!'

Bolton wrote:

> … some people in the Queensland Police Force appear very naive, deceitful or just plain stupid … Their leaders – right through to the Minister [Hodges] and Commissioner [Whitrod] – persist in saying publicly there were no warnings of the dreadful club disaster which cost 15 lives in Brisbane last week, yet there is ample evidence that warning after warning was given.

Despite the debate over Whitrod, police had issued vital information about a lead they were following and asked the public for help. The State Government had offered a $50,000 reward for the capture of the offender or offenders. Particularly, the police wanted to know the whereabouts of a certain black car.

> A shiny black sedan, possibly a Holden, has become a major lead in investigations into the massacre … Homicide detectives urgently require any information about the car, which was seen driving away from the Valley nightclub's Amelia Street entrance before two drums of petrol ignited in the club's foyer at 2.10 a.m.

A young couple told police yesterday they saw the shiny black car drive off just before the club burst into flames. They said the car drove off without lights and turned right into St Pauls Terrace.

It was a description that perfectly matched the car seen pulling up outside the club by witness Kath Potter. The hunt was on.

An extraordinary series of allegations by Whiskey manager John Bell then followed in the newspapers. He claimed Stuart had walked into the Whiskey at about 10 p.m. on the night of the fire and spoken to both Bell and Brian Little. Bell told the newspaper:

Stuart told me that these criminals would throw a hand grenade through the window or drive a burning car into the front foyer. He said there were four young Sydney criminals trying to make a name for themselves. He mentioned the name of two brothers involved in the gang. Stuart told me they had asked him to arrange a protection racket in Brisbane with the clubs and to collect the money.

It was unknown to Bell, and indeed the *Sunday Sun* at that point, that days before the fatal fire Stuart had accidentally bumped into Peter Hall and Tommy Hamilton of the Clockwork Orange Gang in the street, and had made a joke to a witness that here were the 'two Sydney gangster brothers'. Hall and Hamilton were often mistaken as brothers because of their red hair. Had Stuart simply used the gang as the basis for his fictional Sydney gang, set to extort Brisbane clubs?

There were more revelations to come. 'Stuart said that these criminals had firebombed the Torino but had not had enough publicity from it,' Bell added. 'Just before he left he said the crime would be done when there were people about and that the innocent would suffer.'

At the time Stuart made these allegations to Bell, investigators had no idea who was behind the Torino fire. And while rumours would circulate years later, it wouldn't be until the murder trials of Garry 'Shorty' Dubois and Vince O'Dempsey over the McCulkin killings that the true culprits behind Torino's were revealed. Gang member Peter Hall would finally confess to the Torino firebombing in 2016, telling a court that it was he, Shorty Dubois and Keith Meredith, who committed the crime, which was organised by Vince O'Dempsey and Billy McCulkin.

Was the so-called Sydney crime gang Stuart was talking up actually the Clockwork Orange Gang?

Stuart knew who was behind the club fires when he told Bell that the Sydney gang 'had firebombed the Torino', but it would take more than four decades for Stuart's fabric of lies to be unpicked.

Caught

John Andrew Stuart's long discussions with his friend, Inspector Basil Hicks, did not keep him immune from the Whiskey's myriad police investigators, who had come from three States – Queensland, New South Wales and Victoria – to assist investigations into the Whiskey firebombing. Despite all Stuart's attempts to shore up an alibi for the Whiskey fire – the Sydney gang stories, the tip-offs to police, creating an alibi at Flamingos, the notes left with journalist Brian Bolton, and his lengthy rambling to detective Basil Hicks – police still considered him a serious person of interest.

'We got a call from [Stuart's brother] Danny saying Stuart and Finch were at his house …' officer Pat Glancy would later say. 'There was a barbecue on at the house. A couple of carloads of us went out there. As we arrived, a woman came out of the house. She said, "I'm getting out of here, it's going to be a bloodbath." I was the first one in and I saw that Stuart had something behind his back.'

According to Glancy, when police swooped on Dan's place at 12 Mankinna Street, Jindalee, Stuart was brandishing a hunting knife. It was known among his friends and associates that he often carried a knife in his boot. Glancy said he raised his gun and threatened to shoot Stuart if he didn't drop the knife. Glancy said Stuart threw the knife across the room. 'When we drove into headquarters, Stuart, who was in the back seat, wouldn't shut up,' Glancy added. 'He had his head down and shouted that everyone was trying to kill him, that the police were trying to kill him.' Finch was nowhere to be found. According to newspaper reports the next morning, Sunday 11 March, police received another call to return to the Jindalee house.

Finch had gone back to the house but fled again. By 11 a.m. he was captured in the area. Both men were interrogated through that Sunday, and at 8.55 p.m. were formally charged with murder.

'I am very pleased at the work of the police team,' Commissioner Whitrod announced. 'They have worked long hours and have done very well. In this instance police mobile crews played an important part. We have received great co-operation from the public. People have phoned in many leads which we have worked on.'

Even Premier Joh Bjelke-Petersen weighed in on the back-slapping. 'I would like to commend the police on their very excellent work on a difficult problem,' he said. 'I have often said that we in Queensland are fortunate to have the police force we have got.'

Both Whitrod and Bjelke-Petersen were condemned by the Bar Association of Queensland for their words of praise. President J.D. Dunn said it was a fundamental principle of law that no one is presumed guilty until a court makes that decision. He said the comments bordered on contempt of court.

On that Sunday evening, Billy McCulkin rang Ellen Gilbert's house to let his wife know that Finch and Stuart had been arrested for the Whiskey firebombing. 'She received a telephone call and she told me that she was relieved, and she said her husband had called and that John Stuart had been arrested for the Whiskey Au Go Go fire,' Gilbert later recalled to police. 'She borrowed some money from me for a cab and then left. Mrs McCulkin informed me that John Andrew Stuart was a friend and that he had stayed with her and her husband at their home on occasions.'

On Monday 12 March, with Stuart and Finch safely in custody, the inquest abruptly ended. Coroner Birch said: 'Yes, gentlemen, well, it's quite clear that my function at this stage is to adjourn the inquest ... to a date and time to be fixed ...'

The inquest into the mass deaths at the Whiskey was never resumed.

The Verbal

When Finch was interviewed, on the evening of Sunday 11 March 1973, there were plenty of police interested in the proceedings, from the lead interviewers to young constables on duty down at headquarters. When the typed record of interview was done and handed to younger officers to produce copies, a number of extra copies were made and the juniors pocketed them as 'souvenirs'.

The interview was conducted by then Detective Senior Sergeant Brian Hayes, and present were Detective Sergeant Syd 'Sippy' Atkinson, as well as New South Wales police officers – Detective Sergeant Noel Morey and Detective Senior Constable Roger Rogerson. The interview commenced at 5.45 p.m. The typist for the interview transcript was Detective Sergeant Ron Redmond.

The police pulled a standard line – they told Finch that his mate Stuart had willingly confessed to the crime. It was a ruse. Everyone who knew Stuart and Finch were adamant they would never confess to coppers.

Hayes asked Finch how long he'd been back in Brisbane and Finch told them Stuart had written to him the previous September with a business proposition. Finch arrived in Brisbane on 27 February, just over a week before the Whiskey fire. He conceded that he and Stuart had been friends for years.

Hayes then informed Finch that police were investigating the fire at the Whiskey, which had resulted in the loss of 15 lives, and proceeded to read out the names of the dead.

Finch asked them to stop reading the names, claiming he had been 'sick ever since it happened' and had dry-retched for a day when he found out about the fatalities.

'Are you admitting that you were involved in the deaths of these people?' Hayes asked.

'Yes unfortunately,' Finch supposedly replied. 'It was not intended to be this way. It was intended to intimidate them so as Johnny could get what he wanted.'

Hayes asked him what he meant by saying 'Johnny could get what he wanted'.

Finch said it was all 'Johnny's idea' and that the idea was to 'start a bit of a fire' in the foyer of the club and 'frighten' people. He said it was all part of Stuart's plan to extort money from Brisbane nightclubs. He wanted to 'tie up' Brisbane just as gangster Lenny McPherson had tied up the Sydney scene.

Finch said Stuart paid for his flight to Brisbane knowing he would 'do anything' to help his mate.

Finch supposedly told police that Stuart had been planning the operation for months and that he'd established an iron-clad alibi for himself. He said he had used a local reporter to plant stories in the newspaper about Sydney gangs coming to Brisbane and extorting clubs. When the fire was set and the extortion racket established, Finch was to slip out of the country.

He said Stuart wanted to be the 'Mr Big of Brisbane'.

Hayes then asked him what his movements were on the night of 7 March, and into the early hours of the next morning. 'We drove in towards town and on the way Johnny pulled up in the bush and picked up two empty drums, he told me he planted them there,' Finch replied. 'Before we got to town, Johnny drove into a side street and there were some cars parked there and we took a drum each and a piece of tubing – Johnny filled his first from a car parked in the street and then I put my drum under the tank and as I was filling mine a dog barked and we decided to give it away. We put the two drums of petrol in the back of Johnny's station wagon.'

He said Stuart dropped him at the entrance to the Whiskey at about 1 a.m. and he hid the petrol drums in the shadows at the side of the club.

'... Johnny said he had been at the club a few times and there would only be a handful of people there at about 2 o'clock and that they would soon get out the fire escape,' Finch continued. 'Oh God why didn't those people get out, why did they stay there. Johnny said around about 2 o'clock I was to take off the caps of the drums and roll them into the entrance and then light a full packet of folder matches – you know the ones, like you get at the hotel and clubs and all.'

Finch admitted he had lit the fire.

He refused to accompany police back to the site of the Whiskey in Amelia Street.

'Are you prepared to read this record of interview over aloud and sign it if it is a correct record of our conversations,' Hayes supposedly said. 'You are not obliged to sign it unless you wish to do so.'

Finch refused to sign the document.

The interview had lasted just two hours and eight minutes.

Also present for the interview, as noted at the start of the record typed by Redmond, was the famous Sydney detective Roger Rogerson, whose notorious career would in the end see him found guilty of murder and imprisoned for the rest of his natural life. 'John Andrew Stuart kept saying it was Sydney criminals, Mr Bigs, Lenny Mc[Pherson], George Freeman, he was dropping a lot of names,' Rogerson said. 'And there was a journalist up there writing up stories about Sydney crims taking over the Valley … It was a way of setting up an alibi. It was all crap. Stuart had been barred from returning to Sydney. He was a ratbag. It was all a story organised by him.'

Still, had Finch been verballed?

Jack 'The Bagman' Herbert, supreme organiser of the corrupt Queensland police system of graft known as The Joke, was at CIB headquarters the night Finch was interviewed by police and made his so-called confession. Herbert would reveal before his death that he had seen investigators Atkinson and Hayes later washing blood from their arms in the washroom. He said Finch and Stuart had been dragged into the washroom at some point and severely beaten. Herbert said the 'Sydney police' were also involved.

'[They] dragged the two of them down, gave them a wash up and that's all dead-set what I know,' he would confidentially tell his biographer, Tom Gilling. 'But I've never told another soul. I'll tell you why. At the time everybody was incensed at these bastards doing what they did. I wasn't going to get them out and lose all the bloody sympathy of the public. I remember that was my feeling at the time. That I couldn't afford to [intervene], so I thought about it a lot and I can't do anything about it. Because what's it going to do?'

Gilling asked Herbert if he'd seen police drag the two suspects out of the washroom.

'Oh, yeah,' he said.

'They'd taken them in for a wash?' Gilling asked.

'Yeah.'

Fifteen years later, in the 22 November edition of *The Bulletin* magazine, Roger Rogerson, present at Finch's interrogation that Sunday, would tell journalist Bruce Stannard:

'He [Stuart] was like a bloody wild animal when they brought him into the Watchhouse. All he had on was a pair of briefs and I remember he stood at the charge desk with his feet well back and his arms stretched out, leaning on the desk and snarling like a bloody animal.

'He was a pretty fit little bastard. I remember all the muscles on his chest and stomach rippling like a bloody weightlifter. Stuart never made a statement. He was too smart for that.

'So, when they lumbered Finch, we said, right, this bastard is going to talk. Syd Atkinson brought him into Roma Street after a bit of a chase on the Sunday morning and he was given a terrible hiding. He was handcuffed to a chair and we knocked the shit out of him. Siddy Atkinson was pretty fit then and he gave him a terrible hiding. We all laid into him with our fists. The old adrenalin was up.

'The blokes were yelling at him, "You fucking cunt, Finch. You fucking murderer: you killed 15 fucking people, you mongrel."

'But I've got to say this for him. I admire the way he kept his trap shut. He was as guilty as sin but he didn't want to give us the satisfaction of hearing it from his own lips. The bastard didn't utter one bloody word. He just sat there and copped an almighty hiding.

'I've seen a lot of blokes get biffed and, believe me, Finch got a real going over but he didn't even whimper. That takes real guts in my opinion. Some blokes, you kick them in the balls and straight away they start squealing and they'll tell you everything.

'But not Finch. The bastard sat there like a dummy.'

Drama in Court

On Monday 12 March Stuart and Finch were transported in a convoy of four carloads of detectives, many armed with shotguns, to the magistrates court where charges were read against them. The two men were separated, and were led into Number 1 Magistrates Court. They were manacled and surrounded by a scrum of police. True to form, Stuart caused pandemonium. He shouted his innocence and had to be restrained by six police officers. He had to be dragged and pushed into the dock. At one point, Detective Pat Glancy had Stuart in a headlock.

As the murder charges were being read by police prosecutor Senior Sergeant F.G. Donaghue, Finch interrupted. 'Can I say something?' he asked. 'When I was being brought in the police put a record of interview in my pocket and one of them said, "Cop that." I made no admissions. I was beaten up by the police a couple of times yesterday. I am innocent.'

Stuart later shouted out in court: 'Let go of my arm. What do you think I'm trying to do? Beat 40 coppers. You're breaking my arm and I'm not even struggling.'

Neither were granted bail and both men were remanded until 20 March. They were taken to Boggo Road Gaol.

With Finch and Stuart under arrest and awaiting trial, the press and the public now turned on the authorities in shock and rage, demanding answers. Were the notoriously corrupt Queensland police not telling all they knew?

The Sydney *Tribune* – the official newspaper of the Communist party of Australia – fired a salvo that did more than hint that there may have been a conspiracy afoot.

> Behind the fire-murder of 15 in Brisbane's Whiskey Au
> Go Go nightclub, and the current hasty prosecution of two

police-selected culprits lies one of the greatest police and inter-
governmental scandals ever seen in this country. Before the full
story is finished, it will reveal much more of the ill-concealed
rot and corruption that has featured for years in the police force
under the Bjelke-Petersen Country-Liberal Party regime.

Was this simply a 'commie rag' taking the opportunity to
savage one of the nation's most conservative State governments?
Could the newspaper really link the death of 15 innocent people
to 'how indifferent the State machine of capitalism can be towards
human life'?

There may have been liberal lashings of hyperbole, but the article
joined some interesting dots that would still be puzzling decades
later. The *Tribune* said evidence was already emerging, just days
after the fire, which pointed towards 'police and State government
negligence and indifference'.

> The Bjelke-Petersen government during passionate scenes last
> Thursday in State Parliament clamped the gag on an attempt
> by the State Labor Opposition to probe police and government
> negligence over the fire, only hours after it had occurred. They
> rightly demanded an immediate Royal Commission into the
> increase in crime, extortion and other rackets.

The report repeated the denials by Commissioner Whitrod that
there was no evidence that the fire was the result of extortion attempts
by Sydney gangs to set up rackets in south-east Queensland.

> But in a suddenly-called, special press conference [on the
> Saturday] … Whitrod angrily confirmed the correctness of a
> statement made on Friday in Canberra by the Commonwealth
> Police that they had warned the Queensland Police two weeks

beforehand that the Whiskey Au Go Go nightclub was a target for underworld violence. Whitrod – himself a former ASIO officer and Commonwealth Police Commissioner – sought refuge in the claim that he personally had not received the warning until two days after the bombing [Saturday 10 March], when he 'found confirmation on his desk'.

This was an extraordinary situation. An explicit warning from a Commonwealth Police officer, having gathered credible information from an informant about an impending and potentially huge tragedy, had not been passed on to Whitrod until it mysteriously appeared on his desk a full two days after the mass murder. The *Tribune* asked:

> … clearly some people in [the] Queensland State government police regime are interested in suppressing Commonwealth Police advice and warnings about impending crime in Queensland.
>
> If the Commonwealth Police DID OFFICIALLY inform the Queensland Police of the danger of firebombing, why was that information not put on Whitrod's desk … until TWO DAYS AFTER the bombing?
>
> Was it simply inter-police rivalry, dislike of Whitrod by some of the Queensland police hierarchy, or was it that some police (backed by the State Government) wanted to protect a corruption-ridden relationship between police and criminals?

Or indeed was it a murky combination of all three? The *Tribune*'s speculation about a cover-up, and the damage to Whitrod, was further underlined by Stuart's own assertions to Inspector Basil Hicks, that the torching of the Whiskey was 'politically' motivated, and that Whitrod and Hodges would 'cook' for it. Why had Voigt and Hicks not passed on their concerns about the torching of the Whiskey, separate from the Commonwealth Police warning?

One former Queensland police officer explained that the ranting of police informant Stuart may at the time have been seen as just that – wild, improbable conjecture from a known liar who would do and say anything to suit his purposes. Indeed, Stuart's long-winded stories to Hicks, which placed Stuart as a lifelong criminal now trying to assist police and avert what might develop into a tragedy, must have seemed fantastical at the time.

How did Stuart know so much about this impending attack from Sydney gangs if, as he claimed, he had nothing to do with the detailed extortion rackets?

The former officer said it would take a more tangible evidence, apart from just Stuart's word, to see those allegations move up the investigative chain to the point where priority dictated action by police.

But that didn't explain how the formal Commonwealth warning, on paper, had been kept from Whitrod until two days after the tragedy. Who, on Whitrod's staff, had the access and power to physically withhold that information? That singular act proved to be extremely damaging to Whitrod's reputation.

The *Tribune* demanded action on the whole sorry saga, and said it was time for 'a Federally-conducted public enquiry into the Whiskey Au Go Go murders, the failure of the Queensland Police to stop it, despite ample warning, and the Queensland Government's attempt to smother the whole tragedy up'.

The newspaper's calls went unanswered. It had been shouting into the wind.

The Man in the White Suit

It was around the time of the Whiskey Au Go Go tragedy that Vincent O'Dempsey began to show his entrepreneurship and started a small business with a number of branches. This was the lucrative 'massage parlour' game. Perhaps taking a leaf out of the book of Sydney heavyweight Stewart John Regan, O'Dempsey started running a couple of prostitutes out of two rooms upstairs in the Mayfair Hotel in Palmerin Street, Warwick.

The old pub had a bar downstairs and accommodation upstairs. 'It was across the road from the post office,' one local said. 'Vince used to have a couple of girls working for him there. The police knew about it but I don't think they were game to touch him. I used to drink with a few of them when they were off-duty, so if we knew what was going on upstairs at the Mayfair, then they knew.

'Vince was good friends with one particular police officer anyway. They used to drink together and played rugby league together. They might have had some businesses together going on the side.'

A few decades earlier, O'Dempsey had stood out on the Warwick streetscape when he dressed as a bodgie. By the 1970s he had changed his attire entirely, although it didn't make him any less conspicuous. 'He always wore a white suit,' says one acquaintance. 'It stuck out like signs beside a road. Back then you dressed up a little bit more. But that was Vince. A white suit.'

The acquaintance said he was in a Warwick pub one day when some locals were welcoming a new resident, a young woman, who noticed the white-suited stranger across the bar. 'She asked who that suave gentleman was. One of the girls had to take her to the toilets and explain to her that it was Vince O'Dempsey.'

At this time, too, according to family friends and former criminal business partners, O'Dempsey was running some prostitutes on the Gold Coast. 'He was always going back and forth to the Gold Coast,' said one source. In the not too distant future, O'Dempsey would also open his 'health studio', Polonia, in Brisbane.

Meanwhile, after the Whiskey went up the Clockwork Orange Gang quickly dissipated. One associate says several of them moved from their rented share house in Chermside to a house in nearby Geebung. 'This was the start of the run,' the associate remembers.

Another associate says the Clockwork boys were understandably quiet after the Whiskey horror. 'A couple of police said to us, there is no interest in you guys, for the Whiskey,' he recalls. 'We heard that from the guys [corrupt police] at Nundah. The higher powers communicated with Nundah to start with. I got a request to come into the CIB. I went in there ... and that's when he [the copper] dropped the bombshell ... He said, "How you feeling about helping us out? Giving us information about what's going to happen and helping us out?"

'I said, "Turn it up, I'm already paying you money, I'm not going to start giving you information ... forget about that ..."

'After a while, especially after we were told there was no interest in us, it was back to square one again.'

The gang quietly moved around Brisbane, then further afield. 'From the Geebung house they went and stayed in a shed near Rocklea for a little while. I helped find that for them. I took their suitcases and stashed them ... They were at that shed for only about a day and for some unknown reason they just took off. They jumped on a bus and off they went.'

[Keith] Meredith went to Darwin. Dubois headed to Adelaide where he had relatives. Hamilton and Hall went over to New Zealand and they stayed there for a while.

In time most of the gang would return to a farmhouse at Caboolture, north of Brisbane. 'They came back and settled in the farmhouse,' the associate says. 'They were laughing at Stuart and Finch's predicament. If you rob a bank with me and you get caught and I get away, that's just bad luck for you. I'm not going to hand myself in. I might send you a Christmas card and sign it Joe Blow or something, but I'd never laugh at you and the predicament you're in.

'That's what Tommy and the gang were doing. They were laughing at Stuart and Finch. They were laughing their heads off.'

Evidence and Amputations

Given the histrionics displayed during Finch and Stuart's brief court appearance on the day after their arrest in early March, there was much more to come in the weeks leading up to, and during, their committal hearing in Brisbane. A number of police who had taken witness statements from Finch and Stuart testified to both men being guilty, as did Stuart's brother Dan, who had in fact given his own brother up to police on the day of his arrest.

The Little brothers joined the witness fray, as did the mysterious John Hannay, albeit briefly. Brian Little told the court he was on good terms with Hannay, the Whiskey's former manager, but they had had a dispute over money. 'There was a large amount of money missing from the company and there were certain records that John Hannay had in his offices in Brunswick Street that were either misplaced or destroyed,' Little said under questioning. He said the missing money could have been about $20,000.

Hannay, who listed his address as the Grosvenor Hotel in Rockhampton, said he had been the manager of the Whiskey until November 1972.

Why did he leave Little Enterprises, he was asked.

'I got belted up,' Hannay said in court. He said the bashing occurred in a laneway near Chequers Nightclub in Fortitude Valley. He said he was given his letter of dismissal from the Little's nightclub business the next day. Hannay said he had been attempting to get an explanation for his sacking.

On 21 June 1973 Stuart and Finch were committed for trial and so began the predictable skirmishes, medical emergencies and delays leading up to the trial that would grip the nation. Within days of being committed, Stuart was taken to hospital complaining of 'severe abdominal pains'. X-rays revealed nothing. (Finch had earlier tried to amputate one of his fingers as a way of delaying his court appearance.)

In mid-August, Stuart was then remanded on charges of having assaulted three prison officers. It was alleged he had thrown a bucket of urine through the bars and struck one officer. Two officers who went to their colleagues' aid were also assaulted.

In a separate matter, it was also alleged that Whiskey owner Brian Little was further threatened as the trial loomed. (During the committal Little was approached by an 'intermediary' at his other club, Chequers, and issued a threat. The man told him that Billy McCulkin was not 'very happy' about his best mate Stuart being charged over the Whiskey fire. Little was told hitman [Frederick] 'Paddles' Anderson would be coming into the club 'to have a chat' and John Bell would be knocked off.)

The trial opened on 10 September before Justice George Lucas. Preliminary legal debate lasted almost two days before the jury was empanelled. Only then did Crown Prosecutor L.J. McNamara read a list of 131 prospective witnesses. It was set to be a long trial.

After those early delays, Chief Crown Prosecutor L.G. Martin opened the Crown case, describing Stuart in the lead-up to the Whiskey fire as the 'distraught prophet of doom'. He said Stuart's warning to police and the press was nothing more than Stuart sowing fear and building an alibi for himself.

Within days, the trial was rocked by two things. Stuart abruptly dismissed his legal counsel, and then he swallowed four pieces of metal and was taken to the Royal Brisbane Hospital for treatment.

It was expected he would be operated on, and confined to hospital for 10 to 14 days. For a moment, the future of the trial was in jeopardy. But in the end, after careful consideration, Justice

Lucas was having none of it. He ordered the trial continue in Stuart's absence. Justice Lucas said he was convinced this was part of Stuart's plan to either stop the trial or prevent him from being tried jointly with Finch. The judge said Stuart would be provided transcripts of each day's proceedings.

One of the early trial witnesses was Sydney gangster Leonard 'Mr Big' McPherson. McPherson denied Stuart's claim that he and Stuart had arranged to meet on the Gold Coast in September 1972, where McPherson had a holiday house. McPherson admitted he knew a man named [Stewart John] Regan. He said he had nothing to do with any attempt to set up extortion rackets in Brisbane.

Underworld figures Frederick 'Paddles' Anderson and Regan also made star appearances. Regan was described in court as a 'company manager'. He testified he had no interest in Brisbane nightclubs.

Detective Senior Sergeant Brian Hayes came under fire over the questioning of Finch and the unsigned record of interview. Was it a police verbal?

'It was not a fabrication. That is how it happened,' Hayes replied.

Given there were a number of detectives present when the so-called record of interview was generated, did he think that if the record was ever challenged there'd be safety in numbers?

'No,' he shot back. 'If a jury would not believe one detective senior sergeant it wouldn't believe six. The six men were not there by design. They just happened to be present at that time.'

Syd Atkinson backed up his colleague, Hayes. When asked whether Finch had been bashed by police during his interrogation in the city CIB offices, he emphatically denied it. 'There were no thumps in that room,' he told the court. 'There were certainly shouts and bumps but no one was thumped.'

On 4 October, Justice Lucas heard medical evidence about John Hannay and whether he was fit to appear as a witness. It appeared Hannay had recently fallen from a horse and suffered brain damage. Hannay's doctor was of the strong opinion that mental tension had aggravated Hannay's condition and that any cross-examination might permanently damage his health.

In the end, Hannay was brought in to give evidence, accompanied at all times by his doctor. Hannay said he bore no grudges against the Little brothers and denied he had anything to do with the Whiskey fire. He also denied that he had made a phone call from Rockhampton to his Brisbane solicitor at 2 a.m. on 8 March, just minutes before the fatal fire. Hannay would go on to say that it was Johnny Bell and two other men who had bashed him in the alleyway, rendering him unconscious.

Then, in what must go down as one of the most unusual interludes in any major criminal trial in Queensland, more than a month into the trial the jury, legal counsel and others were taken to the Royal Brisbane Hospital to visit defendant John Andrew Stuart, recovering from swallowing the metal pieces at the start of the trial.

The Brisbane *Sunday Sun* described the bizarre scene. 'Rarely could there have been a hospital visit more strange,' it wrote. 'For five minutes 43 men sat, their eyes glued on the pale, frail figure in the portable bed. For five minutes John Andrew Stuart lay in the bed, silent, almost deathly still. The room at Royal Brisbane Hospital had the air of a death scene.'

Stuart had taken a second bout of wire in hospital while he was recovering from the first, and given it was a very real possibility he would not see the inside of the courtroom for the duration of the trial, Justice Lucas had made the decision to take the court to Stuart.

Stuart remained silent. Finch, watching from the sidelines, was recorded as saying: 'I thought they only done this in Russia.'

In the end it took the jury just two hours to find Stuart and Finch guilty of the Whiskey atrocity. On 23 October, Stuart was transported from hospital for his sentencing. He was accompanied by his doctor and was under heavy guard.

According to the Brisbane *Telegraph* he looked 'wasted, pallid and frail'. Just prior to sentencing he spat in the face of Chief Crown Prosecutor Martin, QC. 'You'll never wash that off,' Stuart said. 'You'll have it on your face until the day you die.'

Stuart continued his outburst. 'The jury's verdict is wrong,' he said. 'I would know that better than any man. I wish to say that because of the evidence presented in this case the jury's verdict was correct on what they heard. But as I said, only I would know that that was false.'

Justice Lucas, in summing up the trial, told the court that Finch's theories about this whole thing being a conspiracy concocted by police who were prepared to perjure themselves in court over a false record of interview would amount to a conspiracy of the first order.

'Finch's defence is that the unsigned record of interview is a complete fabrication and that a large number of police officers have entered into a conspiracy to defeat the course of justice; thus, the six police officers present at the taking of the record of interview have given perjured evidence ... It has always seemed to me that the larger a conspiracy becomes and the more policemen involved in it, the less likely the story of a conspiracy is to be true.'

John Andrew Stuart was sentenced to life imprisonment. As was James Richard Finch.

Mrs Dulcie Day, mother of Whiskey victim, the musician Darcy Day said: 'I know that boy's soul is in torment, but I can't feel sorry for him. I'm not bitter at him [Finch]. I don't think he meant to do it. I feel sorry for his mother ... I think he and his friend John Andrew Stuart are hard boys. They chose that life.'

Stuart's mother, Edna Watts, said that although her son was 'no angel', the family would continue to fight for his freedom and that the trial was 'a farce'.

Brisbane journalist Mick Barnes attended the next State Parliamentary sitting expecting to hear robust debate about the

Whiskey. He didn't. 'There will be no Royal Commission into the Whiskey Au Go Go tragedy,' he wrote:

> There will be no judicial inquiry, no Cabinet investigation, not even a Ministerial inquiry. The public demanded and was promised a Royal Commission into whether police were warned of the tragedy and whether it could have been prevented. The Government has since reneged on this promise.

When the matter of the Whiskey was actually raised during the sitting, it was ruled out of order. It was sub judice. Appeals were pending. Barnes concluded:

> I was reminded that many years ago Emile Zola, the great French writer, brought a similar government down with an article entitled, "I Accuse". I do not accuse the Queensland Government. I pity it in its egomania. I pity it that it can put party politics before the death of 15 hapless people. And I pity the people of Queensland that they accept this with equanimity.

Officially, the saga of the Whiskey Au Go Go was over. But it was just the beginning of Barbara McCulkin's problems.

Where There's Smoke

Barbara and Billy had reached the point of no return in their marriage. And there was the baggage she carried from what she learned about his and his friends' criminal enterprises. Particularly the fires at the beginning of the year.

Her brother, Graham Ogden, who lived in Strathpine on Brisbane's northside, was also getting strange vibes from his sister.

'We visited her quite a few times over the years [at Dorchester Street],' he recalls. 'My wife was always impressed about the sewing, and Barbara looking after the kids and doing a really good job.'

On one visit Ogden says McCulkin pulled up in Dorchester Street driving a white van. This put paid to McCulkin's curious lifelong insistence that he couldn't drive a car, let alone a truck. 'We were standing in the front door facing the street,' Ogden recalls. 'Bill drove up in a white Mazda bongo van. A blind van ... there were no windows in the side just the front and back ones. And Barbara said, "Where'd you get that from?"

'"Oh," he said, "a mate of mine that lives around town." He did know how to drive and that's all there is to it.'

Ogden also remembers the last time he ever saw his sister alive. He and his wife paid another visit to the ramshackle Queenslander in Dorchester Street towards the end of 1973.

'That shocked me – last time I saw her she was terrified,' he says. 'We both believe to this day that she stopped saying [to us] what she wanted to about Billy. And we now believe Billy was [involved] in the Whiskey fire. Had she said what she wanted to we could have been in danger. We both feel she stopped there. But she was terrified ... He was standing behind her. That old house ... is like an old drum inside. It echoes like mad. And he was watching Barbara. I'm sure he heard everything.'

Ogden asked her what was wrong. 'I can put him away with what I know about him for a long time,' Barbara told him. Ogden was positive she was referring to McCulkin. 'And we left them and it was the last we saw of her.'

Barbara was also tired of Billy's endless philandering. (He was seeing another women, Estelle Long, at this time, and was about to move into her flat in Juliette Street, Annerley, just south of the Brisbane CBD.) Barbara was ready to get on with her life. She was booked in for surgery to remove stretch marks around her breasts and stomach. She wanted to meet someone else, and secure some stability for herself and her girls. And to do that, she wanted to look ship-shape. She was also considering leaving the snack bar and getting a new job. Perhaps in one of the big department stores like Myer. It was a beginning, of sorts.

Barbara McCulkin couldn't know she and her girls had just a few months to live.

Polonia

Only days after Stuart and Finch were sentenced to life imprisonment, Vince O'Dempsey and his de facto wife, Dianne Pritchard, opened their own 'health studio' in Lutwyche. The studio was a part of a small clutch of offices at 518 Lutwyche Road. A large office fronted the road, but down a small driveway to the right was another separate cream brick block of three smaller, adjoining office spaces. The front of the offices was all glass and aluminium, illuminated by neon lights. Inside each office was a small waiting room at the front, a large room to the left and a small kitchen with a sink at the back. The décor was painted besser brick and carpet.

The lessee of the space that would become the Polonia Health Studio was Ernest Latima Watkins of 34 Cordelia Street, West End. Watkins in fact managed the Vogue Private Hotel there; a refuge for many of the city's prostitutes. Pritchard kept a room at the Vogue to store clothes and belongings. As did Margaret Grace Ward, a young woman from the Gympie region who had originally trained as a nurse and arrived in the big smoke of Brisbane to broaden her horizons. Somehow, she had been lured into prostitution. She also worked with Pritchard at the new Polonia. According to police records, Polonia opened its doors on Friday 19 October 1973.

Had O'Dempsey and Pritchard been given the green light by corrupt members of the Licensing Branch to hang out their shingle in the competitive world of prostitution? Were they expected to pay massive kickbacks to police? And where did they get the money to set up the health studio in the first place?

Given that O'Dempsey and Pritchard had failed to register Polonia as a business name, was this a case of a health studio flying completely under the radar of all checks and balances? Was it a coincidence that the brothel had opened its doors for business just after the conclusion of the Stuart and Finch trial? As the Whiskey killers festered in Boggo Road, O'Dempsey was off on a new venture that, if successful, and despite the downside of the tax to corrupt police, could be a licence to print significant amounts of money.

One criminal close to O'Dempsey at the time said the timing of the opening of Polonia was important.

'The way I saw it, it was Vince's reward from the corrupt coppers,' he said. 'The Whiskey is wrapped up, Finch and Stuart go down, that's the end of the story. The whole thing is contained. There is no way in the world Vince could have done what he did without being protected by police. He just couldn't have. He was close to Murphy. The question is, what did Vince have on Murphy that allowed him to do pretty much what he pleased?'

Keith Meredith of the Clockwork Orange Gang remembered being invited over to Vince's new brothel when it opened. 'I was with [Garry] Dubois and [Tom] Hamilton when I first saw O'Dempsey, who at the time was working for Paul Meade at an auction house run in Queen Street, Brisbane,' Meredith later told police. 'I later saw O'Dempsey when he had the massage parlour on Lutwyche Road. O'Dempsey's girlfriend, Dianne Pritchard, was running the massage parlour for O'Dempsey. O'Dempsey and Dubois were close and I believe they were both in gaol at the same time [in the 1960s].

'When the massage parlour first opened up O'Dempsey had invited Dubois to come and have a look. I went with Dubois, [Peter] Hall and Hamilton to the massage parlour. I got a massage and it was the first and only massage I ever had.'

Curiously, Vince's Polonia was just a block or two north from one of Simone Vogel's brothels, Napoleon's Retreat, and both would have operated according to the age-old rules and stipulations of the corrupt system known as The Joke. Those rules ensured that only the Licensing Branch could sanction such an outfit, and they were specific on location and the number of girls working in each parlour. The kickbacks were to be paid on time once a month. Warnings were given on any impending raids, and occasionally one of the girls was 'written up' to maintain the facade of vigilant policing.

Parlour proprietors like Vogel and O'Dempsey knew the rules, but events didn't always go to plan. Despite the optimism surrounding this new venture, O'Dempsey had one of those strokes of ill-fortune. He and his new brothel had come to the attention of CIU Inspector Basil Hicks. Within weeks of Polonia starting its operations Hicks knocked on the door.

'Part of my duties at the unit was to investigate any organisation behind prostitution in massage parlours,' Hicks later told a coronial inquest. 'I would visit the various massage parlours in Brisbane and interview the people working there ... I can remember seeing a woman there [at the Polonia] named Dianne Pritchard who also went under the name of Cheryl Evans.'

Hicks proceeded to interview Pritchard. 'She told me that she was carrying on prostitution at that parlour,' Hicks said. 'She said she was living with a man named Vince O'Dempsey ... [he] was known to me as a convicted criminal. I can remember seeing the man O'Dempsey in a back room ... it was a little kitchenette there. I did not speak to him. He was standing just inside the door and it appeared to me that he was hiding so he couldn't be seen ...'

Hicks also saw someone else at Polonia – a young woman by the name of Margaret Grace Ward. Hicks said: 'I passed information to the Licensing Branch that Pritchard and Ward were operating as prostitutes at the Polonia and both women were interviewed by the Licensing Branch on 9 November 1973.'

The Licensing Branch acted on Hicks's information and went out to inspect the so-called health studio. One of the officers involved was Kingsley Fancourt. 'We went out and did a walk-in on a brothel in Lutwyche,' he recalls. 'O'Dempsey was there and I didn't know him from bloody Adam. Later that night I'm back at the office and Merv Hoppy Hopgood asked me what I'd done during the day. I told him we were out doing a walk-through in this parlour … who was there? Bloody O'Dempsey.

'He asked, "Do you know about O'Dempsey?"'

'He told me Vince O'Dempsey had buried two people on a fenceline in western NSW, and he had a body in the dam wall at Warwick, that he was a knife man, that he'd swore to kill a copper, and he was warning me to be careful of him.'

Both Pritchard and Ward were charged with prostitution at the brothel on Lutwyche Road. In her statement Ward claimed Pritchard had forced her into prostitution against her will. She claimed she had innocently responded to an advertisement in *The Courier-Mail*: 'Masseur required. No experience necessary.'

It was a minor setback for O'Dempsey and his new business venture. Somehow Detective Hicks, the cleanskin in Commissioner Whitrod's corruption-busting CIU, had slipped past O'Dempsey's cordon of police buddies. He had, for years, enjoyed the protection of none other than Rat Pack big wheel, Tony Murphy.

One of O'Dempsey's associates confirms the relationship, and says Murphy once paid a visit to the police in Warwick to set the ground rules – O'Dempsey was not to be touched.

The associate says that years later he was sitting around a campfire one night at a property outside Warwick when Tony Murphy's name came up. A number of criminal associates were present. One witness said: '[criminal] Dennis Ide was carrying on about Murphy, and Vince said, "We don't have to worry about fucking Murphy. Murphy's not going to come out here and bring us undone. He's been to the Warwick coppers and told them to fucking pull up."

'It's like everybody needs someone to do their dirty work, don't they? Dennis had an issue with Murphy, and Vince just, with a little cheeky grin on his head, he said, "He's already been out and told them fucking don't even touch me and leave me alone."'

Before the Deluge

The rain seemed to go on forever in the spring of 1973. Billy McCulkin was enjoying his first regular employment in years, working as a dogman on the construction of a high-rise office block at 444 Queen Street. The site was just around the corner from the notorious National Hotel, owned by Jack, Rolly and Max Roberts. The National was the drinking hole of choice for corrupt police. Billy, naturally, spent a lot of time drinking there with his mates after work. As he did in the other 'copper's pub' in Queen Street, the Belfast, which was a regular haunt for Detective Tony Murphy. McCulkin was also a regular patron of the Treasury Hotel, where his girlfriend, Estelle Long, worked.

They had begun a relationship earlier that year but lately things had started getting serious. He decided to move into Long's flat in Annerley. But first his new mistress laid down some ground rules. She was aware he'd been involved in various crimes in the past. Long told him she wanted him to 'get away from that', and she didn't want his old friends hanging around the flat, just as they had done at 6 Dorchester Street, Highgate Hill.

'The reason for me leaving the family home was because I could not get on with my wife, and she could not get on with me,' Billy would reveal in a police statement, '… well I don't think she was sort of overjoyed [at him leaving] but I don't think she was ready to burst into tears, you know, it was just sort of accepted, I think.'

With Billy out of the house, Vince O'Dempsey – despite living with his de facto, Dianne Pritchard – began showing interest in Barbara McCulkin. He would sometimes drop her off to work at the Milky Way snack bar in his distinctive 1972-model orange and black-striped Valiant Charger (PYM908). Sometimes he'd pick her up after work and drive her back to Dorchester Street.

It was during these meetings that O'Dempsey told Barbara of her husband Billy's numerous affairs, including details of his relationship with Estelle Long. Barbara, in turn, told her workmate Ellen Gilbert that O'Dempsey had taken her to his flat in 'Nethercote Court' at 66 Elizabeth Street, Rosalie, but 'nothing happened'. He would often take her on 'drives' in his Charger.

Billy McCulkin's lover, Estelle Long, later told police: 'I recall that at the time Billy knew that O'Dempsey was showing interest in Barbara, there was reference to O'Dempsey taking her for drives and Billy was aware of his interest in her.'

Barbara said she had no great affection for O'Dempsey, and told Gilbert she had heard a story that he had on occasion tied up his girlfriend, Dianne Pritchard, in the place they were living and went out. Barbara herself had no personal safety issues with O'Dempsey. She knew that her husband, Billy, had trusted Vince, and to a degree so did she. It was Billy she was more afraid of.

In fact she had relayed her concerns to her neighbour, Peter Nisbet, who lived with friends in the house next door at number 4 Dorchester Street. Nisbet's bedroom was in the front right-hand corner of the house, and overlooked the McCulkin's yard and kitchen. The houses were physically close. When Billy McCulkin was still living in the house, Nisbet couldn't help but notice that he was physically violent to his wife. Billy would later admit to 'hitting' his wife.

After Billy moved in with Long, Nisbet observed Vince O'Dempsey's distinctive car parked often in front of the McCulkin property. He deduced that O'Dempsey 'had more than a passing interest' in Barbara McCulkin.

Barbara liked Nisbet. They would talk over the fence when he mowed the lawn. Towards the end of 1973 she confided to Nisbet that she was frightened of Billy and wanted to get away from him. 'On occasions Mrs McCulkin spoke about John Andrew Stuart and the Whiskey Au Go Go nightclub fire as well as the Torino nightclub fire,' Nisbet later said in a statement to police. 'She stated that she was in a position to put her husband away in gaol for offences which he had committed of which she knew about.'

He also told a coroner's court in 1980: '... the context in which Bill is mentioned in it [the fires of early 1973] is that, you know, that he'd given her a hard time at certain stages and, you know, she wanted to get away and if she could, you know, it'd be a way out, by putting him up the creek.'

Nisbet said Barbara seemed to think Stuart wasn't involved in torching the Whiskey and that 'he'd been set up for it'.

Nisbet later elaborated in another statement to police: 'I can recall one conversation with Barbara where we spoke for an hour to an hour and a half. Barbara told me that her husband was associated with criminals and she had enough on Billy to put him away for years with what she knew.

'In the same conversation Barbara told me that her husband, Billy McCulkin, had something to do with the Whiskey Au Go Go fire and that if the cops had asked him the right questions they would have found out more people were involved in the Whiskey Au Go Go fire.

'Barbara indicated that Finch and Stuart were not the primary movers of the Whiskey and that they were just collateral damage or an easy get for the cops. She seemed to think Stuart was set up for the Whiskey Au Go Go fire.'

Margaret Grace Ward Goes Missing

Following the Licensing Branch raid on O'Dempsey's little 'health studio' at Lutwyche, his de facto, Dianne Pritchard, and young worker Margaret Grace Ward were issued summons' on prostitution charges. They were due to appear in court on 16 November 1973.

Ward was terrified about her court appearance, and extremely worried that her parents would discover she was being prosecuted for prostitution. On 15 November, the day before her court hearing, Ward, with Pritchard and O'Dempsey, saw a solicitor in the city about the imminent case. Ward was going to have to give evidence against Pritchard, and in turn, O'Dempsey.

The next day, Ward failed to appear in court and was convicted in her absence. Pritchard was found guilty of keeping a premises for the purpose of prostitution. She was given a fine.

On Saturday 24 November, Ward was reported as a missing person by her stepmother. A police investigation was launched into her disappearance. All of Ward's clothes and belongings had remained untouched in her room at the Vogue Private Hotel.

Margaret Grace Ward was never seen again.

The End of the Affair

Barbara McCulkin was admitted to St Andrew's Hospital on Wickham Terrace, on Friday 7 December 1973, for cosmetic surgery to remove stretch marks from her stomach and her breasts. She'd finished up work at the Milky Way café the week before.

Workmate Ellen Gilbert said: 'Mrs McCulkin informed me that her husband was extremely jealous of her and she further informed me that she had particularly severe stretch marks in the abdomen area and ... that she was very conscious of these stretch marks and would not have an affair with another man owing to her appearance and had arranged to have the operation to remove the stretch marks and so begin a new life for herself as her husband had deserted her.'

She was operated on by plastic surgeon, Dr William Everingham, on Tuesday 11 December, to 'excise stretchmarks on the abdomen' and for breast augmentation, according to a statement he later provided to court. The operation went 'without complication'.

While Barbara was in hospital, Vicki and Leanne McCulkin were looked after by one of Barbara's friends. According to police statements, Billy McCulkin asked Estelle Long to help pay for Barbara's operation.

'I'm not sure why but Billy said it was an operation Barbara "had to have" and so I assisted with the money,' said Long. 'I don't remember the amount but I remember it was a fair bit.' (It was a ruse by Billy. Barbara would go on to claim the cost of the surgery from Medical Benefits of Australia.)

Barbara was discharged from hospital around 14 December 1973. Billy collected her from the hospital and took her home to Dorchester Street. He later claimed he had visited her every day in hospital and taken her flowers and chocolates. Billy was giving his wife and children a lot of attention after the operation.

'I knew that Billy was going back and visiting Barbara and the children and that he spent a lot of time at the house when Barbara was first out of hospital,' Long said in a statement.

Around this time, Nisbet, the neighbour, was awoken at around two o'clock one morning by lights in the McCulkin's kitchen shining on his bedroom window. His first thought was that Billy McCulkin had turned up at the house to give Barbara 'a hard time'.

'... so I went over to check to see if she was okay and Mr O'Dempsey was there then, on that occasion and I was ... I spoke mainly to Barbara and she said, "This is Vic O'Dempsey or Vince O'Dempsey" ... and I said, "Good day" and went home again,' Nisbet later said. 'That was it. She was okay. There was another fellow there as well.'

Billy McCulkin was no longer living at the house but he visited often, and O'Dempsey's regular presence ensured that a criminal milieu still orbited 6 Dorchester Street. Shorty was occasionally there, as were Tommy Hamilton, Keith Meredith and Peter Hall.

Still, the life of the family rolled on, and Barbara began making preparations for the New Year. Schoolbooks were bought for the girls. And despite the wet summer – south-east Queensland was saturated from constant rain, not helped by tropical Cyclone Wanda pushing monsoonal troughs south – the McCulkin girls made the most of their vacation, playing with the Gayton girls who lived across the road at 7 Dorchester Street. Janet, 13, went to Yeronga State High School with Vicki McCulkin, and Juneen, who was about to turn 10 on 16 January 1974, was good friends with Leanne McCulkin.

Barbara continued taking her children and the Gayton sisters to the Red Hill Skate Arena in Enoggera Terrace most Saturday nights. She continued to put out food for the stray cats of Dorchester Street. She was still recovering from her surgery, and had to wear special medical brassieres. Barbara was due to meet her surgeon, Dr Everingham, in his offices at Morris Towers on Wickham Terrace in Brisbane's Spring Hill later that month for a check-up.

Meanwhile, Billy was still splitting his life between Estelle Long at Annerley and his family in Highgate Hill. While he had a job for once he was still drinking most of it away. There was no evidence he was giving Barbara any regular cash to upkeep the house and feed the children, though he claimed he paid the rent on the Dorchester Street house.

Billy spent most of Tuesday 15 January with his wife at Dorchester Street. They discussed the state of their marriage. It was decided that Billy McCulkin would leave Dorchester Street, and the marriage, for good. He packed most of his belongings into two large, battered suitcases that he left in one of the back rooms of the house.

The next day, McCulkin by chance saw Barbara on a council bus in the city. The bus was travelling down Queen Street towards Fortitude Valley. 'She waved to me and I waved back to her, and I mouthed out to her, "I might come over tonight",' Billy McCulkin later told police, '... she nodded her head and the bus took off and that's the last I ever seen her.'

The Vanishing

The last day of Barbara McCulkin's life was a busy one. At about 11.30 a.m. on Wednesday 16 January 1974, she telephoned her good friend, Carole Quiller, who lived at Yeronga, and they discussed one of Quiller's children visiting the McCulkins the next day. Quiller told Barbara she'd bring her over either the next day or Friday.

Barbara told her friend she was heading into town to see the Medical Benefits of Australia about her $200 refund for the operation. She also said she was popping into Myer to see about getting a new job. (She was interviewed and told they'd call her when they had a vacancy.)

During the middle of all this activity, her bus by chance passed the building construction site at 444 Queen Street, where Billy was working, and they had their brief exchange.

Later that afternoon, Barbara was hard at work at her sewing machine, making clothes for herself and the girls. Billy McCulkin never came to the house that night. Instead, he got drunk after work and ended up back at Estelle Long's flat.

Then at about 6.30 p.m., the Gayton girls were on the verandah of their house at 7 Dorchester Street when they saw two men entering the McCulkin property across the road. One of the men was carrying a half-carton of XXXX tallies.

The sisters then crossed the road to get the McCulkin girls. They were having a tenth birthday party for Juneen, and the cake and candles were all ready. 'While I was standing near the front gate of their home, I saw a man playing with Ginger Meggs,' Janet Gayton would tell police less than three months after Barbara McCulkin and her daughters vanished. 'Ginger Meggs' was one of the McCulkin family cats. 'I also saw another man standing near the stove in the kitchen and he was talking to Mrs McCulkin. I knew that man as Vince because I had seen him there before.'

Janet whistled for her friends and Vicki and Leanne came out of the house. Juneen asked: 'Are you coming over? The cake's on the table.'

'Yes,' Vicki said. 'Vince and Shorty are here.'

'What's Shorty's real name?' Janet asked.

Vicki told her. 'Shorty is a mate of my father,' Vicki added.

Vicki was wearing blue jeans with yellow stars on the flared cuffs, a tight-fitting red jumper with a zipper up the front and a Zodiac chain around her neck – she was a Scorpio. Leanne was dressed in a pink smock decorated with flowers and stripes, and pink stretch shorts. The McCulkin girls then crossed the road with the Gayton sisters for the party, leaving Barbara alone with 'Vince and Shorty'.

At some point after this, Clockwork Orange Gang member and Torino arsonist Peter Hall said in a statement to police that Shorty

Dubois had turned up at his house at 24 Nielson Street, Chermside, where Hall said he was living with Carolyn Scully, the sister of Tommy Hamilton.

'On this day Carol and Jan Stubbs, Shorty's partner, were out at the gym,' Hall alleged. 'I was babysitting the kids at the house, and Keithy [Meredith] was with me. Shorty came back in Vince's car to pick up Jan and take her home to his mum's place. When he got to the house it was dark; Shorty told me that he and Vince were at the McCulkins' on the piss and were going back to McCulkin's to have sex. He didn't say who with specifically but he asked me and Keith if we wanted to come along for the fun.

'He told me that O'Dempsey was still back at the McCulkin house and he was going back there after he dropped Jan off home. I told him I was not interested and Keith didn't want to go either. Shorty left the house to drop Jan home and I didn't see him again that night.'

Back at Dorchester Street, Leanne left the party at around 7.30 p.m., feeling unwell. Her older sister, Vicki, got home at around 10.15 p.m. Both respectively told the Gayton girls, when they left the party, that they would see them the next day.

As promised, Janet and Juneen popped over the road to the McCulkin house the next day – Thursday – but found no one at home. They checked repeatedly throughout the day but failed to make contact with the McCulkin girls or their mother. It wasn't until about 6 p.m. on Friday 18 January that Billy McCulkin arrived at 6 Dorchester Street, having worked all day at 444 Queen Street.

'On arrival at the house, I found that it was locked up and I could not rouse anybody,' Billy McCulkin told police in a statement just weeks after the disappearances. 'I then went to the shop on the corner of Dorchester Street and Gladstone Road, where I spoke to the store-keeper, Mrs Swanston, and I asked if she had seen my wife and children, or if she knew where they were.'

Mrs Swanston did not, so he returned to the house and sat on the front steps waiting for his family until nightfall. Later, he saw Janet Gayton walking to the shop.

'Have you seen Vicki or Leanne?' Billy asked her.

'No, they haven't been there all day,' Janet said. 'They weren't there yesterday either.'

Worried, Billy smashed the glass on the front door and gained entry to the house. The scene was described by one eyewitness as 'eerie'. Billy immediately made a chilling inventory. None of Barbara's clothes or personal effects were taken except for the blue dress with white and yellow spots she was wearing when Billy saw her on the council bus two days earlier. Her cosmetics and the sunglasses she always wore were still in the house.

None of the children's clothes were missing except those they wore on the Wednesday. Barbara's change purse containing $8 and personal papers was found on the top of the refrigerator. There was food in the fridge as well as bottles of beer. The children's two pet Siamese cats – gifts to the girls from Estelle Long – had been locked in the house with no food. A dress Barbara was making was still in the sewing machine, and the machine's light was still on. None of the beds in the house had been slept in.

In the letterbox Billy found a letter from Medical Benefits of Australia with a cheque for $210, and another for $170 made payable to St Andrew's Hospital. It was as if the house was frozen in time. He began a frenzied search for his family, hailing a taxi to Barbara's friend Carole Quiller's house in Yeronga. She had not seen or heard from Barbara and the kids. Having kept the taxi running, he then headed to his sister's partner's house at Wynnum.

'What's wrong?' they asked him.

'Well, she [Barbara] has just disappeared or something, because she hasn't been there for a couple of days,' Billy informed them.

His sister Eileen and her boyfriend volunteered to help him

search. Billy left in the taxi and they promised to meet him soon in Dorchester Street. Later, the three of them drove to the Red Hill Skate Arena for a look around. They weren't there. Billy McCulkin then entered the phone box outside the skating rink and called Vince O'Dempsey's brothel, the Polonia, at Lutwyche.

Dianne Pritchard answered the phone. 'Do you know where Barbara is?' Billy asked. 'She hasn't been home for a couple of days, her money purse and everything is left there.'

'No I don't,' Pritchard replied.

'Is Vince there?' he asked.

'No,' she said.

'I'm worried about her.'

The trio travelled to Barbara's brother Graham's place at Strathpine. Nobody had seen Barbara and the girls. Billy then headed back into the city and reported his wife and the children missing to the CIB in the city and the Woolloongabba police station. It was now late in the evening and Billy was dropped off at the Treasury Hotel where he waited for Estelle Long to finish work. She then drove Billy back to Dorchester Street.

The search continued into the early hours of Saturday morning. Billy was due to work at the Queen Street construction site that day but he called in and arranged to have the day off. He caught a taxi to the Carina home of a friend, Norman Wild, and asked if he'd help him search. Given Wild had a car, he agreed, and they returned to Dorchester Street. Frustrated and tired, McCulkin again saw his daughters' friend, Janet Gayton, across the road. He went over to talk to her. 'Are you sure they weren't here?' he pleaded with her. 'Was there anybody else here?'

'Yes,' the young girl said, 'Vince and Shorty were here. They were here on Wednesday night.'

Estelle Long, who was living with Billy McCulkin at this stage, remembered him as being distraught. 'I recall the night when Billy first told me that Barbara and the girls were missing,' she later told police, '... he appeared genuinely shocked.' He told Long he had found beer and dried fruit at the house. He knew O'Dempsey, a vegetarian, ate a lot of dried fruit.

When Billy discovered that Vince and Shorty were seen at the house in Dorchester Street, he feared the worst. 'He [Billy] told me straight away that he knew they had done something to them,' Long recounted. 'He told me that O'Dempsey had killed someone and had a brothel at Lutwyche and talked about the other man [Shorty] being charged for rape.

'I remember there was a time ... Billy thought O'Dempsey and Dubois were going to shoot him and he had my shotgun ready at the flat. I think Bill was frightened of O'Dempsey but after the girls disappeared he was more so.'

Shortly after, Estelle Long got a phone call from O'Dempsey at the hotel where she worked. 'It was just on the normal hotel line,' she said. 'He said, "I just want you to know I have had nothing to do with Barbara's disappearance." I was shaking and told him, "Don't phone me again, I'm not your friend, [am] never likely to be your friend, so don't ring."'

She remembered Billy McCulkin talking about the disappearances every day. 'What happened to his family haunted him,' she said.

When the Sun Came Up

Billy McCulkin and Norman Wild immediately raced over to Garry Dubois's mother's home at 19 Allan Street, Kedron. The property was a raised housing commission–style home set well back from the street. Norman Wild went around the back of the house while Billy knocked on the front door.

Shorty answered the door.

'Have you seen my wife?' Billy asked.

'No, why?' he replied.

'The kid across the road told me that you were there on Wednesday night.'

'I don't know your wife,' Dubois supposedly replied. 'I'm surprised you asked me.'

'Alright, fair enough,' Billy said.

He got back in the car with Wild and they headed back into the city on Lutwyche Road. By chance he saw O'Dempsey's orange Charger parked outside the shopping arcade where he ran Polonia's. Soon after he saw O'Dempsey walking across Lutwyche Road and approached him.

'Have you seen Barbara?' Billy asked.

'No, why?'

'She hasn't been home for a couple of days. The kid across the road said you were there on Wednesday night with Dubois.'

O'Dempsey supposedly hesitated.

'Was Shorty with you?' Billy pressed him.

'Have you seen Shorty?' O'Dempsey asked.

'Yes, I've just come from his place. Was Shorty with you?'

O'Dempsey again supposedly hesitated.

'Well was he with you or wasn't he?' Billy insisted. 'If he wasn't with you, then who was?'

'I forget,' O'Dempsey said. He suggested they both go back and see Shorty.

Back in Allan Street, McCulkin sat down with O'Dempsey and Dubois in the kitchen. It was time to get down to brass tacks. Billy had known O'Dempsey for about eight years and they had had some criminal adventures together. Billy was also aware that O'Dempsey's reputation was not a savoury one. Allegations that he murdered people who got in his way or threatened his freedom swirled around him. He had briefly lived in their house when he got out of gaol in late 1970. And Billy knew that in recent weeks O'Dempsey had shown some physical interest in his wife, Barbara.

As for Dubois, he was largely an unknown quantity who had served a long prison stretch for rape, even though Shorty had helped Vince and himself pull off the Torino insurance scam bombing.

Billy went on about his missing family. 'If you know anything about it, tell me,' Billy said, 'I've had to go to the bobbies about it. I'm worried about them.'

Both Vince and Shorty assured him that they would like to help.

Then Billy turned to Vince and asked: 'What were you doing there [at Dorchester Street]?'

'I wasn't there,' O'Dempsey said according to McCulkin's statement to police.

'Well I don't care if she's run off with anybody or anything like that, all I want to do is find out if she's alright.'

'We don't know anything,' O'Dempsey and Dubois told him.

'Well look,' Billy said, 'if anything has happened to them, I'll just blow the heads off the person whoever done it.'

The next day – Sunday 20 January – Detective Basil Hicks was telephoned by Billy McCulkin, who asked to see him urgently.

'I met him at the Ampol Service Station at The Gap [in the city's west],' Hicks said in a statement. 'At the time, McCulkin was very upset. He told me that his wife and two children were missing and that he feared that they may have been murdered.'

Hicks met McCulkin at Dorchester Street the following day. McCulkin informed him that the girls across the road had seen 'Vince and Shorty' at the house the previous Wednesday night.

'He [Billy] said that he was sure that they were responsible for his wife's and children's disappearance,' Hicks added in his statement. 'McCulkin said that he knew O'Dempsey as a vicious criminal and that he was capable of committing any offence, including murder. He said that he knew Dubois as a sexual pervert who was always talking about having sex with very young girls. He said he was convinced that they had gone to the house to rape his wife and two children either there or away from the house, and afterwards murder them.'

McCulkin reiterated to Hicks that if he found out that Vince and Shorty were definitely responsible, he would 'shoot them both'.

'I am telling you now, I don't want it to go any further than you,' Billy told Hicks. 'If I find out that Vince and Shorty have done anything to Barbara and the kids I will fuckin' blow them both apart. I won't do them one at a time. I will fuckin' blow them both apart at one time.'

Hicks concluded, in his CIU report, that he believed if Billy found any evidence that Vince and Shorty had something to do with the disappearances, he would 'murder them without any hesitation'.

On Monday, O'Dempsey telephoned McCulkin and told him not to worry about his wife and children – he was sure they would all be back in time for the children to begin the school year. During this conversation he also asked McCulkin if he had a gun. Perhaps someone was trying to 'square up' with Billy McCulkin over something that happened in the past, O'Dempsey suggested. McCulkin was positive O'Dempsey was just sounding him out to see if he had an available weapon.

McCulkin assured him that he had a shotgun ready. McCulkin confided in Detective Hicks that he in fact feared that O'Dempsey might harm him.

What Billy McCulkin – frantic about his missing family – did not know about were the conversations that were going on between members of the Clockwork Orange Gang.

It was the morning habit of Peter Hall, living in Chermside with Carolyn Scully, to cruise by Shorty's mother's house in Kedron, where Shorty was living, pick him up and then sort out 'what jobs we could find' that day, namely break and enters and general theft.

But Shorty was nowhere to be found on the morning of Thursday 17 January, the day after the disappearance of the McCulkins. Hall told police in a statement decades after the event: 'When we got there [Allan Street, Kedron] Shorty was not there and we were told he had not come home the night before; neither his mum nor Jan [Stubbs, Shorty's partner] knew where he was. It was unusual for him not to come home, but more so for us not to know what we were all up to.

'We checked all the usual places, we checked in with Tom [Hamilton]. We did not know where O'Dempsey lived so we could not go there to see if Shorty was with him. This was unusual and Keith [Meredith] and I went to try and find him.'

As it transpired, Dubois turned up at Scully's house later that day. According to Hall: 'He initially wouldn't say where he had been the night before, he said he got tied up with something, he was pretty vague, but I could tell something wasn't right. He didn't even want to come out cruising. It was also strange that he didn't want to talk about the night before. Shorty was not himself after [that] night. He could not settle down.'

Either that day or the next, O'Dempsey turned up at Allan Street and sat in his parked car. Dubois went outside to talk to him then O'Dempsey left. Hall was convinced 'something had gone on' with the two men but Shorty said nothing.

On that weekend the gang convened in the kitchen at Allan Street with O'Dempsey and Dubois. Tommy Hamilton asked O'Dempsey directly if he had anything to do with the disappearance of the McCulkins. 'He denied it saying that he was being set up by the coppers for things he'd done in the past,' Hall recalled in his statement.

Then, as Billy McCulkin was racing around Brisbane looking for his family, and sought help from Detective Basil Hicks, the gang – Peter Hall, Tommy Hamilton, Keith Meredith and Shorty

Dubois – were in one of their cars just shooting the breeze when Dubois allegedly opened up about what had really happened on the night of Wednesday 16 January.

'He told us they took the girls for a drive,' Hall said in his statement. 'He said he didn't know what was in O'Dempsey's head at first, but Vince tied them up. He said he drove them to the bush and that's where it happened.

'He said Vince took Barbara away into the dark and strangled her. He said that Barbara was not raped; he thought that's what it was going to be but he just killed her. He said he couldn't see it but he could hear the gurgling sound. He said he felt sick and it seemed to take forever. He said he knew then that the kids were going to be killed.'

According to Hall, O'Dempsey raped one of the children and told Dubois to rape the other. 'He said he didn't want to but was not game to refuse,' Hall alleged. 'He said that Vince then killed the girls. He said O'Dempsey asked him to kill the other one but he couldn't do it.

'He didn't say specifically how the girls were killed but he was clear he didn't kill anyone. Vince killed them all. He said they were buried. He said that they had both been digging. Shorty said he felt even worse when the sun came up and he had to look at them, they were laying there …'

Shorty now feared O'Dempsey, Hall said, and the gang kept a keen eye on O'Dempsey. 'We knew what he was capable of, and were wary of him having some strange thoughts, and that he might want to tie up loose ends,' Hall said.

For the first time, some members of the Clockwork Orange Gang began to suspect that O'Dempsey may have been 'protected' by corrupt police.

'Looking back at it now … and realising that for many years O'Dempsey may have been a protected species – I have no doubt police were involved somewhere along the line,' one former gang member says. 'He got away with stuff for so long. How they were never convicted to start with [after the coroner's recommendations at the 1980 inquest] … I didn't even know that they'd hauled him and Shorty in for trial. Why wasn't I dragged in to give evidence then?

'Then I hear the stories about files going missing and different stuff going missing … I'd say he worked for Murphy. What he did for Tony Murphy I don't know … [or] who disappeared under Murphy's orders to him …

'He definitely got away with things he shouldn't have. If Murphy had some control over him, he would have been an ace in his pocket for sure. We all knew around town that McCulkin was an informer. We didn't know with who, but I heard later it was a guy named Hicks. Apparently he [Hicks] was also getting information off O'Dempsey too. They were at one stage fairly close, McCulkin and O'Dempsey.

'Then later we started to realise that Murphy was maybe mixed up in [the McCulkin disappearances]. We could not work out how, after witnesses saw them [Vince and Shorty] there [in Dorchester Street] … Vince must have felt pretty safe, that he wasn't going to be dragged into it, and if he did get dragged into it, that nothing was going to happen.'

On Monday 21 January, as Billy was giving Detective Hicks a tour of the empty house at 6 Dorchester Street, O'Dempsey telephoned Ross Stephens Car Sales at Newstead and arranged for a salesman to come to the flat in Rosalie and make an offer on his beloved Valiant Charger.

As Detective Hicks pointed out in his official investigation into the McCulkin disappearances in 1974, O'Dempsey treated that car 'like a baby'.

'It is suggested that if O'Dempsey could possibly love anything it was this car,' Hicks noted. 'He would cover it each night with a sheet of silk and it was a standing joke with all persons who knew him that it was the only thing he really cared for.'

O'Dempsey sold the car on the spot for $2900.

The next day his de facto, Dianne Pritchard, turned up at the Polonia massage parlour. A co-worker reported that she 'appeared to be particularly worried at this time'. Soon after she headed over to the Vogue Private Hotel in South Brisbane and picked up some belongings she had stored there. That evening, a couple living in the flat next door to O'Dempsey and Pritchard in Rosalie observed men taking household goods and personal items to a car parked outside.

'Shorty asked us to help Vince leave town [and] we agreed to help,' Peter Hall later told police in a statement. 'Shortly after we went to Vince's unit ... Vince was not there when we got there, but his partner, Dianne, let us in ... I recall we were carrying heavy stuff down some stairs and putting it in the car. We transported it all to a relative of Dianne's, maybe her parents. I remember Dianne was really upset and angry that she had to move. She was pretty drunk at the time and was blowing up because everything was in turmoil.'

Hall said he knew O'Dempsey was leaving town because of the McCulkin investigation. On Tuesday 22 January Adrian Burton, the owner of the 'Nethercote Court' block of flats, was at the property doing the gardening when he saw O'Dempsey leave.

'... he arrived back an hour later,' Burton later told a court. 'He had three gentlemen with him.' He observed the men removing garbage bags of items.

The next day, while collecting the rent from tenants, he noticed that the occupants of Unit 8 had gone.

'It was empty,' he said. 'There was nothing there other than coathangers.'

Hawks Nest

Just north of the working-class town of Newcastle, then a rough and tumble port town, is Port Stephens, and on the northern tip of its inlet is the village of Hawks Nest. Popular with holidaymakers since the 1950s Hawks Nest was just a thatch of streets facing Bennetts Beach, and despite the seasonal crowds, it was a fine place to lie low. It was also a convenient bolt hole for anyone who might have pulled a job in Sydney or Newcastle and needed to disappear fast.

It also happened to be the temporary base for a handful of Queensland criminals in January 1974, and it was where Clockwork Orange Gang member, Peter Hall, chose to shack up until the dust settled over the McCulkins' disappearances. Not long after, in late January or early February, Hall was staying with a mate when they received unexpected visitors.

'While I was there O'Dempsey and Dianne Pritchard turned up …' Hall later told police. 'They had their own place … there was no discussion or conversation with Vince while we were in NSW about the McCulkins other than that he was laying low for a while. Nothing was ever said to him about what Shorty had told us.'

Another associate says he remembers O'Dempsey and Pritchard arriving at Hawks Nest. It was more than a week after the McCulkins vanishing, and in the back of his mind he had an idea that O'Dempsey and Pritchard, as well as Dubois and his partner, Jan, might have had some time away together before O'Dempsey turned up down south.

'At that point I never heard a thing about the McCulkins, I never heard a thing about it, nothing. Then Vince rung a mate's place and my mate asked him, how did he get his phone number, or something, and he said Shorty gave him the number. He [O'Dempsey] was ringing from Newcastle … and my mate arranged to meet him in a suburb called Hamilton, in Newcastle, outside the post office there.

'O'Dempsey said he was sick of it up in Queensland and he wanted a good place to stay down here,' the criminal remembered. 'He said he definitely didn't want to stay in the city. It was suggested he might want to settle in Nelson Bay, across Port Stephen from Hawks Nest, on the southern side. O'Dempsey said he'd drive around and take a look.

'I watched a fight with my mate and O'Dempsey on the 28th, I think it might have been [in] February, with Tony Anthony, no Tony Mundine and Bennie Briscoe,' he recalls. (Middleweight Australian champion Tony Mundine fought tough Philadelphia fighter Bad Bennie Briscoe at the Palais des Sports in Paris on the night of 25 February 1974. Mundine lost by knockout in the fifth round.)

Anyone who observed O'Dempsey at Hawks Nest noticed his unusual living habits. 'He was a nut case, he'd stay in his room all day,' one witness said. 'He bought a fishing rod because someone esle bought one and we could go fishing and he couldn't fish, he'd try it out and it'd go backwards. And Dianne would say, you fucking idiot, and all this sort of stuff.

'He'd be fucking reading ... drawing maps ... "I could rob this bank and do this and do that ... that's Warwick, the bank there, somewhere else ... I know this area, we could get straight into the bush." By then, you know, we got to know what happened in Brisbane with the McCulkins. O'Dempsey said Billy McCulkin had been looking for him and Shorty ...

'Someone said to Vince, what's this about the McCulkins?

'"Oh," he said, "she's most likely run off to her sister's or something," which I thought that sounds more like it. No one in their right mind would think that what happened to them happened to them, you know. Then we started to have a bit of a look at him, [and] I thought, oh fuck, there's a big fight in this cunt.'

Everyone who came into contact with O'Dempsey began to keep a cautious eye on him.

One acquaintance of O'Dempsey at that time in Hawks Nest noticed that he had a moderately sized hunting knife. The acquaintance borrowed it to go fishing, and promptly lost it. O'Dempsey was enraged, and scoured the local fishing spots for the missing knife. 'He went insane, lost his mind over that knife,' one witness says.

However, there was also some time for fun. Peter Hall and his cohort were clowning around and decided to play some jokes on Vince. 'He's colour blind and me and Peter Hall done a menswear store ... there was a heap of stuff there he [Peter] was selling and he said, "Take what you want Vince", you know, it's all on. Peter urged him to pick something out.

'Peter said, because we were the same size, you know. Vince said he didn't want any loud colours, I don't know what ... there was probably hundreds, there was pink there, pink pants and a fucking green shirt or something. That's what Vince took. He was colour blind. Didn't know what he was choosing. I used to try not to laugh and it was hard not to. Peter said, "He'll wake up, you know, he'll fucking kill you." He was roaring with laughter.'

Meanwhile, back in Queensland, after weeks of heavy rain, a catastrophic flood would inundate Brisbane. Fourteen people would lose their lives. Almost 8000 homes would be destroyed.

The great flood would, seemingly, sweep away any further interest in the disappearance of Barbara, Vicki and Leanne McCulkin. When the sun finally came out again in Brisbane, it was as if they had never existed.

After the Storm

In the chaotic aftermath of the floods, it would take a full 17 days before the local press would report on the disappearance of the

McCulkins. On Saturday 2 February a story on page three of the *Courier-Mail* expressed 'concern' for the safety of Barbara and the girls. 'Police said they had no clue as to the whereabouts of the missing trio who appeared to have simply disappeared from the house,' the story said.

'Up to now we've been treating them as missing persons,' a police officer said, 'but by now we've had to start to think about something else happening to them. We just hope we have not got another murder on our hands.'

The next day, the *Sunday Mail* escalated the drama surrounding the disappearances. Inspector J. Ryan of the Brisbane CIB said: 'We have the strongest suspicion that there has been foul play,' he said. 'We are deeply concerned for the family's safety.'

And there the stories ended.

One close associate of O'Dempsey's wanted to see him after news broke of the disappearance of the McCulkins. 'When that hit the papers I cruised up to Vince's place ... but the place was deserted. Little did I know at the time that when it hit the newspapers he'd been on the run for about three weeks. It was not until February that the coppers reported it to homicide and the media.'

It was beyond fortuitous for the perpetrators that the media had not picked up on the story for a full two and a half weeks. Public pressure through the press was usually followed by increased police attention to a case. In the matter of the McCulkins, by fate or otherwise, the case had been allowed to languish for a significant amount of time. It wasn't until Tuesday 5 February, that police photographic and forensic experts combed 6 Dorchester Street looking for clues.

The disappearance and presumed murder of the McCulkins effectively ended the Clockwork Orange Gang and its operations, though some of them remained in contact. As Hall would later say, 'it was never the same' after the McCulkins.

O'Dempsey and Dubois, however, remained in touch even if they didn't risk being seen together. By April 1974, most of the Hawks Nest gang – including Peter Hall – had settled back in Brisbane. So too had Garry Dubois. Vince and Dianne were still moving around.

During this time, for whatever reason, O'Dempsey acted entirely out of character and wrote a letter to Shorty Dubois. He wanted Shorty to do two specific jobs for him. 'This was just a few months after the McCulkins disappeared,' a witness says. 'I saw that letter. Vince wanted Shorty to get rid of the Gaytons.'

The Gayton sisters who lived across the road from the McCulkins, had identified Vince and Shorty outside the McCulkin home on the evening Barbara and the kids disappeared. 'I'll tell you exactly what was in the letter,' the witness says. 'He wanted to blow the fucking Gayton house to pieces with gelignite and petrol. He said don't bother lighting the petrol because the fucking gelignite would ignite it. He had specific instructions about how the fuel and gelignite were to be placed at the front and back doors of the house so that nobody escaped, including the girls' parents.'

The other component of the letter was instructions on how to exhume and destroy 'the bodies', presumably those of the McCulkins. 'He wanted Shorty to go and dig the bodies up, take drums, empty drums and drums of acid, put the bones in the acid and let it run down a fast flowing stream,' the witness says. 'I never told the police that, I don't think I could say that, I couldn't say that in a court of law. Of course Shorty didn't do any of that. It was insane.'

He says Tommy Hamilton was 'filthy' when he'd heard that Vince and Shorty had raped and murdered the McCulkin children.

As for O'Dempsey, those around him didn't know what to do about his growing menace. 'Peter Hall used to sit up at night and wonder, you know, somebody has got to stop this cunt,' one witness says. 'But what could you do?'

Port News

It was not exactly *The New York Times*, but in turbulent Brisbane in the mid-1970s a small magazine was making huge waves in the criminal underworld. The *Port News* – the official journal of the Storemen and Packers' Union (Queensland Branch) – was published every two months and was edited by Mr William 'Billy' Stokes.

Stokes had done a stint in Westbrook Farm Home for Boys with Stuart and was familiar with members of the Clockwork Orange Gang. Stokes had gotten into some trouble in New South Wales, and taken off to New Zealand in the early 1970s. He worked selling advertisements into small magazines and on his return to Brisbane, secured the editorship of the *Port News*.

In a series of explosive articles Stokes claimed he could expose the truth behind the nightclub fires. Stokes knew that Tommy Hamilton, a local champion boxer, and his gang (including Peter Hall, Keith Meredith and Garry Dubois) were supposedly paid to bomb Torino nightclub in Fortitude Valley, prior to the Whiskey fire. He claimed he had witnessed them bragging about it. Stokes wrote that he knew gangster Billy McCulkin and some members of the gang also had a hand in the Whiskey fire. He also published details about the vanishing and murder of the McCulkin girls.

In February 1975, Stokes wrote in an editorial: 'The following report is very real in all details, but because of the many legal consequences involved, it has been necessary to use only nicknames ... and aliases ...'

According to Billy Stokes the primary suspect was someone he called 'The Loner'. 'He is considered a very violent man capable of violent acts ... at present The Loner is hiding out in Sydney, wanted by police for questioning for five murders ... [including] "Mrs X" and her two children.'

Next was 'Mr X'. Stokes wrote that X was a leading character in arranging both the Torino and Whiskey firebombings. 'Because of an association that his estranged wife, "Mrs X", had formed with "The Loner"... she and her two children were eventually to suffer cold blooded, premeditated murder.'

Stokes claimed to have inside information on what happened the day 'Mrs X' and her two daughters vanished.

> The day came when 'Mrs X' was visited by 'The Loner' and 'Shorty' [Dubois]. On the surface it was just a typical social visit amongst friends. When [they] suggested a drive to break the monotony indoors, she accepted, and suspecting nothing took her children with her.

Two months later, in the *Port News* April edition, Stokes continued his extraordinary series, with one page dedicated to the 'killing of Mrs X'. The page was illustrated with a photograph of Barbara McCulkin.

> Whatever happened to Mrs X and children? I believe that she and the family have been sexually assaulted, cut open with knives, raped and degradedly abused when dead. I believe this because the Clockwork Orange Gang told me that that is what they did. The gory details came to me across the phone, and I taped all the calls. I wouldn't print the details because of the depraved butchery that they contained.

In the June edition of *Port News*, with the story still running, Stokes identified 'The Loner' as Vincent O'Dempsey and 'Shorty' as Garry Dubois.

Then, Tommy Hamilton was abducted by a masked intruder on the night of Friday 10 January 1975 from a house near Hamilton.

He disappeared without trace and was never seen again. There was no suggestion that O'Dempsey was involved in Hamilton's abduction. As Stokes was publishing his damning series of articles, O'Dempsey was arrested in Sydney and charged with the unlawful possession of explosives, possession of Indian hemp and use of an unlicensed pistol. In the end he was sentenced to two years in prison with a non-parole period of one year.

During an inquest into Hamilton's disappearance in January 1978, witnesses implicated Billy Stokes and he was committed for trial and later found guilty of Hamilton's murder on the basis of circumstantial evidence. Stokes was sentenced to life in prison.

'How could you?' he reportedly asked the jury.

Stokes was the first defendant to be found guilty of murder in the absence of a body in Queensland history. He has always maintained his innocence.

Stokes claimed that publishing the stories at the time was a way of protecting himself. 'It wasn't as dangerous as doing nothing, publishing those stories.' He said, 'If I do nothing, they're [the Clockwork Orange gang] only going to get stronger and stronger in their momentum ... If I do nothing, the position is more dangerous. If I'd just sat back and ignored all of this ... someone would have made a move on me.'

Stokes and his little publication were also the source of enormous angst down in the offices of the CIB. One intelligence officer remembered: 'There was some sort of fight going on between Vince O'Dempsey and Billy Stokes. I used to get the *Port News* delivered to my desk. Because of what Stokes was publishing in the *Port News* about the Whiskey and the Clockwork Orange Gang, we were expecting a gang war to break out.'

In September 1976 O'Dempsey was released from prison in New South Wales and made his way home to Queensland.

More Heat

Not long after his release from gaol O'Dempsey once again found himself too close to the spotlight for his liking. In 1977, interest in not only the McCulkin disappearance but the presumed murders of Margaret Ward and Tommy Allen was ignited once again when Queensland police decided to reinvestigate the cold cases.

It was in fact Inspector Tony Murphy, back in Brisbane as the head of the Consorting Squad, who ordered that the cases be looked at again. Murphy was back in his element in the city after his old friend, Terry Lewis, was elevated to commissioner in late 1976 following Whitrod's resignation. And the wily detective loved nothing more than getting his teeth into a gritty murder.

This situation, however, may not have been all it seemed. By initiating a cold case murder investigation into O'Dempsey, Murphy was seen as proactively seeking a resolution to the unsolved murders. But at the same time, by triggering a new investigation Murphy could retain control of the outcome of such an investigation, and ultimately ensure that nothing would come of any subsequent charges that may be recommended by a coroner.

After all, Murphy had successfully avoided prosecution over allegations of corruption when a royal commission was called into sex workers at Brisbane's National Hotel in 1963. By reopening the investigations into the McCulkins, Ward and Allen, and any lingering doubts about the Whiskey Au Go Go firebombing, Murphy could contain the speculation about O'Dempsey's involvement and the involvement of others, including corrupt police. In this scenario, Murphy could say, there was simply not enough evidence to proceed through the court system.

To the criminal underworld, however, these actions pointed more and more towards the reality that O'Dempsey was a protected species, and most probably by Tony Murphy himself.

Still, Murphy chose two young guns – Alan Marshall and Trevor Menary – to look into the five disappearances and see what they came up with. 'Billy McCulkin was known to Tony Murphy,' Marshall said years later. 'All those characters – Brian Aherne [owner of the Lands Office Hotel], Estelle Long. He knew all of them. And he liked to do unsolved murder investigations.'

Both Marshall and Menary worked meticulously for about two years. They gathered statements from many of the leading players and joined some dots. They paid Billy McCulkin a visit. He was then married to Estelle Long.

'We went out to their place,' Marshall said. 'He was ranting and raving [about] fucking coppers … He'd reported his kids missing and the coppers didn't do the right thing, he said. They were stupid comments. Billy was a shit. He's not the sort of person you'd have as a friend. But he really missed the girls.'

They had enough material to see the instigation of a coronial inquest into the five disappearances. 'I did think we had enough,' Marshall said of the case they'd put together.

The police thought there was a chance that McCulkin might roll over and tell everything he knew about the Whiskey Au Go Go and his missing family. 'Trevor Menary didn't drink,' recalls Marshall. 'But I would go there and I would sit down and we'd sit there for hours and I'd drink with Bill. We thought, one day he's going to slip, he's going to say something …' Marshall says they were looking into McCulkin's connections with the Whiskey firebombing, they thought if McCulkin implicated himself and those involved they could get him an indemnity. 'We'd be drinking beer and whatever and trying to get him [Billy] to make a faux pas. Never happened. He stuck to his story.'

At one point, Marshall took Billy McCulkin into police headquarters. Head of the CIB, Detective Tony Murphy, wanted to see him. 'I took him into Tony Murphy's office and sat him down.

And Tony said to him, "Look Bill it's your wife and kids. We don't have ... what we can see as being a watertight motive. But if you want to tell us what you were involved in that may have led to O'Dempsey killing your wife and kids, maybe we can sort of work it out with [lawyer] Des Sturgess and see what can happen." But even as far as an indemnity, it never worked.'

Meanwhile, O'Dempsey and his de facto, Dianne Pritchard, had settled temporarily at 9 Rise Street, Holland Park, with a friend he'd met in Boggo Road during the 1960s. Both O'Dempsey and his friend were working 'straight' jobs, as house painters. His friend had started the business and had his own crew. O'Dempsey would turn up to work in immaculate white KingGee overalls. There was not a tattoo in sight to 'scare off the old ladies'.

'Everyone in that crew was terrified of O'Dempsey,' says one acquaintance, familiar with the house painting operation. 'On the days they were spray-painting houses, you had to be finished by 3 p.m. so that Vince could clean the spray guns. Vince would pull the guns completely apart. He had tools of all sorts to keep every inch of the spray guns clean. He had all the parts laid out meticulously in the back of the ute. Then he'd put it all back together. No one was allowed to go to the back of the ute when Vince was doing his cleaning. He had all the parts laid out like a body.'

Another time, the crew was on a job at Woodridge, south of the Brisbane CBD. O'Dempsey helped the lady of the house select the colour scheme for the painting job. 'We all knew he was colour blind. Anyway, the colours picked out were mission brown for the main body of the house and burnt orange for the trims. From then on, the place was known as "The Jaffa".'

O'Dempsey also told friends about another botched job, courtesy of his eyesight. They were painting a woman's house when his friend wanted to pack up early and go to the pub. 'Because O'Dempsey didn't get on the drink, he stayed behind to finish the touch-ups himself. Vince is fucking colour blind, so he's got the fucking thing, the paintbrush, and started … doing the touch-ups. Well, the woman's come home and she's fucking distraught. She said, "What's going on with my house? It looks like a fucking hyena!" And he said, because he's heard the other boys say, "What happens is, it just goes on wet and looks like that, but it'll dry and then you won't notice it." Apparently O'Dempsey's friend got back and went, "Oh fuck, here we go" … it was a story they did talk about, and that was hilarious.'

Life in Rise Street was good, except when Pritchard hit the bottle. The friend's wife remembered in a statement to police: 'I recall one time … Vince said that he had tied Dianne up and left her on the bedroom floor. They had just finished painting a house and came home for tea … O'Dempsey wasn't drinking but he would fire up when the boys drank. He was talking about tying Dianne up. I remember he said he left her tied up on the bedroom floor at the house. I was shocked by this.

'I remember Vince said to me, "I've tied up people and put them in shallow graves all over Australia." He kind of laughed when he said it but the way he said it, he meant it. The comment scared me.'

According to the friend's wife, as the house painting venture continued, another scheme was cooking around the same time. '[My husband] set up an insurance fraud with Medibank,' the wife told police. 'He got me and other people to take in another person's Medibank forms and get money for it. There were about five of us doing it … I told my mother what [my husband] had made me do and she rang the police and then Inspector [Tony] Murphy came and saw me about it. I knew who Inspector Murphy was, I had heard [my husband] talk about him a lot. [My husband] could not stand him.'

Murphy interviewed the wife at her mother's house in Nundah, and she became aware that he was taping their conversation. 'I stopped talking then and left the room,' she recounted. 'I believe that tape was later played to Vince O'Dempsey. I think the tapes were given out over the legal system for him to hear what I said that day in my mother's kitchen.'

The couple were arrested in 1978 over the fraud. The wife eventually got six months' gaol for her part in the fraud. Her husband and others got twelve months. According to O'Dempsey's associates, he too had admitted his part in the Medibank scam, but he did no prison time. (At the end of 1979 he was issued a paltry fine for his involvement.)

Why did Tony Murphy, back in Brisbane from his exile in Longreach under previous police commissioner Ray Whitrod, get personally involved in the Medibank con? And how did O'Dempsey evade prosecution altogether?

It at least appeared that since his release from Boggo Road Gaol in Brisbane in late 1970, Vincent O'Dempsey had tiptoed through a minefield of crime, including allegations of murder, and come through relatively unscathed, despite his year in prison in New South Wales.

According to criminal associates, O'Dempsey was 'dropped' by his Sydney cohorts following the McCulkin murders, and in particular the deaths of the two children, Vicki and Leanne. If O'Dempsey had committed the crime, he had broken the sacred code among criminals of not harming children.

'After the McCulkins, the work for Vince in Sydney dried up, they dropped off him,' says one acquaintance. O'Dempsey's criminal activities would now play out a lot closer to home.

The Lady Vanishes

Detective Sergeant Keith Smith of the Brisbane Homicide Squad could have been forgiven for thinking his shift on Sunday

18 September 1977 was going to be a quiet one. He had clocked on to work at around 9 a.m. and was joined by his good friend and policing partner, Detective Robert Cassidy.

It was expected to be a fine day, and soon more than 37,000 football punters from across the city would congregate at Lang Park for the Brisbane Rugby League premiership grand final between the Easts Tigers and the Redcliffe Dolphins.

Smith and Cassidy were settling into their shift in Forbes House in Makerston Street, North Quay, when the phone rang. It was the senior sergeant on the front desk. 'You'd better come out to the counter here, we've got the uniform police,' he said. 'They've got a woman, a missing person case, you might have to look into.'

The uniform police were there with a woman called Marcia Barnard, and the officers explained the background to the situation. 'So we took Marcia into our office and sat her down and took a statement off her. She was very distressed, Marcia, she was genuinely distressed.'

The detectives would soon learn that this appeared to be much more than a run of the mill missing person's case. Barnard wanted to report that her boss, Norma Jean Pavich, also known as Simone Vogel, had not been seen since Friday afternoon.

Vogel, it turned out, ran an empire of massage parlours in Brisbane and on the Gold Coast, and this disappearing act was hugely out of character. She was married to a Gold Coast plasterer and builder called Steve Pavich, and had one child – Mark Baptiste – to a previous marriage. He was set to turn 21 in less than three weeks and she was very excited about planning his upcoming party in Sydney.

'Marcia was the overall manageress of all the parlours, she was at Stones Corner and that was the head office of Simone's massage parlours,' Smith says. 'Marcia was a friend, a good friend to Simone, so she reported her missing.'

The official one-page Missing Person Report stated that Vogel, originally from Sydney, was 42 years old, 152 centimetres tall, of medium build with a fair complexion and blonde hair (she often sported a wig). She was wearing blue jeans, a multi-coloured jumper and sandal-type shoes.

Vogel had last been seen at one of her parlours – the Kon Tiki Health Studio at 91 Gympie Road, Kedron. (She also owned: Beau Brummel in Beckman Street, Zillmere; Napoleon's Retreat at 454 Lutwyche Road, Lutwyche; Golden Hands at 1145 Ipswich Road, Moorooka; Saunette at 144 Adelaide Street, Brisbane city; the Coronet Parlour in South Brisbane; and her headquarters, New Executive Suite, at 431 Logan Road, Stones Corner.) She had a mighty empire, and one you wouldn't think might be troubled by O'Dempsey's little Polonia operation on Lutwyche Road, with its tiny rooms and kitchen out the back.

The report said that on Friday 16 September 1977 Vogel had travelled to Brisbane from her Gold Coast home. Barnard saw her at the Executive Suite at Stones Corner where Vogel received a telephone call from her son, Mark, in Sydney. Vogel showed signs of relief after the call. She then received another call at about midday, and Barnard heard Vogel say, 'You name the place and I'll meet you there.'

The report continued: 'The Missing Person [Vogel] went away and returned at about 3.30 p.m. She received a telephone call at 3.45 p.m. during which the following conversation was overheard by the Inquirer [Barnard]. "I'll meet you in the same parking spot that I met you at before about half past six."'

Barnard told police that when Vogel got off the phone she asked for $3000. A cash cheque was produced. Vogel then left the New Executive at 5.10 p.m. and went to her Kon Tiki massage parlour at Kedron, where she picked up another $3000. This was the last seen of the missing person,' the report said.

Simone Vogel, Brisbane's largest brothel madam, socialite, and mother, had vanished off the face of the earth. Unbeknown to anyone, that quiet Sunday morning was the beginning of a complex 40-year cold case murder mystery.

The High Life

Norma Jean Beniston, born on 4 April 1935, grew up as part of a sprawling family in West Ryde, 13 kilometres north-west of the Sydney CBD. Frank Beniston, a plumber, and his wife Kathleen, married in their teens and went on to have seven children – six girls and a boy. Norma was the oldest.

Her brother, Bob Beniston, remembers a crowded household and a hard-working father who tried his best to provide for his children. 'Dad was the sole bread winner and he really looked after us,' Beniston remembers. 'Every time there was a school holiday, because he was a plumber that worked for himself all his life, and you know … as soon as the school holiday started on the Thursday, we'd be off … the whole car or ute would be packed. I can remember Norma coming with us when I was really young.'

At 17, Norma married Kevin Frederick Tayler, but the union was short-lived. By 1955 she had hooked up with a man named Raymond Eugene Baptiste (also known as David Marshall). Less than two years later she began her peripatetic career as a prostitute on the streets of Kings Cross. Between 1957 and 1966 she accrued 170 convictions for street prostitution. There is no doubt she crossed paths with former Queensland prostitute and brothel madam Shirley Brifman, who was operating out of the Cross at the same time, as was Dianne Pritchard, who later become de facto to O'Dempsey.

Bob Beniston, though young, remembers his oldest sister's comings and goings early in her career. 'Well, she'd come home and

185

live with us for a little while, like Mum and Dad and me and our little sisters. And then sort of go again,' he says. 'And I know at one stage she said she was going somewhere and she didn't come back for about nine months. Nobody knew where she was. Whether she went to gaol or not, and that was the story I got, I've got no idea.'

By 1965, Norma had married Baptiste, and the following year she began work for notorious inner-city brothel king, Joe 'The Writer' Borg. Borg, a Maltese immigrant, invested heavily in The Lanes – a 'red light' precinct of townhouses off Palmer Street in inner-city Darlinghurst, just east of Sydney's CBD – where about 130 prostitutes worked in shifts. They would rent rooms off the landlord.

When Norma went to work for Borg, he had about 20 houses under his control. Off the game, she found that she had a striking head for business. 'Actually, a lot of people used to say she was a business woman,' her brother Bob Beniston says. 'She really had her brains on the business. And yeah, she did make a lot of money, for sure.'

She was also living the high life. Beniston remembers heading over to her home in Newport, on Sydney's northern beaches. 'We used to go over there for a weekend,' he says. 'You know, I'd finish work and my partner would finish work and then we'd drive over there and stay the whole weekend and go out on a boat and just party with the people that she knew. It was the life of luxury for me, being 17 years old.'

For Norma, the party didn't last. Late morning on 28 May 1968, Borg, 35, left his house in Brighton Boulevard, North Bondi, and hopped into his Holden utility parked in the street out front. He had with him one of his treasured Alsatians. Borg turned the ignition and a huge bomb planted beneath the car exploded, throwing him onto the footpath. Both his legs had been almost completely severed. The murder was thought to be related to a factional turf war over Sydney's prostitution rackets. Three men were later arrested over the killing.

As for Norma, who was using the alias Yvonne Miller when working for Borg, her job vanished. According to a Queensland CIU report on Norma, she opened her own brothel with Baptiste on Barrenjoey Road at Newport after Borg's death, but soon headed north to Brisbane.

'When Joe Borg got blown up ... I can actually remember the headlines and I can remember when that happened ... there was a big argument between Mum and Dad,' Beniston says. 'And I think Norma came around and told Mum and Dad that she knew him or something like that, you know? And that's when she left Sydney. Because I think she might have been the next on the list, you know?'

By the end of 1971, Norma and Baptiste were renting a house in Mount Ommaney, 14 kilometres west of the Brisbane CBD, under the fake names of Louise and Ron Shepherd. Norma also opened her first Brisbane brothel – the Costa Brava at 491 Stanley Street, South Brisbane. It was the start of a new life, and the beginnings of an extremely lucrative business empire. With her Sydney experience she would revolutionise the sex industry in Brisbane, dragging it from a disorganised cottage industry to a huge money-making network. Her great innovation was disguising brothels as health clinics and massage outlets.

When she arrived in Brisbane she was likely aware of corruption within the Queensland police force, but perhaps not its depth and breadth. She would become known in police, criminal and social circles as the brothel madam Simone Vogel.

Her business savvy repaid her with immediate success, and she soon lived the life of a wealthy socialite. Her brother, Bob Beniston, remembers frequent trips to Brisbane and later the Gold Coast where Vogel moved to in 1976 following her divorce from Baptiste. 'The whole lifestyle, to me now looking back, is mind-boggling,' Beniston says. 'I used to see the diamonds and you know, the cars ... and I'll tell you ...'

In February 1976 Vogel purchased a house on a canal at 13 Alma Street, Coral Gables, on the Gold Coast. She also continued to expand her business. By now she was in a long-term relationship with Steven Pavich. They would marry in August 1976, in a civil ceremony at their Coral Gables home.

In early 1977, however, despite her wealth and power as Brisbane's leading brothel owner, she was starting to tire of the game. It turned out Vogel was not immune to crooked police and the system of corruption known as The Joke – a vast system of kickbacks from prostitution, SP bookmaking and illegal gambling. And she would have been acutely aware of how Sydney and Brisbane corruption worked. In her old home town, gangsters did their own thing with the assistance of corrupt police, but in Brisbane, the corrupt police ran the show. To open a massage parlour required permission from police, in particular the shady Licensing Branch, and it meant monthly kickbacks to stay in business. Vogel loathed the entire set-up.

'I know that she promised Mum, because Mum knew what she was doing, that she wouldn't be in it much longer,' says Beniston. 'That was possibly early '77. She might have just had enough and decided, bugger it, I'm not going to give them [corrupt police] any more money. I'm getting out of this.'

Investigating Officer Keith Smith had a similar theory. He was convinced Vogel was fed up with her businesses being so entangled with corrupt police. 'She was frustrated with the whole deal and drugs were creeping into the parlours by then,' Smith recalls. 'But the main thing with her was her business and she was just being blatantly ripped off by the bloody [Licensing Branch] detectives. She was stood over by those rotten corrupt detectives and it would be on a weekly basis, every week handing out $3000. She must have thought, "They're getting more out of it than me. This has got to come to a stop." Why would you want to stay in a business like that?'

Bob Beniston confirms he discussed the corrupt payments with his sister. 'I don't know how it came up but she was telling me she was paying $3000 a week to them,' he says. Police records revealed that Vogel was earning in excess of $4000 a week from the brothel empire, so the police cut was more than substantial.

After seven years in Queensland, there was little Vogel didn't know about corrupt police and The Joke. She was a central cog in the machine. With all that dangerous knowledge, what if she did want to extricate herself from the system? What if she decided to blow the whistle like brothel madam Shirley Brifman just five years earlier, a decision that cost Brifman her life?

Undercover Licensing Branch officer Kingsley Fancourt interviewed Vogel in the mid-1970s. 'She was a very, very attractive woman, a $2000 a night job,' he recalls. 'She was well-spoken. She conducted herself in a very stately manner. I was starting to … get information. It was well known she was going to start name-dropping and all the rest of it. The heat was on her.'

Bob Beniston remembers one of the last conversations he ever had face to face with his sister. 'I was plumbing,' he says. 'I was a plumber [like his father]. And I just wanted to be a cop. I joined the Commonwealth Police in March 1977. She [Norma] looked at me and she said, "Do not ever be corrupt." And I said, "No, I won't be, I won't be." And she said, "Well just make sure you never accept a penny and do everything right." I won't say it hit me in the face. But I always remember that last talk with her.'

Yet Another Missing Person

After Vogel was reported missing on Sunday 18 September 1977, Smith and Cassidy telephoned their superior, Detective Inspector Ron Redmond, who was in charge of the Homicide Squad. He summoned the young officers to the Breakfast Creek Hotel where they explained the scenario. Redmond said 'this could be serious', and he ordered them to investigate immediately.

Early in the investigation the officers learned from Pavich that when his wife had gone missing on the Friday he had engaged the services of a private investigator – former Gold Coast detective Greg Bignell. Pavich believed the Gold Coast police lacked interest in her disappearance and had hired Bignell to get some answers.

On the Saturday, Bignell discovered Vogel's Mercedes SLC convertible in the car park at Brisbane Airport. The car was unlocked and the keys were in the ignition. Presumably at Pavich's request, the car was towed back to Coral Gables. 'Bignell's finding of the vehicle and the removal of it from the airport aroused our suspicions but after speaking with Bignell and Pavich our suspicions were allayed a little,' Smith later noted.

Smith travelled to Sydney and interviewed Vogel's family, friends and former associates. 'Whilst they believed that [her] marriage was on shaky ground they were adamant that Simone would not have planned her disappearance and just vanish without letting her mother, sister, or her son, Mark, know,' Smith later wrote.

While Smith chipped away at his investigation, Vogel was also never far from the thoughts of her younger brother, Bob Beniston. Then, about six months after Vogel vanished, Beniston received a phone call at home.

'Is that First Constable Robert Beniston?' the caller asked.

'Yeah, yep,' Beniston replied, thinking it was a mate making a prank call.

'I'm going to tell you this once and once only.'

'Oh yeah, yep, no worries,' Beniston said.

'Don't ever set foot in Queensland again.'

'Who's this?' he asked.

'Superintendent Syd Atkinson,' the caller answered.

Still thinking the call was a hoax, Beniston made light of the situation.

'Do you understand what I said?' the caller asked. 'It's Superintendent Syd Atkinson here. I just told you don't ever set foot in Queensland again or you're dead.'

Atkinson had been superintendent of the Gold Coast region since February 1977. He was close friends with then commissioner Terry Lewis as well as other senior police of that era including Tony Murphy. (More than a decade later, allegations of corruption would be levelled at Atkinson during the Fitzgerald inquiry.)

Beniston, still not convinced of the caller's legitimacy, said he would phone Atkinson back, which he did. He was put through to Atkinson's phone.

'I ... told you,' Atkinson allegedly replied. 'Don't set foot in Queensland again or you're dead.'

Eighteen months after his sister vanished, Beniston was called into Commonwealth Police headquarters in Canberra and interviewed about Simone. 'These two dudes sat me down and did the full-on interview,' Beniston says. 'I asked them what the statement was for. They said [Queensland Police] Commissioner Lewis has asked for this statement ... they want to know what you know about it all. Of course, looking back now, I was an idiot to even open my mouth.'

At about that time Beniston compiled his own report into Vogel's disappearance and concluded that there may have been Queensland police involvement in her disappearance and likely murder. He had interviewed many of Vogel's employees and came up with the names of four Queensland police officers. He submitted his report to his own commissioner at the Commonwealth Police and heard nothing further.

After more than two years, Smith, in Queensland, compiled an official report of his investigation. He too concluded, in part, that there may have been police involvement in Simone Vogel's disappearance.

Superintendent Tony Murphy, in charge of the Criminal Investigation Branch (CIB), read the report and called Smith and Cassidy into his office. 'He told us we were on the wrong track,' Smith remembers. 'He said we weren't putting enough effort into Pavich as the main suspect. Murphy always wanted Pavich. Murphy said we couldn't see the woods for the trees.'

Murphy took both Smith and Cassidy off the investigation and appointed two other detectives to the job. Smith knew Murphy's decision couldn't be overturned, so he produced another report along the same lines as the first and gave it to a friend and fellow officer he believed he could trust.

'At some stage or other there was going to be a coronial inquest … or a breakthrough on this investigation one way or another … and I wanted to secure this report of mine and I wanted it to remain, naturally, confidential,' says Smith. 'Then, I forget how much later it was … they decided to have an inquest. So I thought to myself, I'll go and get that report. I thought it was safe where it was. I didn't even tell Ron Redmond I was doing it … if that report got out I was in bloody serious trouble.

'I rang my friend up and asked him about my report which he had secured in a safe. He said my report came up in discussions with Commissioner [Lewis] and Tony Murphy somewhere along the line about that investigation. He said somehow or other my name came up … it must have come up about my suspicions … he said what I put in that report was discussed at length by the Commissioner and Murphy and they decided none of it could be substantiated, there was nothing there by way of solid evidence. He told me it was decided that that report would be shredded.'

In 1980, the Vogel case earned a mention at the inquest into the disappearances of Brisbane mother Barbara McCulkin and her two daughters in 1974, and the disappearance and suspected murder of prostitute Margaret Grace Ward in late 1973. Ward had worked briefly for Vogel at the Coronet parlour in South Brisbane.

The formal inquest into Vogel's disappearance began on 24 August 1981. It ran over 26 court days and concluded that Vogel had disappeared under circumstances which showed she had not vanished of her own free will. The coroner, Mr C.E. Webster, declared Norma Jean Beniston, also known as Norma Jean Baptiste, Norma Jean Pavich and Simone Vogel, officially dead.

Her murder occurred at the heart of a volatile period in Queensland criminal and police history. Corruption was rampant. A dozen prostitutes, madams, associates to criminals and criminals themselves were killed or went missing in the 1970s, many of the cases suspected to have been linked to corrupt police.

At the time of Vogel's disappearance, O'Dempsey's partner, Dianne Pritchard, was working occasional shifts for Vogel, hitchhiking down the highway from the Christian compound where they sometimes stayed, near Mount Tuchekoi (about 150 kilometres from Brisbane). 'Vince was so tight he made her hitch,' says one associate. 'He told me the woman Dianne was working for was giving her some trouble.'

It was well known during the 1970s that O'Dempsey was the strong arm for the Brisbane vice scene. 'He used to drive through [Brisbane] and he'd say, "Oh there was a brothel there years ago. I closed it down", and, "Oh yeah, there was a brothel over there. There used to be, but I closed that one down, too,"' an associate says. 'He ran the scene with an iron fist ... what O'Dempsey used to do is, anyone who was fucking playing up, he'd go and sort them out.' The associate says O'Dempsey was in charge of who ran what brothel businesses and where. 'You had to get his permission.'

At one point the associate decided to get into the prostitution game. 'I told a mate that I had these two women and I was going to take them down to Brisbane and get started,' he said. 'I was arrogant. I decided I didn't have to go through Vince. I'd just do it myself. My mate said, "You'll end up in the fucking Brisbane River. You can't do that mate. You're not allowed to. You keep your head out of it, you don't know what you're doing. You should go to Vince and get him to help you, or don't do it at all." That was the advice I was given. I talked to Vince about it and he said he knew someone in Brisbane and he'd help set it up, but I didn't end up doing it.'

He said he was discussing guns with O'Dempsey one day and the discussion prompted another story from the past. 'I wanted to put a silencer on a .357 Magnum and O'Dempsey said, "You can't do that … you need a low velocity bullet … a .357's got too much punch",' the acquaintance recalls.

'And he said, "I let a shot go in Queen Street [Brisbane], and nobody heard a fucking thing. Nobody heard a thing, and we dropped her."

'He said, "We put her on a mattress … you've got to burn the mattress … make sure you don't leave any blood."

'Now we've gone complete somersault from … all I'm talking about is a silencer to he's just knocked a sheila. That's what I've got in my head. He's let a shot go in the main street, in Queen Street, and dropped her on the mattress … and nobody heard or saw a thing. So … like today it'd be difficult, with cameras and everything. But back in them days, there was nothing like that there.'

Could this have been Simone Vogel, who had been giving Vince's partner, Dianne Pritchard, grief before she disappeared for good?

Another close acquaintance recalled: 'There's something in the back of my head that that murder had something to do with cash and a lot of jewellery.'

Either way, Vogel had joined the ranks of several other unsolved cold case murders.

Innocent

On Saturday 26 November 1977, John Andrew Stuart was given a pass to the reception store of Boggo Road Gaol, having complained that some of his personal property had been stolen, namely, photographs of his mother and a personal diary. It was 8.20 a.m. and Stuart was not accompanied by a guard. Returning to his wing of the gaol, he scaled the partially demolished brick wall of the prison's old A Wing – it was unused and due to be pulled down – and onto an awning before he shimmied up an external drainpipe and onto the roof.

Once up there, he began tearing off sheets of corrugated iron and prised out bricks with a crowbar. He then spelt out in bricks the message – INNOCENT VICTIMS OF POLICE VERBAL. F + S (Finch and Stuart).

During his protest, which could be seen from Brisbane's south-east freeway, Stuart became something of a local attraction, with sightseers gathering outside the gaol. The Comptroller-General of Prisons, Allen Whitney, said: 'He can stop there as far as I'm concerned. He got up there by himself. He can get down that way too. He can't get anywhere from where he is.'

The Prisons Minister, John Herbert, ordered warders to leave Stuart where he was. He lasted 52 hours. At 12.45 p.m. on the Monday, an exhausted Stuart was having a rest near one of the cavities he'd created by removing the roof iron, and was snatched by two warders. In the melee, Stuart yelled out for his fellow prisoners to riot.

They didn't.

'After a brief, violent struggle, he was brought to the ground as fellow prisoners cheered,' the *Courier-Mail* reported. Stuart was locked up in solitary confinement for five days as punishment. He was given just bread and water.

His mother, Edna Watts, berated him for his 'silly' stunt. 'I went really crook at him,' she said. She prayed that he wouldn't get extra gaol time for his rooftop protest, and was elated that he was only given days in solitary. 'I've heard it's like the Black Hole of Calcutta,' she told reporters. 'You can't see your hand in front of your face. Next they'll be cutting off hands for thieving and splitting tongues for lying. I think it's terrible.'

Years later, his friend and criminal accomplice James Finch revealed the true nature of the missing 'personal diary' and why Stuart had reacted so strongly to its theft. The coded black book was in fact stolen by a corrupt prison warder who had befriended Stuart. He managed to con Stuart into deciphering the code before he lifted the small black book.

Sun journalist Dennis Watt would later write: 'The book, in which Stuart used tiny cryptic writing, detailed the planning and execution of the nightclub firebombing. It named the police mastermind who ordered the firebombing, known criminal Vincent O'Dempsey as that officer's partner in a protection racket, torchman Tom Hamilton and Bill McCulkin as Finch's accomplices.

'Finch said the book also listed the names and activities of corrupt senior police and prison officers. Stuart ... had worked for a secret group of dissident police known as the "Committee of Eight". One of the Committee's leading figures was CIU detective Basil Hicks, who had worked with Stuart on and off for years. Stuart's so-called codename was Emu.

'The Emu file was one of 400 missing when ... commissioner Terry Lewis took office after the resignation of Ray Whitrod in November 1976,' Watt further wrote. 'All details contained in the missing [Emu] file, some of which related to police involvement in vice and gambling rackets and armed robberies were duplicated in Stuart's black book.'

Hicks would later confirm that on the orders of Whitrod, he had destroyed 'about six sacks full' of files when Lewis got the top job. He said Whitrod was trying to protect police informants by getting rid of the documents and Whitrod feared that former assistant commissioner Tony Murphy would try to secure the files. 'He wanted anything destroyed that could be used to sue anybody, or to be used to the detriment of anybody at all. He told me to destroy them ...'

Two years later, at 8.45 p.m. on Monday 1 January 1979 Stuart was found dead in cell 317, in maximum security C-wing. His body was discovered during a routine cell check. The Government Medical Officer and police were immediately notified. Prison sources told a newspaper that Stuart's face 'had a contorted expression'. He was found face down on his prison bed, with his left hand holding a pillow behind his head, and his right arm tucked under his body.

Prison authorities stated categorically that no unauthorised person could have had access to Stuart. And despite the fact that Stuart was on yet another hunger strike at the time of his death, an autopsy would discover traces of digested food, and traces of a prohibited drug. Bowel samples suggested Stuart may have eaten the day before his death.

The official cause of death was later given as an inflammation of the heart caused by some virus. Pathologist Dr A.J. Ansford said there were numerous surgical scars on Stuart's body, but no evidence of any recent injury. At the coronial inquest into Stuart's death a few months later, his mother, Edna Watts, said that she had received a series of telephone calls leading up to her son's passing, telling her his death was imminent, and that a man could be poisoned with dingo bait given over a long period of time, and no traces of the chemical could later be detected. Mrs Watts said she told nobody about the calls because she didn't think she'd be believed.

Others also held on to theories that Stuart had been murdered or committed suicide. Carolyn Scully, sister to the missing Tommy Hamilton, says Stuart was poisoned in gaol. 'Johnny Stuart killed himself because he couldn't handle gaol any longer,' says Scully. 'And it was McCulkin who took the poison up there that he took. He killed himself and I know that for a fact because Vince told me.'

At the time of Stuart's death, Scully was living in a house on Turner Road that ran across the back of the Lutwyche Cemetery in Lutwyche. 'We were standing in my yard watching [Stuart's funeral],' she recalls. 'Vince got out of gaol that day. It was really funny. Vince said, "Oh, I'm trying to keep a low profile and I walked through the cemetery so nobody will see me, and here's all these people, the police, the cameras." He was laughing.

'He said, and this is coming straight from the horse's mouth, he said it was McCulkin took the poison up the gaol and Stuart took it, because they bashed him shitless. Two of them [prison guards] got demoted and the rest of them just got a slap over the knuckles. And they gave him a hell of a hiding, that's why he was in the hospital.'

However, one senior prison officer who was working at Boggo Road at the time of Stuart's death said any talk of poison being smuggled into the prison was impossible. 'I wouldn't believe that,' he said. 'Stuart had abused his body so badly over the years and there's no way in the world a prison officer would risk everything to do that. There's no way in the world Stuart met with foul play in the end.'

John Andrew Stuart was buried in a narrow grave in a portion of the cemetery close to Kitchener Road and not far from the cemetery's honoured war graves. The humble marble plaque simply read:

DAVID J. STUART / Died 21-11-56 / Aged 49 years. JOHN A. STUART / Died 1-1-79 / Aged 38 years. AT PEACE WITH THEIR SAVIOUR.

Onward Christian Soldiers

For many, it must have been a measure of relief that the bloody 1970s were drawing to a close. The decade had seen unprecedented violence and bloodshed in Queensland that had left dozens of bodies in its wake. Many of those murder cases remained stone cold, and some would stay that way for decades to come.

Although the McCulkins had been missing now for more than five years, the police tasked to reinvestigate the triple murders had collated an enormous quantity of material and were getting close to bringing the case to court through a coronial inquest. In fact, Detective Sergeant Trevor Menary had interviewed O'Dempsey about the disappearance of Margaret Grace Ward at the Gympie police station on 29 June 1979.

He had put to O'Dempsey: 'I suggest that you murdered the girl Ward to prevent her giving evidence against your de facto, Pritchard.'

The noose appeared to be tightening around O'Dempsey.

On 5 July, Queensland police announced that they would be seeking an inquest into the deaths of Barbara McCulkin and her two daughetrs, along with Margaret Grace Ward and Raymond Vincent 'Tommy' Allen, and were hoping to bring charges against a 'strong suspect'.

Incredibly, the next day the Brisbane *Telegraph* published an interview with O'Dempsey written by reporter Peter Hansen. The headline was: 'I'M NO KILLER'. The story did not mention O'Dempsey by name. 'The man, aged about 40, works near Gympie,' the report said. 'A clergyman who sees him regularly fiercely defended the man yesterday. "He has seen the light," the clergyman said. "He and his wife have made God their partner."'

O'Dempsey was described as 'bearded, fit and muscular in work clothes'.

Extraordinarily, O'Dempsey also issued a typed statement to the newspaper:

Recently … I was asked certain questions in relation to certain matters by the State police. I gave my name, age, birthplace, address and type of work. I was asked would I read the statement of interview through. I said no.

I was asked questions in relation to the five people named – Mrs Barbara McCulkin, Vicki Maree McCulkin, Barbara Leanne McCulkin, Margaret Grace Ward and Raymond Vincent Allen.

The questions were all relevant to that. They were trying to ascertain their whereabouts. I made no comments to any of these questions. This was in conformance with a legal directive which has been sent by my solicitor some years ago to the Police Commissioner in Queensland. I shall not be making any further comment to the police regarding these matters.

O'Dempsey wrote that police had a search warrant 'purporting to be looking for a firearm at my residence', and that he possessed no firearm. He then provided brief summations of the circumstances surrounding the five victims, as far as he knew it.

The only comment I'll make on these matters is that Raymond Vincent Allen to my knowledge at the time of his alleged disappearance had to appear in court about a matter with which he was charged. Whether this is the reason for his disappearance I do not know.

Margaret Grace Ward – she also had to make an appearance in court about a matter with which she was charged and she also failed to do so as far as I know.

Regarding Mrs McCulkin, I am not fully aware of what the set up is but there was disenchantment with her husband because of alleged irregularities of his appearance on the home scene and the fact that he was keeping company with a hotel proprietress. He was living with her around the time that Mrs McCulkin left the matrimonial home. There was also another defacto wife, but Billy McCulkin could elaborate on that.

It was interesting that O'Dempsey had summarised Barbara McCulkin's disappearance as her leaving 'the matrimonial home'.

O'Dempsey continued:

> I will not be making any further comment to the police nor to other members of the media. If it had not been for the fact that I had contravened some of society's laws in the past I doubt very much if these suggestions regarding these matters would have ever been made.
>
> I have given away my former lifestyle and have become an active Christian and I don't wish to be bothered with this matter again.

The clergyman added his further support to O'Dempsey and his partner, Dianne Pritchard. 'I don't care what a man has done in his past,' the clergyman said. 'God is his life from now on and the future for him and his wife. He has been an inspiring and untiring worker here. He is often trusted with our cars to do jobs well away from here. No one could say he has been in hiding. I think everyone should get a fair deal.'

Since he was a boy, O'Dempsey had had a peculiar relationship with religion, steeped in Catholicism from a young age, he was also immersed in the family's ancient Irish roots, replete with great warriors and a clan at war with any authorities that challenged it.

He could quote any passage in the Bible, yet vowed to those around him that he hated the church, and yet he had brothers and other relatives who went on to serve God as priests and Christian Brothers. It was a constant internal struggle, this question of faith.

Even so, throughout his life O'Dempsey did not hesitate to use the church and disappear into its fold when he was in a pinch. Such was the case in the late 1970s when he and de facto, Dianne Pritchard, were still moving from place to place following the disappearance of the McCulkins in January 1974.

As the cold case police investigation into the deaths of the McCulkins, Ward and Allen gathered pace from 1978, O'Dempsey and Pritchard spent considerable time at the Christian Outreach Centre at remote Mount Tuchekoi. O'Dempsey would give occasional sermons, and committed to manual labour and fixing machinery around the centre.

It was where Detective Sergeant Menary caught up with them during his investigation into the McCulkin murders. Menary had the bit between his teeth and couldn't let it go. When he finally interviewed Dianne Pritchard, she had recently become Mrs Dianne O'Dempsey, married by the centre's pastor, even though she was known at the centre as Cheryl Jackson.

While she was being interviewed in one of the police cars Pritchard said: 'I was a prostitute. I've found God now. I'm a Christian. These people here are wonderful. I've even seen them make legs grow. I went close to the stage to have a look before I'd believe it.'

Menary offered her some pristine logic – if she was now a committed Christian, she could answer questions from police truthfully.

'Yes,' Pritchard agreed.

Menary then informed her that they were seeking information about the disappearance, and presumed murder, of Margaret Grace Ward in late 1973.

Ward had worked with Pritchard in O'Dempsey's brothel Polonia. Both Pritchard and Ward had been issued summons' to appear in court in November of that year to answer charges that they were working as prostitutes, and that Pritchard was managing a brothel. Ward had visited her solicitor in the city before the court appearance. After that meeting, Ward vanished.

'I can't remember anything about that,' Pritchard told Menary, 'that's all in the past. The past has all been forgiven. It's too long ago. I don't remember anything about that.'

Menary said to her: 'God just left you … he flew out the window.'

He informed her he believed Ward had been murdered and Pritchard quickly changed her tune. 'Vince told me not to talk to you,' she said. 'I've said too much already.' She admitted to police she had once worked for missing brothel madam Simone Vogel.

Menary told her he believed her husband had murdered Ward to prevent her from giving evidence against Pritchard in their pending court case in late 1973.

She later told police of her new home on the mount: 'We don't have any guns here. We are Christians now and we don't need them.'

She said she and Vince had only left Brisbane because she was being harassed by police at the massage parlour.

Despite the police circling ever closer, O'Dempsey still had to earn a quid, and was in the process of growing one of his first cannabis crops in bushland on the eastern side of Cunninghams Gap and the Main Range on the way to Warwick. While O'Dempsey was diligently trying to make a buck on the outside, his name was mysteriously popping up in criminal circles.

One ex-con serving time in gaol for car theft and false pretences, met a fellow inmate called Leslie Smith. The ex-con knew many of Brisbane's criminals including James Finch and John Andrew Stuart, and had been a long-time phiz-gig, or informant, to a number of Queensland police officers, including detective Tony Murphy.

Leslie Smith, according to the Costigan Commission into the activities of the Federated Ship Painters and Dockers Union, was a member of that union. Interestingly, the Brisbane meeting rooms for union members, located in Cairns Street in Kangaroo Point, had been under surveillance by police in mid-1979. An officer tasked with scoping the union office says, 'there were literally hundreds of people coming and going who were either criminals or associated criminals'. He says, 'There were crims out of Victoria turning up in Cairns Street … and it was a hub for Queensland criminals.'

'Smith told [the ex-con] that he could arrange his escape but that it would need to be from another prison,' the Costigan report said. '[The ex-con] was thereafter moved to Palen Creek.'

How he managed to get himself so conveniently moved to the prison farm at Palen Creek was not explained. However, in a statement years later to the Fitzgerald inquiry into police corruption, a document was tabled in Queensland State Parliament that shed some light on the ex-con's role in these strange events.

The ex-con said that in 1979 he was approached in prison by police Inspector Ron Redmond and another police officer. Redmond, of course, had been one of the six police officers present when James Finch was interrogated at CIB headquarters days after the Whiskey Au Go Go firebombing in 1973. Redmond had typed Finch's unsigned record of interview.

Now, according to the ex-con, Redmond needed a favour. The ex-con said the police wanted him to make contact with Vince O'Dempsey, who was lying low given the gathering intensity of the McCulkin reinvestigation. Redmond wanted the ex-con to pass a message on to O'Dempsey. The inspector said O'Dempsey might be charged in relation to the McCulkin murders, but 'he would not be convicted'.

The ex-con added in his statement: 'Redmond said to me words to the effect of: "Just tell him everything will be OK. There'll be a hearing but he won't be convicted."'

The ex-con's amazing story alleged that he had been secretly removed from solitary confinement by police in order to make contact with O'Dempsey. He did indeed escape from Palen Creek, as arranged, in November 1979. He immediately made contact with Stewart Bridges, also a member of the Painters and Dockers. They met at the union rooms in Cairns Street. 'A change of clothing, money and a car were provided on the following day during another meeting at the Rooms,' the Costigan report said. Frank Costigan's royal commission into the Federated Ship Painters and Dockers Union between 1980 and 1984 was set up to examine the criminal activities and associated violence of the union. Costigan uncovered the story of the ex-con when he focussed on the union's activities in Queensland.

'[The ex-con] was directed to people in Newcastle who would arrange his continued concealment from the law. No consideration for this assistance was sought from [the ex-con] although, as will appear, there was to be in due course some quid pro quo.'

The ex-con hooked up with two Painters and Dockers union members in Newcastle. One criminal source confirmed that he turned up in Newcastle driving a stolen car. 'Everyone felt sorry for him at the time,' he said. 'No money. Nothing. We took him on a job and got him $500, but he went through that straight away gambling.'

According to the Costigan report, the ex-con was then 'ordered' to 'help Vincent O'Dempsey plant and tend a cannabis crop on a property outside Warwick in Queensland'.

Here was another coincidence. The ex-con had been moved to Newcastle and then offered a job on a crop run by O'Dempsey, the very man Inspector Ron Redmond wanted him to see and talk to. '[The ex-con] wasn't ordered up there,' the criminal source said. 'He went with a bloke up to O'Dempsey's crop and didn't last long. He took off.' The ex-con was to be the cook on the crop. Instead, he surrendered himself back into police custody and was returned to solitary confinement. But not before he had given up O'Dempsey and his illicit crop.

'Vince was howling on him when he dogged to the copper,' the criminal source said. 'If Vince could have got [the ex-con] that man would have suffered a terrible death.'

Another associate of O'Dempsey's said: 'Vince was filthy. He said if he caught the dickhead he'd strap him to a tree and feed him dog biscuits for a week, then he'd work out what to do with him.'

It appeared that police were looking for any possible way to keep O'Dempsey incarcerated once the call for the inquest gathered momentum. In July 1979 he was charged with seven counts of conspiracy to defraud that stemmed back to the Medibank fraud the year before. O'Dempsey was convicted but only fined and ordered to pay restitution costs. Then in March 1980, just as the inquest was kicking off, O'Dempsey was charged with cultivating a prohibited plant, possession of a prohibited plant and possession of an unlicensed concealable firearm. It was the ex-con's tip-off to police that had led to O'Dempsey's arrest. 'They caught Vince with a ridiculously small amount of dope seeds, it was pretty rough,' said one criminal colleague.

Nevertheless, police had him in custody when the inquest began in Brisbane in early 1980.

An Overdue Inquest

It had already been a summer of cyclonic winds and bushfires when Brisbane magistrate Robert William Boujoure finally opened the coronial inquest into the disappearance of the McCulkins, and others. The hearing would focus on five unsolved homicides stretching back to the early 1960s that invariably intersected with the underworld and its vicious and violent cast of characters. The victims were the McCulkins, along with Raymond Vincent 'Tommy' Allen – the young Pigott & Co. jewellery store robbery accomplice of O'Dempsey; and Margaret Grace Ward – the reluctant prostitute working out of O'Dempsey's Polonia Health Studio in Lutwyche in the early 1970s.

The inquest would look into whether these murders were the handiwork of one man – Vincent O'Dempsey – who was strongly connected to the Sydney underworld as well as the local franchise. As for Shorty Dubois, his co-accused in the McCulkin disappearances, he had gone AWOL. There were several warrants on drugs matters and the McCulkin murders out for his arrest. He had been elevated to one of Australia's ten most wanted criminals.

The inquest was held in the Holland Park Magistrates Court – a dour, single-storey concrete and glass rectangle – south of the Brisbane CBD. Eight police, including detectives and an inspector, were assigned to guard the court. They were instructed to use two sets of handcuffs to chain O'Dempsey to the bottom of the bar table. Even so, he was omnipresent in court. He was infamous already as a man of few words, and by 1980 had a towering reputation. 'Everybody said at that time that he was the most feared man in the Australian underworld,' says one criminal associate.

Nobody could foresee how O'Dempsey might react under intense questioning when Garry Forno, assistant to Coroner Boujoure, began quizzing him about the disappearances.

'Mr O'Dempsey,' Forno began, 'your full name please?'

'No comment.'

'Well, is not your full name Vincent O'Dempsey?'

'No comment.'

'Would you tell us your present address please?' asked Forno.

'No comment.'

'Are you married or single?'

'No comment.'

'You're aware, Mr O'Dempsey, are you not, that these coronial inquiries are into the disappearances of firstly Raymond Vincent Allen, secondly, Margaret Grace Ward, and thirdly, Barbara May McCulkin, Vicki Maree McCulkin and Barbara Leanne McCulkin?'

'No comment,' O'Dempsey replied.

'First of all, do you know a Raymond Vincent Allen?'

'No comment.'

'Do you know Margaret Grace Ward?' Forno asked.

'No comment.'

Forno asked if he knew the McCulkin women.

'No comment,' said O'Dempsey.

And so the tone was set for the inquest. Forno tried various lines of questioning to prompt a response from O'Dempsey, all to no avail. 'Mr Forno,' the coroner said after some time, 'in view of the attitude of the witness, it might be wise if you did not pursue the matter further at this stage'. He was stood down.

Then it was Billy McCulkin's turn. Having been a close acquaintance of O'Dempsey since 1966, McCulkin was called as a witness at the inquest on 13 February. He, too, was cross-examined by Garry Forno, who was interested in a conversation McCulkin had with O'Dempsey about six months prior to the disappearance of Barbara and the girls in January 1974.

'It was in a hotel,' McCulkin said of the conversation. 'We were having drinks and some mention of a story about people being put in a dam in Warwick ... two people were allegedly put in a dam at Warwick. I said no, I didn't really believe that story because of the ...'

'This came up in the conversation with O'Dempsey, did it?' Forno asked.

'O'Dempsey brought the matter up, yes,' McCulkin went on. 'And I said I didn't really believe that they could put people in a dam wall because having worked on construction sites myself I realised that the work was inspected pretty thoroughly and usually right up to the point that you're pouring concrete … you have got a Clerk of Works present.'

'I see,' said Forno.

'But we were talking away about things and he mentioned about a … it got round to giving information to the Police,' Billy continued. 'He made a statement to me that there was a person in Warwick or near Warwick … that wouldn't be talking to the Police anymore. I asked what he meant by that and his reply was, "Old Vince [Tommy Allen] won't be talking to anybody anymore."'

'And in what manner did he say that?'

'Well, you know,' Billy replied, 'sort of a sneaky manner I suppose you might say but then again I didn't take a great deal of notice at the time. Sort of a secretive manner.'

Forno asked McCulkin a number of questions about his marriage to Barbara, the children, and then about the day they vanished and events following their disappearance.

McCulkin told the court that when he was searching for his family he confronted O'Dempsey and Dubois. '… I went into the kitchen and spoke to Dubois and O'Dempsey,' McCulkin added. 'I said something to the effect, you know, "What were you doing there [at Dorchester Street]?" And he [O'Dempsey] said, "I wasn't there."

'I said, "Hang on a minute … five minutes ago, you inferred that you were there" … and he said, "No, well, I wasn't there."

'I said, "If they've run away or anything like that, just let me know and, you know, as long as they're safe I'm not worried if they've gone anywhere. If they need any help, well, I'll help them."'

McCulkin was then tested by O'Dempsey's legal counsel, C.D. Thompson Claire, and was asked about his friendship with Vince O'Dempsey.

'Now, you've known Vince O'Dempsey since about 1966, that was some years after your marriage, which was in 1960,' said Claire. 'That's the situation, isn't it?'

'That's basically it,' McCulkin said.

'And you have seen much of Mr O'Dempsey over those years up until the time of the disappearance of your wife, I mean, did you see him constantly over all those years or just from time to time?'

'When he wasn't in gaol I seen him quite a bit.'

'Did you regard him as a friend?'

'… I regarded him as a friend,' said McCulkin.

Claire then focused on the McCulkin marriage. 'How did you get on with the children?' he asked.

'I got on with them alright,' Bill said.

'At the time were you fond of them?'

'Yes.'

'Had you not hit your wife in the past at all?' Claire asked.

'Yes. I certainly had.'

'You had hit her?'

'Yes,' Billy repeated.

'And assaulted her?'

'I didn't assault her, no,' he qualified. 'I didn't run at her with a baseball bat or anything like that. Perhaps we had an argument and she might have struck me and I might have struck her.'

Then Claire dropped a bombshell question: 'Have you ever had sex with any of your daughters at all?'

'I certainly have not,' McCulkin answered.

'Has there been any reason for your wife to complain to anybody else that you may have had oral sex with your daughters or one of your daughters?'

'I certainly have not.'

'Have you been aware of any complaints, even if not true, have you been aware of any complaints of that sort of thing coming from your wife?'

'I certainly have not.'

'You've not?' said Claire.

'I would say that they would be a figment of whoever's imagination told you that,' McCulkin responded.

'Did you ever persuade your wife to attend husband and wife swapping parties at all in the past?'

'No,' he said.

The questioning moved on to a letter that O'Dempsey had sent to Billy McCulkin in 1975, the year after Barbara and their daughters disappeared. Claire said the letter, on the surface, appeared friendly enough.

McCulkin disagreed. He said it contained 'an implied threat'.

'You think there is?' asked Claire.

'I thought so at the time or I wouldn't have given it to the police,' McCulkin replied.

'Is there any particular ... part of the letter which you feel is a threat or did you just think the whole thing was an implied threat?'

'Well, I think ... if I persisted in my enquiries and seeing the Police that perhaps your client might endeavour to do something about my life.'

'That was the impression you got from the letter, was it?' asked Claire.

'Well, he seems to have done it before, so I thought, why stop at me?'

It was an extraordinary moment in the infant stages of the inquest. O'Dempsey, a former friend with whom he'd once robbed and cracked safes, among other things, was now chained to a chair at the bar table in the courtroom. To discredit McCulkin's evidence about the disappearance and presumed murder of his family, O'Dempsey's counsel was now asking him about incest with his daughters. Claire also asked McCulkin whether or not he had taken part in Australia's then worst mass murder at the Whiskey. McCulkin denied any knowledge of the Whiskey.

Where had the information about McCulkin allegedly having sex with his own daughters come from? O'Dempsey had briefly courted Barbara McCulkin in late 1973 and into 1974 when Billy McCulkin had left the family home for Estelle Long. Had the allegations come from O'Dempsey?

And what of Billy's association with the Whiskey firebombing? Were the allegations from Claire simply based on articles that Billy Stokes had published in the *Port News*? Or had these, too, come from O'Dempsey? And if so, how would O'Dempsey know if McCulkin was in on the Whiskey tragedy or not?

There is no honour among thieves, and McCulkin's credibility and character were being severely tested. If he was involved in the Whiskey mass murder, and had sexually assaulted his own children, how could anything he said about O'Dempsey and Dubois be believed?

It appeared his former friends in crime, O'Dempsey and Dubois, were happy to tip the bucket on him to protect themselves.

Then again, if Billy McCulkin had been part of the crew that torched the Whiskey, he could hardly implicate himself in 15 murders. In many ways, McCulkin was snookered. He believed he knew that Vince and Shorty had killed his family. But how far could he go before his possible connection to the Whiskey was exposed?

After McCulkin gave his evidence Boujoure adjourned the inquest until 10 a.m. the following day.

Mad Dog

As the presumed murders of the McCulkins and others were being picked over in a Brisbane court, Detective Senior Constable John Attwood and Detective Sergeant James Munro of the Major Crime Squad in Adelaide were staking out a house in the suburb of Christies Beach, south of the South Australian capital.

Police had information that Garry Dubois, a wanted fugitive from Queensland, had been sighted at a house in Ramsgate Avenue. Attwood, Munro, other members of the Major Crime Squad and uniformed police approached the house at about 6.30 a.m. on Monday 7 July 1980. Munro and Attwood rapped on the front door and received no response. 'I then heard the sound of a person running through the house,' Attwood later recalled. 'The front glass door was then broken ... and I could see Dubois and a uniform policeman Rogers wrestling on the floor of the lounge room. I could see that Dubois was trying to take a shotgun away from Rogers.'

Dubois was subdued, handcuffed and taken to Adelaide police headquarters. At 8.45 a.m. he was transferred to the city watchhouse where he was searched and charged. He was briefly interviewed by Munro at the CIB. 'Now that we're alone can I do some business with you?' Dubois allegedly asked Munro.

'What do you mean?'

'I'm not going real well at the moment,' Dubois said. 'I could get five grand. Yes, five grand.'

'Don't come that rubbish with me,' Munro said. 'You're talking to the wrong fellow.'

'Well, do you blame me for trying?'

Attwood entered the interview room and they continued the interview. 'Do you know the McCulkins?' Munro asked.

'I knew Billy.'

'Is he the husband?'

'Yeah,' said Dubois. 'He knocks around Queensland. He fancies himself as some sort of gangster.'

'Did you know his wife and kids?'

'Aw, not really. I'd met them but I hardly knew them.'

'As I understand it,' Munro continued, 'both Mrs McCulkin and her children have been murdered. Where were you back in that particular time in 1974?'

'I don't know. I could have been anywhere.'

'Were you responsible for their deaths?'

'I don't know anything about it,' Dubois said. 'Anyway, you know me. I don't talk.'

Early the next afternoon, Attwood went to the watchhouse and handcuffed himself to Dubois in preparation for his court appearance. They sat in an interview room. 'Fucking hell, man, this is stupid, murder, I don't believe it,' Dubois supposedly said to Attwood.

'What do you mean?' the officer asked.

'What's the use, no one can help me.'

'You know what you are saying and who you are saying it to, so remember anything you do say may be taken down and later used as evidence,' Attwood reminded him. 'Do you understand that?'

Dubois said: 'Man, I know all about that ... I'm guilty by association, that's it, because I know O'Dempsey, that's it, I hardly knew them.'

'Do you want to talk to me about it?'

'If I blab I'm dead and I'm dead if I don't,' said the prisoner. 'Man, I'll be an old man when I get out ... they throw away the key for murder ... I'm guilty because I know him.'

'There is a lot of difference between a charge for drugs and a charge for murder.'

'Difference ... fucking life, man,' Dubois supposedly said to Attwood. 'If I talk I'm dead. I've [got] to cop it. I'll have to live with him in gaol and he'll get me there if I talk.' Dubois said his situation was 'hopeless'.

In court, orders were issued to extradite Dubois back to Queensland. According to Attwood, Dubois was agitated and close to tears. They both went into the court holding cell after the hearing.

'Fucking murder, I can't believe it, I'm guilty because I know O'Dempsey ...' he remarked. 'He's fucking mad, you know ... I think he likes doing it … he's a mad fucking dog, man. Jesus Christ, I'll never see Jan and the kid again. When I get back there [to Brisbane], it's goodbye world. Jesus, I wish you'd taken me out at the house.'

Dubois was on a roll: 'You know, every time I get with crims, I cop it. Eight years for rape, I served seven and a half, everyone else got bonds and a few months. They reckon I'm a sex deviate because I like young girls. Christ, I met Jan when she was at school and I married her. Not this. Guilty by association, that's that.'

Attwood said there had to have been some evidence if a warrant had been issued.

'I hardly knew the McCulkins,' Dubois continued. 'Fucking hell, man. A bit of dope to make ends meet, but fucking hell, murder, it's not my bag, man.'

When Dubois was extradited back to Queensland, his loyal mother, Hilma, was there to support her boy. His older sister Gail later told police: 'I remember one day Garry was on the TV. He had been brought back from South Australia for the McCulkins. I was horrified because I saw my mother on the camera when they were filming Garry. Garry was kicking the camera.'

Gail later tried to get clarification on the situation from their mother. 'I went and tackled Mum about what was going on,' she said. 'She told me that Garry was suspected of being involved in the disappearance of the McCulkins. I had seen on the news and in the papers about the McCulkins disappearing and I knew it was about a mother and two little girls. Mum told me that she had asked Garry about it and asked if he had done it and he told her that he didn't do it, but he was in the vicinity when it happened. Mum accepted that from him.'

As the inquest progressed in Brisbane, Billy Stokes, in gaol for murdering Tommy Hamilton, was subpoenaed to the Coroners Court hearing but told the magistrate he didn't think the hearing was 'fair dinkum' and refused to answer questions.

Stokes later said: 'Earlier in the prison I had spoken to O'Dempsey and Dubois about the McCulkin family murders and when I criticised Dubois for killing kids he snapped … he just went off. Then when I … mentioned that it had been rumoured that the girls were sexually slain, O'Dempsey held up his hand in a stop sign and said, "We only did what …"'

'He never finished the sentence. During the Coroners Court inquiry, Dubois told me that the matter would be committed for trial and then No Billed, which was more or less what eventually happened.'

In the end, Coroner Boujoure recommended that O'Dempsey and Dubois be arrested and charged with murder in relation to the McCulkins. 'I consider there is a body of circumstantial evidence upon which, taken as a whole, and I emphasise as a whole, a jury could reasonably infer that O'Dempsey and Dubois are responsible for the deaths of Mrs McCulkin and her two daughters,' Boujoure said.

But the case never proceeded.

In December 1980, senior Crown legal officer Angelo Vasta recommended that the charges against O'Dempsey and Dubois be dropped. The recommendation was made after the Solicitor General sought a legal opinion on the charges. 'In my opinion,' Vasta concluded, 'the state of evidence against O'Dempsey and Dubois is such that it is incapable of establishing a prima facie case of murder against either of them … In all the circumstances I am of the opinion that this is a proper case for the filing of No True Bill, and I respectfully recommend accordingly.'

Vasta's opinion received the support of prominent barrister Cedric Hampson QC. Two months later, Attorney-General Sam Doumany announced that the Crown would drop its case against both men.

'Looking back in hindsight,' detective Marshall reflected, 'we did the best job we possibly could at the time. It was a big disappointment. But I suppose you've got to respect the referee's decision.'

The former criminal who in late 1979 had escaped from prison to bring a message to O'Dempsey from Inspector Ron Redmond – that in effect O'Dempsey would be charged with the McCulkin murders but the charges would not make it to court – said in a statement: 'On my release from solitary confinement I learned that an inquest into the disappearance of the McCulkins had been convened and that Garry Dubois and Vincent O'Dempsey had been committed for trial. I also learned that the prosecution against them had been discontinued.'

The ex-con added in his statement that he was later threatened by Queensland police and told to keep his mouth shut. Ron Redmond's prediction had come true. And with that, the McCulkin case went stone cold for another 34 years.

While O'Dempsey and Dubois may have been relieved to put the inquest behind them, Billy McCulkin was not happy about the outcome. For him, the killer or killers of his entire family were still untried and unpunished. He returned to working as a dogman on cranes and on city construction sites.

A co-worker at the time says McCulkin was a quiet person in those years. 'He'd been a pretty hard man, yeah, because he had that tattoo on his old fellow and you know, [he used to] get in the pubs and when he was half-full of piss he'd flash it out in the earlier days ...' the co-worker says.

Following the 1980 inquest into Barbara and the kids, McCulkin seemed like a different person. The co-worker says: 'I'll tell you one thing, Billy, he was a very, very quiet sort of bloke, very quiet when I knew him ... I don't know if he could drive a car or not, but his wife used to drop him off and then she used to come and pick him up in the afternoon every day. When I knew him he didn't go to the pub.'

He says McCulkin was haunted by the death of Barbara and the girls. 'Well, he mentioned it and everyone was talking, you know.

I got the impression that he knew more about it than what he let on. I wouldn't be surprised that he actually set things up to get his wife killed but not his kids. But yeah, he never said anything like that but he was out to get bloody Vince. He was going to fix him up, but I think everyone was scared of Vince O'Dempsey.'

Domestic Entanglements

When Kerri-Ann Scully was growing up in various suburbs across Brisbane's inner-north – Wavell Heights, Geebung, Chermside – the great and painful shadow across her family was the disappearance and presumed murder of her Uncle Tommy Hamilton in January 1975.

Her mother, Carolyn Scully – Tommy's sister – had never gotten over the loss, despite the fact that Billy Stokes had been tried and convicted of Tommy's murder. What the Scully family shared with the McCulkin family was that neither crimes perpetrated against their family members had produced bodies. The McCulkin girls and Hamilton had vanished off the face of the earth.

'Even though he died before I was born, Uncle Tom has been a significant part of my life,' Kerri-Ann would later tell police. 'He was a famous boxer and helped my mum provide for her kids. My mother has been obsessed with finding out what happened to his remains so she can bury him ...'

The Scullys were well acquainted with the Clockwork Orange Gang. Peter Hall had been in a relationship with Carolyn Scully at the time of the McCulkin disappearances in 1974.

In the early to mid-1980s, however, there was a steadying influence around the house when Kerri-Ann was a kid, and that was a man called Vince O'Dempsey. 'I don't recall the first time I met Vince, but recall him being part of our lives as I grew up and he was often spoken about by my mother and our friends ... I recall when I was about ten years old my mother and Vince were in a short relationship. I remember him coming around to our place a lot. He always had lots of money and would buy things for us, he taught us self-defence, like how to flip people. He would always tell us to stay away from drugs. Vince was the only man our mother had around us, she didn't really have boyfriends.'

Kerri-Ann said she knew her mother and Vince had a sexual relationship at one point but they'd had 'a big fight'. Kerri-Ann thought it might have had something to do with Vince sleeping with another woman. 'My mother has since told me that Vince asked her to move with him to Warwick but she did not want her children raised on drug money and refused him,' Kerri-Ann said. 'I remember a time when Vince stopped coming around and I was told he had gone on a long holiday. I knew that meant he had gone to gaol.'

In fact, in March 1985 O'Dempsey was charged in Tweed Heads, just south of the Queensland border, with supplying prohibited drugs and supplying heroin, and was granted bail. On 16 September in the Lismore District Court he was found guilty and sentenced to ten years in prison with a non-parole period of seven years. During the six months between him being on remand and being convicted, criminal associates noticed a different man. One said that he believed O'Dempsey had tried to set him up with police. Other acquaintances were suddenly being arrested and charged. The associate said: 'It was the first time I felt that Vince might have been acting as an informant to police, and helping them out,' he said.

Early in his sentence, O'Dempsey successfully argued for a one-year reduction in his prison sentence. He was due out in 1991.

During this stretch, O'Dempsey would miss the police and political corruption scandal that would become the Fitzgerald inquiry in 1987, the fall of police commissioner Sir Terence Lewis, and the collapse of Sir Joh Bjelke-Petersen's premiership. There's no doubt, however, that O'Dempsey would have been aware of many of the corrupt police who got caught in the inquiry net, and many who evaded it. He may have even tipped his hat to retired Assistant Commissioner Tony Murphy, who while he was named repeatedly during the inquiry, was never charged with corruption or any other malfeasance. Nor, indeed, would O'Dempsey himself feature in any substantive evidence before the inquiry, the terms of reference only reaching back to 1977.

And while the Fitzgerald inquiry didn't specifically touch the Whiskey Au Go Go tragedy, Finch would piggyback off the relentless evidence of corrupt Queensland police and the practice of verballing, to continue to cry out his innocence. In the years after John Stuart's death, Finch had become the focus of any matters relating to the Whiskey firebombing, and he had been revelling in a strange celebrity status whereby he, a reviled mass killer, simultaneously possessed a lurid attraction. First there was his romance with a woman called Cheryl Cole, wheelchair-bound with a debilitating, and terminal, disease. They would become engaged in 1984. During this well-publicised romance, there was a parallel narrative playing out in the press.

Enter Scottish language expert Reverend A.Q. Morton, who used his language-tracing technique – sylometry – on Finch's unsigned record of interview from 1974. Morton concluded that there was one chance in 236,742 that the confession was made by him. Out of Morton's findings came a push to either reopen the Whiskey investigation, give Finch another trial, or secure him a pardon.

The heartbreaking story of the terminally ill fiancée and the move to free Finch somehow got tangled together, giving the story even more power. Suddenly this was a tale of possible redemption. Of forgiveness. Of admitting even the slightest possibility that Finch may have been verballed by police after all, and may or may not have been involved in the Whiskey.

What remained immovable throughout all of this was the roll call of the Whiskey dead, and the grief of the families and friends of the victims. Tom and Dulcie Day, who lost their teenage son Darcy in the Whiskey all those years earlier, posed the simple question: 'Why won't the Whiskey go away?'

In mid-1985 the Days said the State Government owed it to the families of the Whiskey victims to hold an inquiry that might answer some of the questions that kept haunting them. 'We watched it on television last week and it brought it all back,' Mr Day said. 'We still don't know why no real investigation was followed up into the firebombing of the Torino ... shortly before the Whiskey Au Go Go fire. These things don't fit in.

'I'm confused. Why can't they try and give people like us some answers?'

As for the McCulkin murders in 1974, it was as if they had slipped off the map and been forgotten.

Flight of the Birdman of Boggo Road

The years of campaigning for the release of James Richard Finch produced little until, at the beginning of 1988, the narrative of his police verballing, by a sheer twist of fate, was given some solid context. In late January, State Cabinet revealed that it would at last consider parole for Finch. This about-face had come, however, following more than six months of damning evidence that had been produced at the Fitzgerald inquiry into police and political corruption.

Queensland was reeling from the daily revelations of the inquiry, and the exposition of a dangerously corrupt police force under Commissioner Terence Lewis. Evidence before the inquiry also pointed to a State government wracked with cronyism and corruption under Joh Bjelke-Petersen, who had been punted as Premier just a couple of months earlier, in late 1987.

In this light, the police verbal supposedly inflicted on Finch in a small room in CIB headquarters on a Sunday night in March 1973 could no longer be seen as simply a convicted mass murderer's ruse to be released from prison. Queensland now had a new Premier with integrity – Mike Ahern – and the reformative winds of change could already be detected across government and the community as a whole.

Finch was granted parole, after 15 years in gaol, on 1 February 1988. Corrective Services Minister Russell Cooper said Cabinet had approved a unanimous recommendation from the Parole Board that Finch be released. 'God sure answers prayers,' said Cheryl Finch. She had married Finch in the women's prison chapel in February 1986. 'I have been praying a lot. It's like a dream come true.'

A condition of Finch's parole was that he was to be immediately deported back to the country of his birth, the United Kingdom. The decision on Finch instantly sparked renewed press and public interest in the Whiskey case, and it was in the news for weeks. The families of victims said they hoped the Fitzgerald inquiry could get to the bottom of what really happened that night at the Whiskey. It was speculated that the inquiry might take on the task of reinvestigating the fatal fire.

On 7 February, a week after the news of Finch's release, the *Sunday Mail* published an extraordinary story about the Whiskey and who might have been behind it. The story carried no by-line.

> A 1973 report by a group of senior police known as the Committee of Eight, which names a former senior Queensland police officer as having approved the Whiskey Au Go Go firebombing, will be given to the Fitzgerald Inquiry. A Gold Coast solicitor, Mr

Christopher Nyst, will soon present fresh evidence to the inquiry relating to the conviction of James Richard Finch on murder and arson charges following the blaze ...

The story detailed how Queensland had been pre-warned about the firebombing and had even been given a date when the attack might occur, and no inquiry into the torching of Torino's and the Whiskey had ever been called. The report continued:

> A Fortitude Valley resident has told the *Sunday Mail* that police warned a number of people to stay away from the Whiskey Au Go Go on the night of the firebombing. Mr John Hannay ... with Ken and Brian Little, said last week that nightclub owners bribed police to stay in operation. He also said police were involved in the Whiskey Au Go Go fire. Hannay ... says he dealt regularly with members of the Licensing Branch.

While the Fitzgerald inquiry became an instant vessel for all sorts of new information about the past and present, there was a danger that, on the other side of the coin, its findings could be used by people without pure motive as a way of blaming everything on corrupt police. Solicitor Nyst also revealed that he was preparing a submission to the Attorney–General in relation to aspects of Finch's guilt or innocence, and had fresh evidence from police about the so-called verballing of Finch in 1973.

Finch was deported on 16 February. As he boarded his Qantas flight to London, he gave a V for victory sign and said: 'I'll be back to tell the truth – if I'm allowed to.'

His solicitor, Nyst, read out a prepared statement from Finch: 'Fifteen years ago, Judge Lucas asked me if I had any comment to make before he passed sentence. I said, "I'll maintain my innocence until the day I die." He then did what he had to do and sentenced me to gaol for the rest of my life. Now I am no longer in gaol, but I am not free yet. I will not be free until I am totally exonerated from all involvement in the Whiskey Au Go Go fire. I am innocent of that crime.'

The Boeing 747 closed its doors at 2.45 p.m. and left for Singapore. When Finch landed back in the United Kingdom, he faced one particular headline in the *Daily Mirror*. It read: 'WELCOME HOME KILLER'.

Powderkeg

During the Fitzgerald inquiry the commission received many documents and statements pertaining to the Whiskey – it was a crucible of information, true or otherwise – but the inquiry had not dealt with the fatal fire singularly. It was, like so much brought to the inquiry and its investigators, its own seething entity.

While the Fitzgerald inquiry may not have focussed directly on the Whiskey Au Go Go, the extensive hearings did draw out people who wanted to share what they knew about the incident, albeit 15 years later.

The deportation of Finch, too, loosened some lips. After Finch from the safety of the United Kingdom accused then Acting Police Commissioner Ron Redmond of having verballed him over the Whiskey, other police came forward and named Syd Atkinson as another who contributed to concocting the so-called Finch confession.

The Whiskey hornet's nest had been stirred again. And the *Courier-Mail*, in a firm editorial on 24 February, demanded answers.

Despite the apparent reluctance of the Police Minister to do so, the Queensland Government must reopen investigations into the

convictions of James Richard Finch and the late John Andrew
Stuart for the murders arising from the Whiskey Au Go Go
firebombing.

In the 15 years since their conviction, frequent doubts have
been raised about the value of some evidence given at their
trial ... The public expectation that policemen always operate
on the right side of the law has been demonstrated to be wrong.

Evidence given to the Fitzgerald Inquiry – direct evidence
in the form of confessions or indirect evidence – has revealed
that some members of the upper echelons of the Queensland
police force have been corrupt for a long time. If these officers
can accept bribes from illegal gamblers and brothel owners to
ignore the law and if they can set themselves up virtually as a
controlling authority for the vice and gambling trades, then why
can't their colleagues lie and fabricate evidence in a notorious
murder trial?

Former police commissioner Ray Whitrod backed a reinvestigation
into the Whiskey. Retired and living in Adelaide, he said that
Finch and Stuart might not have been innocent. He said there were
many unexplained events surrounding the bombing and there was a
possibility that Stuart and Finch were acting on the orders of more
powerful criminals.

More ghosts rushed out of the closet.

Then, on 14 April 1988 – two months after Finch had left the
country – the ALP member for Rockhampton, Paul Braddy, made
a stunning address to parliament in relation to the Torino and
Whiskey fires. As a prelude to the powderkeg he was about to light,
Braddy said: 'The public seem to be of the opinion that anything
that relates to police corruption in this State can be dealt with by
the Fitzgerald inquiry. Clearly, that is not so. The terms of reference,
even interpreted widely as they are by the commissioner, must be

the parameters of his investigations.

'So it is a time to look at it and say to ourselves here in the House and to outsiders: what is happening? Are the matters being dealt with adequately and exposed or are there matters that to some extent are associated with police corruption, or potential police corruption, malpractice or failure that should be exposed further?'

Braddy was setting the grounds for the extraordinary information he was about to impart. And he was hinting, not so delicately, that other matters raised by the inquiry merited their own serious investigation. One such matter was, he said, the case of convicted killer James Finch and the Whiskey Au Go Go mass murder.

Braddy told the house that Attorney-General Paul Clauson had received information from the legal outfit Witheriff Nyst about their client James Finch, which included a statement from a former member of the Federal Narcotics Bureau.

According to Braddy, the informant told the now retired narcotics officer that Torino's restaurant was to be firebombed on a certain night and that Billy McCulkin had been paid $1000 to do the job. Braddy said: 'As we now know, as predicted, Torino's restaurant was fire-bombed. It was not stopped, nobody was apprehended and no police action, to my knowledge, has ever been taken in respect of the information provided.

'Of course, the Whiskey Au Go Go fire occurred a short time after the fire-bombing of Torino's restaurant. Suggestions have been made that people involved in the Torino's restaurant fire could also very likely have been involved in the Whiskey Au Go Go fire.'

Braddy informed the House that he had personally spoken to an Officer Russell, who was concerned about the lack of action within the police force to prevent the tragedy. He said that Russell was asked by his superiors to put his concerns in writing, which he did.

'He handed in a written report in which, he tells me, he indicated that the fire-bombing would occur at the particular time that it did. He further indicated ... that he would like to be present and do what he could as a conscientious police officer to protect the building and to apprehend the villains who were about to perpetrate the offence. However, he was told that it was nothing to do with him; that the matter had been detailed to the Valley police and that it would be attended to. He was told by his superior, "I have experienced detectives", and it was indicated to him that his presence was not required.'

Braddy told the House that after the bombing of Torino's, Russell had made further inquiries. The information he was given by Queensland police was that there had been a dreadful mistake. On the night in question, the detectives who had been detailed to protect Torino's and apprehend the villains were supposedly waiting down at the Valley police station for the owner of Torino's to turn up with the key so that they could get into the premises. While they were sitting down at the Valley police station waiting for the key, the perpetrators who did not need a key turned up to firebomb the restaurant.

It was extraordinary, Braddy suggested, 'that it was thought necessary for police officers to have a key to prevent the fire-bombing of a building that obviously could be attacked from the exterior'.

Braddy's assertions about police inaction and their proximity to the fire would be confirmed years later by separate sources. Firstly, Clockwork Orange Gang member Peter Hall would confess to the Torino's bombing, admitting that he and others in the gang did the job at the request of Billy McCulkin, and that Vince O'Dempsey had organised the hit. Secondly, Licensing Branch officer Kingsley Fancourt said that on the Monday morning after the fire, he would bump into a fellow branch member who had worked the overnight shift, and claimed to have actually witnessed the bombing, and that no arrests were made. And thirdly, a relation of one of the firebombers would say gang members actually saw a group of police officers standing around outside the Fortitude Valley police station as they made their escape from the crime.

Braddy tried to stress the seriousness of the inaction by Queensland police. Why had they done nothing to prevent the bombing or arrest the perpetrators when they had all the information to hand?

Braddy then reminded the House that there was substantiated rumour that suggested the deaths of the McCulkins was linked to knowledge Barbara had in relation the Whiskey fire. 'Subsequently,' Braddy said, 'at a coroner's inquiry into the murder of Mrs McCulkin and her two daughters, Mr O'Dempsey was committed for trial … The suggestion is that gangland people had stepped in to protect Billy McCulkin and that, if they had not murdered Mrs McCulkin, the facts in relation to Torino's bombing and the Whiskey Au Go Go bombing would have emerged. Taking into account the inquiries that are now taking place in Queensland, that is a very serious matter.'

Braddy's assertions about 'gangland people' stepping in to protect McCulkin may have been more prescient than he knew at the time, given the circumstances in the wake of that tragic fire.

Within hours of the Whiskey, crooked New South Wales cop Roger Rogerson rushed to Brisbane. Rogerson, for all the notoriety he would later attract, was a 'fixer' with strong connections to Sydney's underworld, including Fred 'Paddles' Anderson and Lenny McPherson.

Had Rogerson been one of those people who had stepped in to protect McCulkin? And if so, was McCulkin indeed the target of the 'gangland people's' largesse? Could it have been Vince O'Dempsey they were protecting, given his links to Anderson and other crime figures? Was O'Dempsey protected as a prize asset of Sydney crime figures?

Stewart John Regan, the feared Sydney hitman, also made a beeline to Brisbane in the hours after the fire. Why? He had also made the extraordinary offer of volunteering to kill John Andrew Stuart as a favour to police. Was Regan also in town, along with Rogerson, to ensure that the true story of who was actually behind the Whiskey mass murder was managed and contained? It's a fact that when Stuart and Finch were arrested a wall seemed to go up around this complicated crime. And remained in place for decades.

At this point in Braddy's speech, government members complained that his subject was irrelevant to the debate at hand. But Braddy had other pressing matters to canvass and would not be put off. 'I ask the Minister: is there a concern that some police officers could themselves be involved with the people involved in Torino's bombing and the Whiskey Au Go Go fire-bombing?'

Braddy wanted to know why the trial against O'Dempsey did not proceed following the inquest. He claimed to be in possession of an affidavit that contained important and worrying information about these events. But where could he take the affidavit?

'If an inquiry was held into all of these matters, I could go to that inquiry with that affidavit. Such an inquiry does not exist.'

Braddy told the House he had tried to obtain and read a copy of the coroner's inquest depositions, in order to ascertain whether matters in those depositions could be sent to the Fitzgerald inquiry and further investigated. However, the information that he received from both the Department of Justice and the Sheriff's Office was that the depositions in relation to Vincent O'Dempsey were no longer on the file and that no copy of those depositions could be located.

At this point the ALP member for Inala, Henry Palaszczuk, interjected with a question about the whereabouts of the despositions. 'Where are they?' he asked.

'Indeed, that is the question: where are they?' echoed Braddy. 'I telephoned the clerk of the Justice Department to inquire whether or not I could obtain a copy of the depositions of that inquest. I was informed that those depositions could not be located. No reason could be given for that. Not only were the depositions missing, but the O'Dempsey file in the Supreme Court also was missing.'

These were extraordinary allegations. Not only had Braddy suggested that members of the Queensland police force may have had some involvement in the Whiskey mass murder, but that important official documents relating to the case had mysteriously vanished.

Where was Vincent O'Dempsey's Supreme Court file? Where were the depositions?

Braddy said: 'The Opposition is concerned that, if there was potentially a cover-up in relation to the O'Dempsey trial, one of the best things to do would be to remove the formal evidence. Indeed, I understand that the official files no longer contain a copy of the depositions which set out in detail the evidence that was given. If those depositions were where they should be, namely, in the Supreme Court file,' Braddy said, 'we would be able to purchase a copy of them to see whether the matter should be pursued further.'

Braddy had more serious allegations to make. 'All of us have been most appreciative, and accept, that the Fitzgerald inquiry has been competent and forthright in the matters which it has been investigating,' he said. 'However, there is some concern in the material that went to the Attorney-General from Mr Nyst about the Finch case and about an officer in the Fitzgerald inquiry.'

Furthermore Braddy claimed to have information about a senior officer in the Fitzgerald inquiry who had interviewed Russell in relation to his statements and that nothing was done about it. 'I have received further information,' Braddy said, 'that this police officer is a close friend of and is in constant contact with Assistant Commissioner Ron Redmond.' Here was Braddy's other bombshell. Redmond, he informed the House, had of course been present at the 'so-called confession of Jim Finch'.

'On reading the materials forwarded to the Attorney-General and on having received the information which I have received, one can only but be concerned about whether in fact there is at least one officer at the Fitzgerald Inquiry who, whilst doing his job in other matters, in fact has conversations with the Assistant Commissioner and is in fact failing to fully carry out his role in relation to matters that are not part of the terms of reference of the Fitzgerald inquiry but which are still touching on it and which are still very serious,' Braddy continued. 'I again ask whether the Attorney-General has done anything about the officer whose name appears in the statement that he received. I ask whether the Attorney-General took any action to see why the officer did not go back to interview the reliable witness with his informant.'

Braddy's main concern was that 'all matters of police malpractice or failure to attend to duty or corruption should be attended to'. Braddy said the government continued to think that the inquiry would be a panacea to all of Queensland's ills. 'The challenge is again before the Government. Why does the Government not inquire into the Torino bombing and the other associated matters? It will be interesting to hear what answers are given in relation to the missing depositions and Supreme Court file.'

The Minister for Justice, Attorney-General and the member for Redland, Paul Clauson, stood in reply. 'I am at some loss as to exactly what the thrust of his speech was,' Clauson said.

'The Honourable member raised a question about Supreme Court files. I am having investigations made into that matter. As he would appreciate, that was an event that occurred long before my time in this place or in this portfolio. However, attempts are being made to locate those files after so many years. I shall keep him apprised of that matter.'

Little was done in relation to Paul Braddy's allegations in parliament and once again, the Whiskey slipped off the radar.

The Confession

Jim Finch settled back into civilian life in the village of Basildon, Essex, with his sister June, thinking he'd put the nightmare of Queensland behind him. His wife, Cheryl, had joined him briefly, but then returned quietly to Australia. The relationship that had worked so beautifully when he was locked up in Brisbane didn't survive in the real world.

In November 1988, as winter began to set in, Finch was paid a visit by his friend and best man at his wedding, Brisbane newspaper reporter Dennis Watt. Watt was a chief reporter for the Brisbane *Sun*, and he'd hoped that Finch might, at last, tell the truth about who was behind the Whiskey tragedy.

Finch sang like a canary. In a series of world exclusives, Watt outlined Finch's story, from his abusive childhood in the United Kingdom to his friendship with John Stuart and the fatal fire of 8 March 1973. Finch made the sensational allegation that a corrupt top police officer was the 'mastermind' behind the planning of the fire and extortion attempt. He said the cop, along with O'Dempsey, was responsible for planning the firebombing as part of a 'Brisbane protection racket'.

'A system of rotten cops and king criminals working together used me and they used John Stuart,' he told Watt. 'John Stuart was the prime manipulator but he wasn't the champion. The bombing was supposed to have thrown a scare not just into nightclubs but all of Brisbane – restaurants, shops, SP bookies – the lot. It wouldn't be much use burning a nightclub if they just wanted to stand over the three or four clubs in town.'

Finch named Stuart, Billy McCulkin and Tommy 'Clockwork Orange' Hamilton as his accomplices in the job. Stuart was promised $5000 to enlist Finch to do 'the dirty work'. He said O'Dempsey 'had to be working in with the copper selling people out ... those blokes don't survive unless they're doing that'.

(An associate of the Clockwork Orange Gang disputes Finch's version of events. 'They were out doing break and enters on the night of the Whiskey fire,' he says. 'Peter Hall, Keithy Meredith, Shorty Dubois and Tom Hamilton were in a car, zooming around. They ended up getting together later in the evening to do a smash and grab on a mag wheel place, yeah.

'Tommy had nothing to do with it. For starters, the boys were apart, as a gang, as a team, running around working, and as far as Tom being involved in anything like that … there's no way in the world they would have got him to do anything like that. I don't even know if he even met Finch. Finch has dropped his name in it. I don't know why he's done that. I'd swear on my life that Tommy had nothing to do with it.')

Finch claimed he and Stuart never spoke about the truth behind the Whiskey because Stuart's mother, Edna Watts, had been threatened. 'They said Mrs Watts would end up like Mrs McCulkin if we spoke out,' Finch said. 'It was always funny how me and Stuart got pinched but nothing happened to the other pair or Vince O'Dempsey. I always had a code of not squealing but nowadays I reckon it's time the truth came out …'

In another story as part of Watt's world exclusive, Finch outlined with eerie precision the murders of Barbara McCulkin and her two daughters, Vicki and Leanne.

'Finch said the offer of money to torch the Whiskey had been made through the driver of the car which took Finch and his accomplice, Thomas Hamilton, on their mission of death.' He named the driver as Billy McCulkin. Hamilton, Finch said, struck the match that ignited the fuel.

'When we got back in the car after setting fire to the place, I noticed for the first time that Hamilton was waving a pistol around,' he said. 'He seemed totally mad in that instant and he was screaming that it was lucky no one came out. He indicated he would have shot them. From what I have seen, and tried twice in gaol, he was on LSD.'

Finch told Watt that Barbara had to be murdered because she threatened to go to the police and tell them about her husband's involvement in the crime. Finch told Watt: 'O'Dempsey and his sick crony Dubois were allowed to get away with murder to hide the truth of the Whiskey Au Go Go. They grabbed Stuart and myself but they didn't get Hamilton and McCulkin and the people behind it.'

He reiterated that he, Hamilton and McCulkin were dressed 'like Black September terrorists', in all black. 'Finch said he had carried the petrol drums and tipped them on their side inside the Valley nightclub while McCulkin kept the engine of a stolen black Holden running,' the report added.

'Finch said he had no doubt the men who murdered the family were the two criminals last seen with them. Vincent O'Dempsey and Gary [sic] Dubois.' He said that only Barbara was to be killed 'but the sexual lusts of Dubois, who was known for his fetish for young girls, took over'.

Even back in 1988, 14 years after the McCulkin murders, Finch wondered why O'Dempsey had never been convicted in the case. 'If we had been O'Dempsey's men I'm certain something would have been done to help us. As it was, we were left there to rot.'

An Unexpected Funeral

Vincent O'Dempsey returned to the world in 1991 following his release from prison in New South Wales on various drugs charges. His wife, Dianne Pritchard, had moved on, and had been in and out of a number of relationships while Vince was in gaol.

'She was on with another bloke and had a daughter to him,' a friend said. She'd been staying at a place that Vince bought for her and the kids at Crystal Creek in the Tweed Shire before he went to gaol. She then started moving around the area, living briefly in the village of Chillingham, not far from Murwillumbah, then Kingscliff on the coast.

O'Dempsey settled back in Warwick. He frequented the National Hotel, or the 'Old Nash', not far from the Warwick railway station. There he met local girl Kim Smith, who was already married with two children. They moved into 1 Myall Avenue, in town, and would soon marry themselves. 'They fought like cats and dogs,' says one friend. 'She threw a knife at him once and cut his face.'

Vince, in the meantime, bought a cattle property in the village of Aratula, 67 kilometres east of Warwick. He improved the property with fencing and other infrastructure, then sold it. 'He was washing some of his money through there, cleaning it,' says one acquaintance.

O'Dempsey then purchased a property close to Warwick township and started breeding alpacas. 'It was a legitimate business,' says one associate. 'Vince used to say, "I'm a legitimate businessman, don't you worry about that." He was obsessed with genetics. The plan was to ship in some camels from Boulia [300 kilometres south of Mount Isa in Queensland's Central West] and embryo transplant from alpacas into camels. Vince was full bore into it.'

O'Dempsey was shocked to learn of his former wife Dianne Pritchard's death in 1995. She had overdosed on heroin in a motel room in Murwillumbah. Even though she drank heavily, friends and acquaintances said it was impossible to believe she had taken drugs.

One long-term friend said he was stunned by Pritchard's death. 'There used to be a sergeant down there at Tweed Heads and I used to give him tips on the horses,' he said. 'I had horses at the time and they were good horses and they run a lot of races you know. And he said [to me] that's bad luck about Dianne. I said, "What happened to her?" He took me into his office and he said, "Read that."

'It was a report into her death. She went to a motel at Murwillumbah with a young prostitute, they got it on together and she was a user ... Dianne never used to use heroin, she must have give it to her and they were all going on, it was a hot shuttle, it was this, it was that.

'It was all there in the report ... they knew who give it to her, who sold the heroin, they knew the lot.'

Friends reported that O'Dempsey was visibly shaken at the funeral. He described his former wife as a good, 'solid' woman.

'Now when Dianne died, Vince was upset,' says one associate. 'And he said, "Mate, you'll never find a woman more solid than her." She wouldn't say a word, she'd go straight to the clink. He was cranky about the way she died.

'Vince was still living in Warwick but it was only a few weeks later and then his wife, Kim Smith, she died of an aneurism in the head. And then it just went around like wildfire [that] he's knocking all these women. Gees, he copped it over that. God, he copped it.'

O'Dempsey was not responsible for either woman's death. In the wake of Dianne's death, he was left to care for their three children. He had no children with Kim. Following the deaths of his two wives, O'Dempsey was 'in limbo'.

It was around this time he visited an old mate from his Sydney days, the criminal Walter McDonald, who had settled with his family in the village of Urbenville, in the Tenterfield Shire in northern New South Wales, near the base of Crown Mountain. It was a long way from the mean streets of Sydney in the 1960s, when McDonald consorted with the likes of gangsters George Freeman and Lenny McPherson.

O'Dempsey took a shine to Walter's youngest son, Warren. 'My father and Vince were long-term friends,' Warren McDonald would later tell police. 'My dad was a man of few words. He did not talk about what he got up to. I knew that he grew pot over the years, but I don't know if that was with Vince. I knew that Vince was a "crim" ... by that I mean that he was involved in criminal activity including drugs and that he was a violent man.

'Dad told me when I was first introduced to Vince that Vince was the most feared man in the underworld. He was a trusted friend of my father's and so I was not overly concerned about Vince but I made sure not to upset him.'

Warren had been working in his brother's supermarket at Woodenbong, just south of the Queensland and New South Wales border in the Kyogle Shire, and a one and a half hour drive to Warwick. Seeing a future for Warren in his criminal enterprises, O'Dempsey took Warren under his wing. Over time McDonald became known as 'The Apprentice'.

'I started to spend a lot of time with Vince ... and he would get me to do things for him,' McDonald later recalled to police. 'I spent a lot of time at [the] Criterion Hotel [in Warwick] with Vince and we would play pool. Vince was a very good pool player. Vince would never drink much ... I have never seen the man drunk.

'Over time we got to know each other quite well and I feel he started to trust me and get me [to] do jobs for him mostly to do with the animals. Vince would also get me to drive him to places. Vince didn't want to drive his own car because he thought it might have been bugged. Vince was constantly concerned about security and being caught by police ...'

McDonald said O'Dempsey often reminisced about his days working at the mock auctions, and his associates in the early 1970s. 'He talked about the group called the Clockwork Orange,' McDonald said in a police statement. 'There was a fella called [Billy] Stokes. Vince called him "The Chicken". Vince would say, be careful, the Chicken would crack. Vince did not like Stokes at all.'

McDonald, knowing O'Dempsey to be an alpaca breeder, initially wanted to get in on the alpaca game. He had dreams of exporting alpaca fleece to China. With this in mind, he bought a property at Karara, 50 kilometres west of Warwick. O'Dempsey, at McDonald's invitation, came and looked over the place.

'My dad and his friends would come out to my property and go fishing in the dam and sit around the campfire and drink,' McDonald recalled. 'There was a shearing shed and another shed which I think has [been] turned into a house now. It was decided that we would do a crop on the place and we started to get ready.'

One O'Dempsey associate, who worked on that first crop, revealed how it worked. 'This property, it ticked all the boxes [for growing cannabis] except the soil was really tough, it was really rough country,' he said. 'But we had more water than you could poke a stick at. One of the crew had a bulldozer and we cleared a little patch here and there. It didn't take us long. We said [to Warren], don't worry about the textile industry and the alpaca fleece, let's get into this. We were like naughty little boys we were.

'Initially there were four patches. The police got the rumour that it was 10,000 plants but that was wrong ... there were about 2400 would be more like it ... Vince had it all irrigated ... it was a brilliant set-up.'

The drug growers got a rude shock, however, before the first harvest. 'We'd be sitting around the campfire at the end of the day ... having a beer and a rum, and they're all talking bullshit you know?' the associate remembered. 'One of the men kept saying the coppers won't come in, they'd be too scared. If they know O'Dempsey's here they won't come in, they'll send the fucking Army in first and then they'll come in.

'So every night sitting around the campfire this is what we copped. Well bugger me dead, one day, here comes the Army. The Army helicopters were coming over. We're down watering the plants and checking everything and the fucking Army's there. I thought we were all fucked. There was no point in running. The helicopters were that low you could see the pilot's bubble on his helmet, and a bit of machine gun out the side. The plants were big, and we just hid ... we're all shitting ourselves. I was expecting everyone to be handcuffed.

'We found out later the Army had a camp about 15 kilometres away ... they flew straight across the crop. Didn't see it because they were doing exercises. They weren't even looking for that sort of stuff. We all needed a rum after that.'

Swami

At some point, Vince O'Dempsey attracted the nickname Swami or Swami the Magician. The Swami knows all. The Swami makes people disappear. O'Dempsey's deceased friend, the hitman Stewart John Regan, was also called The Magician. Criminal associates would swear that the title was self-anointed. But what was the meaning of the moniker?

The 'evil' Swami was a periodical feature in American comic books throughout the 1930s and early 1940s. Artist Stan Aschemeier, also known as Stan Asch, worked for DC Comics and their syndicated comics and created characters like Dr Mid-Nite and Johnny Thunder, and also worked on the Green Lantern and Mister Terrific. A shifty character he created was Swami, or Swami the Magician.

Swami first appeared in *Sensation Comics* in 1944, and was described as someone 'skilled at sleight-of-hand and ventriloquism and was a competent stage magician ... he was a master pickpocket and thief ... [and he] made a killing putting on stage magic performances and robbing the audiences blind as he performed tricks for them. He also made money as a blackmailer using information he gleaned from stolen letters from his audiences.'

In 1946, in *The Shadow* series of comics, the Shadow has an encounter with the evil Black Swami, who is pictured on the cover as a type of monster, with mad eyes and large greenish claws for hands. Had the child O'Dempsey read these tales of thieves with mystical powers, and identified with Swami?

During the late 1990s O'Dempsey spent his time moving between his home in Warwick and various properties tending to his drug crops. Swami knew how to avoid detection when he wanted to, and associates at the time recall various personality traits, including his obsessive paranoia of being followed or observed. People who knew him labelled him as 'eccentric' in his approach to his crops.

'When he was in gaol he read a lot, and declared himself a horticulturalist, a botanist,' says one man who worked on the crop. 'The soil around the Karara area was hard country, but it grew good pot. In the end the plants were so big we had to pull them out with bulldozers. They were as big as trees.

'He was eccentric with the water system. He didn't have regular sprinklers. He developed these water emitters, about the size of a ciagerette packet, that you installed along the hoses, they dripped water. He worked out exactly how many litres per hour would drip out. It was the same system you'd use in a vineyard. It was expensive.'

He said O'Dempsey declared himself an environmentalist. 'He was a greenie,' an associate said. 'He hated feral cats. If you killed feral cats you were a hero. But you didn't shoot a bird in front of him. Or a rabbit. We winged a galah once and didn't he go off. He was spitting chips. He said we were cruel. How's that?'

One of the properties had a large dam and the crop was behind it. A small motorboat was sometimes used to cross the dam. Armed associates of O'Dempsey would patrol the property on motorbikes.

There was another crop on a property near the little township of Yangan, just 20 kilometres east of Warwick. It was a place O'Dempsey knew well. His mother, Mary, had grown up on a farm there. One associate who visited the property said: 'I remember you came in the front gate, the fence was metal chain wire and it was an electrified gate. I never saw Vince arrive or leave ... there was talk of him coming in the back way.'

One woman agreed to work on the Yangan drug crop as a cook. She told police in a statement she remembered arriving at the property's old farmhouse. 'We pulled up on a flat area behind the house. There was a 44-gallon drum and seats in a circle on that flat area. The seats were made out of trees and this campfire was just near the house. The furnishings [in the house] were pretty basic, just a few lounge chairs, beds and stuff. There was a wood heater in the lounge room and I remember a police radio was in the house and was on all the time ... and we all kind of kept an ear out for anything that might indicate police were coming.'

The woman was given a tour of the kitchen. It was well stocked with food, including roasts and corned meat. 'I can't believe you've got all of this set up,' she said to one of O'Dempsey's associates.

'Darling,' he said, 'this is organised crime.'

'I learned after a few days that I would be paid in marijuana or pot. I was being paid a pound a week which we were given at the end of the crop. It was only then that I realised I would have to sell it to get my money, which worked out at about $2000 a week.'

She remembered the ritual whereby O'Dempsey and his workers would sit around the campfire at the end of the day's work. 'Vince was very conscious of his health, and didn't really drink,' she said. 'He was definitely the boss and would keep an eye on everything. I noticed that Vince liked being out there, and was much more relaxed than when I'd seen him in town. Vince would occasionally make reference to things like being a doorman at the brothels in Sydney when he was younger. He would tell us about beating people up. He would talk about being a suspect in some murders, and would laugh and say things like, "Of course, I didn't do that."

'There was something about the guy who had gone missing from Warwick years before who was supposed to have been buried in the dam wall. Vince said he had an argument with him … and the guy disappeared just after the argument. The way he said it gave me a chill, because I believed that he did kill him. There were a few conversations with Vince like this. He would tell us that he was under surveillance by the Federal Police, and had been indicted for murder cases, I think he said nine.'

The woman couldn't help but notice some of O'Dempsey's peculiar mannerisms. 'Vince always had a backpack on in case he had to run into the bush,' she told police. 'He would wear white cotton gloves around the house and was conscious of what he touched. He was the only one who wore them and most of us thought it was a bit silly. He would pull back a chair with his elbow, not his hand. I commented once that it seemed like second nature to him and he responded, "No, it's first nature."

'Vince had sayings like: "What happens at sea stays at sea", "loose lips sink ships", and "a fish that doesn't open its mouth can't get caught" … they were all made in reference to keeping quiet about everything.'

For Warren McDonald, his first crop with O'Dempsey was memorable for another reason. As he grew closer to O'Dempsey, the old man began sharing some of his memories with the young gun. 'Whilst working on that crop I recall a conversation with Vince about the murder of the McCulkins,' McDonald would later say in a sworn police statement. 'It was my job to drive Vince places and to go and collect stuff for the crop site. I remember this day we were in my yellow XF Falcon ute with Vince. We were going back into Warwick … it was while the crop was on and close to harvest time. I think I was dropping Vince off at home in Warwick for his weekend off.'

McDonald distinctly recalled that it was close to harvest time on the crop and everyone was nervous. 'Vince was talking about people giving people up, or talking out of school, and how we have to be careful about it and not let anybody have the crop and that's how the conversation started,' McDonald said. 'Vince said to me: "You need a notch on your gun." I asked him what he meant. He said: "You need a kill, when I was your age I had several notches on my gun."

'He was talking about me getting experience killing someone. He said that he killed the McCulkins and Shorty was nothing but a rapist. I took that to mean that Vince had killed the McCulkins and Shorty had raped them. I asked him if he was worried and he said: "They will never get me because they will never find the bodies."

'At the end of that conversation he said: "If you want to live a long and healthy life never repeat anything that would get you or anyone else into trouble."

'I told him I would never repeat a word of what he said.'

The pair arrived in Warwick, but McDonald couldn't shake what he'd heard about the McCulkins from O'Dempsey. 'I knew that Vince was a suspect for the McCulkins because it had been spoken about generally around the campfire,' McDonald told police. 'I believed what Vince told me because of how he said it.

'I also believed the threat at the end of the conversation because Vince doesn't talk shit.'

The Pool Shark

After the death of his wives within weeks of each other, O'Dempsey eventually started socialising, as he had always done, in Warwick's numerous hotels where he would meet women. While he only occasionally smoked dope, he would never drink to excess.

'In all the years I knew him I never, ever saw him drunk once,' says one friend. 'Three light beers would be a big night for him.'

And O'Dempsey never lost his passion for a good game of pool. Back in his twenties, he would often wind down by playing a few games of pool at The Criterion Hotel in Palmerin Street, Warwick's main drag. In a strange coincidence it was also in The Criterion, decades later, that his attention was drawn to a young woman, Julie Anne Fenton, who was then in her mid-twenties. She too was an excellent pool player.

Julie Anne would later tell police about that initial meeting with O'Dempsey and the subsequent months. 'I was a pretty good pool player and Vince was an absolute "pool shark" and [we] got to know each other playing pool over a few months,' she said. 'It soon became a regular thing. I knew from around town that he had a colourful past. I was aware at that time of the rumours about him being involved in killing the men from Warwick and putting them in the dam wall but I didn't really put much credit in those rumours.

'He was, initially at least, charming, intelligent, funny and good to me. There was a big age gap and he would joke that he had tattoos older than me and that he had been in gaol longer than I had been alive. He had made veiled references to what he had gone to gaol for, but I did not learn much about that for some time.'

O'Dempsey was still residing at 1 Myall Avenue, where he had lived with his wife Kim and her two daughters before she died. It was just four blocks from the old family home in Stewart Avenue. About 18 months after they met, Julie Anne and her daughters moved in.

'After I had lived with Vince for a while, we had a rocky period,' she later told police in a statement. 'I started to see his true colours ... he was very selfish and demanding, expecting me to do everything while he seemed to expect to do very little.

'When I first met Vince I knew he was quite comfortable financially ... there never seemed to be any shortage of money and [I] noticed he would always use cash for almost everything. Once I had been to the crop I knew why.'

Julie Anne also began to learn, over time, about his criminal past. 'He told me little bits and pieces. He was quite guarded in his dealings with people. He was very big on not talking generally and had only passing contact with most people. He had a favourite saying, "loose lips sink ships", he would kind of coach me about it and say you are fine if you don't talk but as soon as you open your mouth that's when you get yourself in trouble. He even asked me about what I would do if I was approached by detectives, and told me to tell them nothing.'

She implied he was paranoid about the police. 'Vince was always very cautious and over the years I remember when police ... pulled him over, he was extremely uncomfortable and on alert,' she recalled. 'Vince would not talk about things he was doing in vehicles or in buildings and would behave as if the police were following, listening ...'

O'Dempsey was also wary of telephones. 'Vince did not like phones as a general rule,' she added. 'He would often lecture me over the years about phones, and I saw him just hang up on people if there was even a hint that they were going up a path of conversation that he wasn't comfortable with, like about the crops ... he would make phone calls from phone boxes, and would use different phone boxes each time.'

Despite a few hiccups, the relationship continued and the couple often travelled down to the Gold Coast. 'Vince liked to gamble and when things were going well we would visit the casino every few months,' Julie Anne later told police. 'There was about six months when we were going roughly every fortnight. Vince had a system of sorts for blackjack, which he taught me. He gave me a book that he had read on it. He would spend a lot of money at the casino. He would have some good wins but also losses. Sometimes he would blow like $2000 on blackjack and just walk away.

'I remember our room at the Sofitel would cost $300 a night, and it would be in my name. We would do a fair bit of shopping while we were there and [that] would also be in cash. I remember they [the casino] approached him at one stage because he was betting big and winning. They were offering him incentives like free parking and things.

'... Vince liked to go to Hamilton Island. It was one of the things he did to spoil us. It was a bit weird because I know he had taken his previous wife there, too.'

O'Dempsey's marriage to Julie Anne Fenton broke down in 2008. They had moved into a new house at Freestone Road, just north of downtown Warwick, but the relationship was over.

'It was a difficult break-up,' Julie Anne later told police. 'I left and went back a few times and during that time I met [someone else]. I was still living in the house with the kids but we were technically separated. I did it because I had nowhere to go and no money to go with. Staying in the house proved to be a big mistake.'

Meanwhile, O'Dempsey was virtually living in a shipping container on his alpaca farm close to town. But he came and went from the Freestone Road house 'like it was his home'. 'When he came there I would try my best to just make myself busy and stay out of his way, but he would nit-pick and niggle and just try to start arguments,' she recalled. 'I knew that he was trying to goad me, and he knows I can be a pretty fiery person. He had told me he and his ex-wife Kim used to fight physically when they were together ... he even told me she stabbed him in the face once during a fight. That was not something that I wanted to happen to me.'

Julie Anne would not tolerate domestic violence, given she had witnessed it against her mother during her childhood. 'There were two times that Vince put his hands on me in that way,' she told police in a statement. 'The first time was at the Gold Coast. We were on holidays but things were not going well for us. I knew he would never leave the marriage because he had the perfect servant, to cook and clean and look after his kids. We had a huge argument. We had joint rooms and all of the five kids were with us. I told him I would go and see a solicitor.

'He just snapped. He grabbed [me] with one hand up under the throat and started to lift me off the ground. I was terrified and thought I was going to die. He leaned in and said, "You know where you'll end up." I knew what it meant. I knew I would be joining the other people he had disposed of.'

The arguments continued. He allegedly told Julie Anne she had come with nothing and would leave with nothing. Then she threatened to bring in the authorities to sort out the mess.

'He just changed,' she recalled. 'I knew it was like threatening him ... his existence relies on the authorities knowing very little about what he does. When I said this he called me all sorts of names and said, "Have you ever seen what acid can do to a person's face? You will never want to leave the house again." It terrified me and from the way he said it, I believed he had seen it and would do it.'

She had, in fact, been worried about O'Dempsey's history of violence for some years. They had occasionally spoken about the murders he had been accused of. She described him as a creature of habit and a 'hoarder'. He had offices at his various properties. 'The office is one of two shipping containers contained within a large shed on the property. Vince has books about crimes and criminals and kept some at the storage shed at the alpaca property and some at the house. There were a few times when he would watch crime-type documentaries and tell me he knew them, or was in gaol with them ... he would laugh and sometimes say they were lying.

'I know he spoke about the Whiskey Au Go Go in general terms.'

A trivial argument over a shirt tipped the marriage over the edge. Julie Anne said O'Dempsey was 'on a rage' and he 'kept coming at me'. She retreated to her 14-year-old daughter's room and stayed awake all night, texting some friends, as O'Dempsey prowled about the house. 'I could not help thinking about the things I knew he had done to people in the past, as well as things he may have gotten away with doing,' she told police. 'I was terrified and knew I had to play it smart. The cold, calculating anger in him that night gave me a chill. In the text to my friends I told them that I was really, really scared and that I thought he might kill me. I told them that if anything happens to me tonight, no matter what you hear, it is him.'

In the end, they came to a financial settlement. 'There were a few times when I really started to question what I knew about Vince at all,' Julie Anne reflected. 'Once was when he made a truly horrible comment about the age of consent for having sex. We were at the farm doing work and I was carrying two buckets. He commented about little girls … "If they are big enough to carry two buckets of water, they are big enough to fuck." It made my skin crawl …'

Around the Campfire

Throughout the 1990s and well into the 2000s O'Dempsey was successfully growing and selling his bush weed around Warwick without being troubled by authorities. Even after his marriage breakdown with Julie Anne, his vigorous sex life showed no signs of slowing down.

'He told me that after Julie Anne he had been with either 53 or 58 women,' says one friend. 'He told me one time he took a cherry, a girl's virginity. You have to remember the man was then in his seventies. He was still jamming hard.'

While O'Dempsey may have sworn by the motto, 'Loose lips sink ships', he opened up about himself – and some of his sexual conquests – on those many nights sitting around the campfire after a long day working on the cannabis crops.

His workers would sit around drinking beer and rum, while O'Dempsey filled the night with stories. 'The tales he told were incredible,' says one crop worker. 'He was an expert in explosives. I don't know where that came from. He probably learned it in the Army. He had one of those old-style Thompson machine guns, the one where you have to wind up the spring. Vince said one day he was on the run and he was up on a hill and the police were down below. The way he described it to me, he was elevated. It must have been scrubby country, and they're all down there, and they're having a meeting saying, "Well, how are we going to catch him?" you know? Like, "Where is he? We don't know where he is."

'Vince was up above them with a Thompson fully loaded and he took the safety off, and he's ready to let them have it and then he thought better of it and put the safety back on. He said he laid there until dark and then bolted. He said, "I was that close." Yeah, he loved that story. He said, "I nearly did it … I nearly bloody wiped out the lot of them."

'We looked at Vince as the most feared man in the underworld. If he said, "You fucking go over there and jump," you jumped.'

The associate said O'Dempsey had confided in the drug crop group about his contact with some of the biggest names in the Australian criminal underworld. He refused to name names for his own safety. 'Vince told someone he'd had a hand in sorting out the Melbourne gang wars in the early days of those wars,' the source said. 'But now we're opening Pandora's box. Like, how far are you going to go with this? It depends how far you're going to go. Yeah, you've got to be careful. But I'd swear on 30 Bibles that he was connected to some of the country's biggest criminals. Yes, no problem.'

The asscociate said O'Dempsey had talked about contract killings. 'He didn't just put an ad in the paper, you know?' he said. 'You had to know the right people.'

How is it that his accomplice Garry 'Shorty' Dubois survived the relationship with O'Dempsey, given everything he knew?

'He came very close to being knocked,' the source adds. 'He come very, very close there once … because one of Vince's children got into a bit of trouble and Vince had the child taken up to Shorty's place, and asked Shorty if he could just put him away for a little bit, until he could get somewhere else for him to stay. And Shorty apparently said no. "No." He said, "I can't do anything." So the kid was brought back and Vince was told that the answer was no.

'And Vince said: "The fucking little rapist arsehole. I should fucking go up and tidy him up … He's nothing but a fucking rapist."'

Sometimes, on the drug crops, talk turned to murder and bodies. One criminal associate said O'Dempsey talked often about the movie, *Snowtown*, directed by Justin Kurzel. The film was based on real-life killings in and around Snowtown, 145 kilometres north of Adelaide. Eleven people were murdered between 1992 and 1999. Police ultimately found several bodies in barrels that had been stored in a disused bank vault. It was known as the Bodies in the Barrels case.

'Anyway, Vince told me that the Snowtown killers had used the wrong acid,' the associate said. 'They used hydrochloric acid and all it did was, it didn't get rid of the sludge or anything. It just got rid of the body, it didn't do anything to the bones or anything. That's what Vince told me. He said you've got to use sulphuric acid, and you've got to grind the teeth, and you've got to pour it in tidal waters so it'll flow away and then you've got to cut up the bins to get rid of them so there's no evidence left.'

Another time, Vince started talking about the McCulkins and

someone asked him if he was worried about getting pinched for the murders. 'He said, "No they'll never catch me. They'll never find the fucking bodies,"' the associate says. 'Well, the only thing I can think of is the acid ... but according to Peter Hall, they were buried. And Vince, being as smart as he is, he'd go back and dig the bodies up and move them. So now Shorty's got nothing on him. But it's also been said that Vince can go and see the people he's killed any time he likes ...'

According to one source O'Dempsey was cautious about speaking about the Whiskey. Whenever the case was revisited in newspapers, he'd 'blow up'. It was the same with any stories published on Barbara McCulkin and her two daughters.

'At the campfires and all that we used to have a talk but ... it was very hard to get a confession out of him ... but he'd put a little snippet into your mind. He'd hurl it into you, to see if you were paying attention or not.'

Did he mention the Whiskey?

'Yeah, shit yeah ... but he never talked about Torino's much, never, you know? Like it was a given, you know? Torino's was a given, like it was only a club, you know?'

At one point it was rumoured that Finch would return to Australia and give evidence against O'Dempsey. A source says a loose plan was hatched for someone armed on a motorbike to shoot Finch if he ever came back. First he was to be blasted with a shotgun in the chest, then the muzzle would be put into his mouth and fired.

'As for the Whiskey, he talked about a bloke called Hannay. He said Hannay wouldn't pay, whatever that means.'

Decades later, when asked about the Whiskey fire, former manager of the Whiskey Au Go Go nightclub, John Hannay, said he couldn't remember a lot of the past, adding that, 'You know some things but you don't know the whole thing.' When pushed for a more specific answer he said, 'It was so long in the past.'

Loose Lips Sink Ships

Life had been difficult for the Scully family of Chermside in north Brisbane since Tommy Hamilton had been abducted and murdered in 1975. His disappearance effectively pulled the pin on the so-called Clockwork Orange Gang and a raft of strong, childhood friendships between himself and Peter Hall, Shorty Dubois and Keith Meredith. Nothing was ever the same again.

Carolyn Scully, Tommy's sister, carried the burden of grief over her brother for years, then decades. Why couldn't she give her brother a decent burial? Where was his body? Why had her children been robbed of their uncle?

Around 2011, one of the Scully girls, Carolyn's daughter Kim, got badly beaten in the watchhouse in Brisbane and sustained serious head injuries. The family tried to get in to see her but were disallowed. They sought legal help. Kerri-Ann Scully, another of Carolyn's daughters, later told police she had contacted Terry O'Gorman – Vince O'Dempsey's solicitor – for assistance. In the end, Kerri-Ann ended up phoning O'Dempsey at his alpaca farm in Warwick. They had not seen each other or spoken for many years.

'I explained that we needed money and he said he would come down and see me,' Kerri-Ann said in a police statement. 'I met him at Chermside Shopping Centre and then he asked me to go to the Gold Coast with him. It was obvious that he was attracted to me and it just went from there.

'When I first met him he talked to me about working on his drug crop. He told me I could work there for about six months and make good money, about $20,000, but I had to live there. He told me I could make this money soliciting because I would be the only girl. He later on decided he didn't want me to do that and he wanted us to be together.'

She said that while they were on the Gold Coast they went to the casino at Broadbeach. 'We had a good time and then I went back to his room with him,' Kerri-Ann remembered. 'He was staying at the Sofitel, but I remember he used a different name because he said he was not allowed in the casino. He told me he would give me half the money he won while he was there. He had a numbers thing he had memorised for blackjack and he did pretty well; he gave me a couple of grand in the end.'

Kerri-Ann said that on their way back to Brisbane she and Vince started talking about her addiction to heroin. He suggested she go to Warwick with him for a couple of weeks to 'detox'. He gave her a further $5000 and said he'd give her more if she came and lived with him.

Two weeks later, O'Dempsey travelled to Brisbane and picked up Kerri-Ann and her children and took them back to Warwick for the school holidays. Meanwhile, O'Dempsey agreed to pay for treatment for her heroin addiction. Scully was determined to get off the drug, and could see a potential new life for herself and her children with O'Dempsey.

'Over time the relationship between Vince and myself developed and we were going to be married and Vince told me he wanted us to have a baby,' Kerri-Ann told police. 'I thought Vince was too old to have a baby but he didn't think so … I grew fond of him and was willing to marry him because of the financial security it would give me and my children, which is something me and my kids have never had.'

She found O'Dempsey 'very intelligent' and a big reader. He knew a lot of facts. She presumed he was in his seventies and knew he had been married several times and had at least six children. He told her he had 26 children. Others close to O'Dempsey said he had 'kids all over the place'. Scully said she was fully aware that he was 'doing something criminal' to get his money.

'I knew his reputation,' she added. 'I knew the crazy names he was known as, Angel of Death and stuff. I knew that if you did the wrong thing by him and he got hold of you, no one would ever find you. I had heard it from Mum and other people. I figured some of it was probably true. There were even times I wondered if he might know how to find out what happened to Uncle Tom, and if I was good to him he might help me find out. I even wondered if he was involved in Uncle Tom's disappearance.'

Scully said their conversation would occasionally turn to O'Dempsey's criminal past. 'One day ... we were outside the back of the house,' she recalled to police. 'I would smoke out there at the sitting area near the pool table and the bar. We were talking about Uncle Tom and what had happened to him. We were talking about Bill Stokes, the man who killed him [Tom Hamilton]. Vince told me how Stokes used to write this thing for the Painters and Dockers called the *Port News*. He said that Stokes was just a clown, and would antagonise him all the time in his writings, and in one of them Stokes said Vince was right for so many murders. The article said 15 or 18 I think. Vince turned around and laughed and said, "He doesn't have a clue. He doesn't know anything. I'm good for this many". He held up three fingers on one hand, and reopened it and made out like the number 33.

'I said, "What, 33? Really?"

'And he said "Yep."

'All I could think of was what a lot of people to have killed. I thought of Uncle Tom and the families of those people.'

She said O'Dempsey's claim to having murdered 33 people wasn't a boast. '[It was] just like stating it matter of fact ... He was cold about it, like he was just used to it, it was second nature to him and there was nothing wrong with it.'

Scully revealed that O'Dempsey enjoyed true crime books, particularly 'the ones he's in'. One of those in particular was

Shotgun and Standover: The Story of the Painters and Dockers, by James Morton and Russell Robinson, first published in 2011. The book outlines the history of the notorious union from its early days at the beginning of the 20th century and beyond. It mentions a cast of infamous criminals who were also part of the Painters and Dockers, from Squizzy Taylor to the Moran brothers, who gained national attention during modern Melbourne's gangland wars. The book also mentions the murder of Barbara McCulkin and her daughters in 1974. Scully said O'Dempsey asked her to buy a copy of the book – he didn't want to be seen purchasing it himself – and that he had obviously read it before because 'he knew the page numbers and everything by memory'.

One night in bed, O'Dempsey, with the book in hand, told Scully: 'I'll show you what they wrote about me.' He then proceeded to read her the chapter aloud in bed. 'He would read bits and tell me the bits that were wrong, and then added stuff about what was written. He told me that he had been handcuffed to the table during the inquest [into the McCulkins et al in 1980], and I remember he told me that Garry [Dubois] took off on bail before the inquest and that he wished that Garry was there with him for the inquest.

'I remember the book talked about both Shorty and Vince being right for the murder of the McCulkins.'

O'Dempsey told Scully that he had answered 'no comment' to every question put to him at the inquest, and that he had earned the nickname 'Mr No Comment'.

'There was mention of Barbara McCulkin, and that she was going to dob in her husband for the Torino's nightclub fire,' Scully continued. 'He told me that Billy McCulkin was molesting his daughters, and I remember I had heard that from someone else before.'

The book proposed theories about where the McCulkins' bodies might be buried – including beneath a high-rise office tower in

Brisbane's CBD – but Scully said O'Dempsey laughed them all off, saying 'it was crazy'.

'Vince was adamant that McCulkin was interfering with his kids and said he had lived there at the house for a while and knew it was true,' Scully added. 'He said Billy was his friend and that he [Vince] had slept with Barbara McCulkin …'

'The book talked about Stokes refusing to give evidence at the inquest and Vince said that was because Stokes was terrified of him. It also said that Vince was serving a ten-year sentence at the time for drug offences and continued to claim privilege. It said that the murder charges recommended by the coroner were dropped. It was then that Vince said, "I'm good for it, but they'll never get me on these murders." Then he laughed.'

'I didn't say anything,' Scully remembered of that moment. 'I was too scared to and what do you say? I was thinking, "What the fuck?" They were two little girls not too different from the age of my kids. I never thought he did it, and I had grown up being told he didn't. I had just found out he was a child killer and my kids were in the next room.'

Scully said the smirk on O'Dempsey's face when he told her about the McCulkin murders showed, in her mind, that he was 'proud of himself'.

'I knew who he was, and what he was, I knew how he got his money. I knew he had killed people but didn't think he could kill two little girls. He didn't say why and I didn't want to know. I didn't want to get in too deep. I didn't want my kids to get killed or hurt hanging around someone capable of doing that. What scared me more than anything was that he was proud of himself, he had this smug smile on his face. He didn't see anything wrong with it. He wasn't joking, he wasn't drunk or on drugs, he was deadly serious.

'That night I did not sleep at all. I was afraid by what Vince had told me. I didn't know why he told me. I had always been told as I was growing up that he had been wrongly accused of the murder of the McCulkins so it was a shock when he told me.

'The next morning I told him I was going back on the bus.'

According to Scully, O'Dempsey sensed something was wrong. She placated him and told him she'd be back. She took the bus to Brisbane with her children and never returned.

Return to Dorchester Street

Not a year would go by without Barbara's brother Graham Ogden religiously telephoning police on 16 January – a date etched in the family's annual calendar and as important as any anniversary – and asking if there had been any developments in the case of his missing sibling and his two nieces, Vicki and Leanne.

As Graham's nephew, Brian Ogden, would later reportedly say: 'You can feel very alone when you have members of the family missing and don't know what's happened to them. Every time someone else goes missing, you feel for them. It's a very dark and lonely place. It's a part of family history that's just blank and that's wrong.'

Meanwhile, that rundown cottage at 6 Dorchester Street sat there virtually unchanged since Barbara and the girls had vanished. There was a newish fence, installed decades later, but by and large the place had remained eerily the same since that long, wet summer of 1974.

On 16 January 2014, however, Graham Ogden would receive news he'd always hoped for but never anticipated. In the lead-up to the 40th anniversary of the disappearance and presumed murders of Barbara and her girls, the State Crime Command's Homicide Squad Cold Case Unit decided to revisit the case. It was, at the very least, a gesture to the McCulkin women and their family that they had not been forgotten. It was also an opportunity to appeal for new witnesses and information after the case had lain dormant for so long.

Homicide Detective Mick Dowie reportedly appealed to members of the public who might know something of the murders. 'If you are sitting at home trying to justify your silence to protect this gang, your ethics and morals are not worth considering,' Dowie said. 'The thing that goes to the heart of this is the children. It is a major threat to murder two innocent children and someone, anyone who has got information that could solve that would have to have had that weighing on their conscience for 40 years.

'These are two young girls who were murdered for nothing … what you believe happened may not be the case, you may be protecting people for all the wrong reasons.'

The public was reminded that a $250,000 reward was still active. In fact, Dowie and Detective Virginia Gray had begun Operation Avow – the reinvestigation into the McCulkin murders – on 3 January and had already set about the laborious task of interviewing potential surviving witnesses and key players, and tracking documents. They followed a similar trail to that of detectives Marshall and Menary more than 30 years earlier. The Cold Case Unit would also work in tandem with the Crime and Corruption Commission (CCC) to extract as much new evidence as possible. Many witnesses were called before the CCC with its coercive powers throughout 2014.

Within a month of leaving O'Dempsey, Kerri-Ann Scully was back on heroin and was gaoled in June 2013 for breaching her probation, and also charged with stealing. She had been writing to O'Dempsey while she was in gaol, and he replied, professing his love for her. In March 2014, having been released from prison, she returned with her children to her home in Chermside.

'I recall being at my mother's house one day … when police came and gave her [Mum, Carolyn Scully] paperwork to attend an inquest into the death of the McCulkins,' Kerri-Ann Scully later said in a statement to police.

'I heard the police talking on the verandah to my mother and she showed me the paperwork after they'd left. Mum was spinning and arranged to see a solicitor. Vince had previously arranged to visit me the next day, which was the day before Mum had to go to the inquest. Vince came to my place at Chermside. When he arrived I told him I needed to talk to him about something and that we needed to go to the park to talk.'

They went to a public park behind the Chermside Shopping Centre on Gympie Road. 'When we got to the park I told Vince about the paperwork that Mum had received the day before, and that she had to go to the inquest the next day,' she said. 'He looked really shocked and went quiet, with this worried look on his face.'

Scully asked: 'Is this going to fuck us up? Do we have anything to worry about?'

He assured her it would be alright and everything would 'blow over'.

'I could tell from how he looked that it was not fine,' she said. 'I was not used to Vince being worried like that. He is usually very confident, even cocky.'

Back in Warwick, the tremors of the new McCulkin investigation were also being felt.

'I remember seeing stuff on the news about the McCulkins in early 2014 and later police doing raids on Vince's place in Warwick,' Warren McDonald told police. 'On 11 August 2014 police came to my place with a search warrant. They seized some documents.

'I was in the main street of Warwick a few days later and I ran into Vince. Vince asked, "Is it true they raided your house?" And I said, "Yes." Vince said. "The CCC is rounding everybody up and you need to keep your mouth shut or else."

'When he said this to me he was deadly serious. I assured him, "There is no need to worry about me, I am solid." I had already received a notice to attend the Crime and Corruption Commission.'

From September 2014 McDonald, on his way to work, would 'run into' O'Dempsey regularly. It was McDonald's habit to pull into the Caltex service station on the road into Warwick at around 4 a.m. and have breakfast and coffee. One morning O'Dempsey was waiting for him. 'Vince was checking in with me to see if I had heard anything,' he recalled in his police statement. 'I brought up [a fellow associate]. I said he is 60-odd and has a young wife and child ... do you think he has rolled?

'I told Vince that I had heard around town that the associate had rolled on him. Vince said, "No, he knows the rules."' McDonald understood that to mean that Martin knew, if he spoke to the police about Vince and his associates, that he would be killed.

His last early morning meeting with O'Dempsey was just prior to O'Dempsey's arrest in October 2014. He alleged Vince told him: 'The police aren't too far off and I have to hit the toe and people will stop talking if they don't know where I am.'

McDonald said, 'I took that to mean that if people didn't know where he was they would be more scared of him.'

This time around, too, the passage of time gave police an advantage. One key witness eventually made a decision to tell what he knew of the era and the fate of the McCulkins, and that was former Clockwork Orange Gang member Peter Hall. He would later tell the court he was a different person now from the one he had been in the 1970s. That he had his own family, and in essence concluded that the old adage of silence among thieves no longer applied.

Other key witnesses followed, and in late 2014 O'Dempsey, then 76, and Dubois, 67, were arrested and charged with the murders of Barbara and the two girls. The long shadow of this crime had finally caught up with both men.

Shorty's Trial

At 9.53 a.m. on Monday 7 November 2016, Garry Reginald 'Shorty' Dubois was brought into Court 7 of the Queen Elizabeth II Courts of Law precinct in George Street in Brisbane. The Correctional Services officers, in their pale blue shirts, directed him towards the glassed-in dock at the rear left of the pale wood courtroom on level four, and secured him inside. He turned and smiled at his wife, Jan, sitting in the public gallery. Compact and fit-looking, with a blunted crop of grey hair, Jan Stubbs, also known as The Pelican, smiled back.

Justice Peter Applegarth took his seat shortly after 10 a.m. Born in Brisbane in 1958, Applegarth attended Brisbane State High and graduated from The University of Queensland (UQ) with a Bachelor of Laws (first class honours) in 1980. He would win a UQ travelling scholarship and completed two years of postgraduate studies at Magdalen College, Oxford. On his return to Brisbane he was an associate to Justice Spender of the Federal Court of Australia, and was admitted as a barrister of the Supreme Court of Queensland in 1986. He took silk in 2000, and was appointed a judge of the Supreme Court in 2008. He was well known in Brisbane circles for his work with Legal Aid Queensland and the Queensland Law Reform Commission.

Standing at the bar table were the Crown Prosecutor, David Meredith, and counsel for Dubois, Dennis Lynch, QC. Meredith, tall and rangy in his black gown and horsehair wig, had a sharp voice that initiated from the back of his throat. It would remain, during the course of the trial, largely monotonal. His manner was consistently fluid and relaxed. Lynch, although similarly formidable in height, gave off an altogether different vibe. He was voluble, blustering, a hive of movement, energy and, at times, emotion. He was the type who stabbed at desks.

Also in the gallery, in the final row of three at the far rear right of the courtroom, sat Barbara McCulkin's brother, an elderly Graham Ogden, with his wife and children. He and his wife commuted from Strathpine station to the CBD each weekday during the trial. They had waited almost 43 years for the trial of Garry Dubois.

At 10.24 a.m. the jury arrived and took their seats at the front left side of the courtroom. They were empanelled by 10.53 a.m. It wasn't until 12.19 p.m. that Meredith rose and opened the case for the prosecution.

'Members of the jury, on 25 February 1973, the Torino – a Fortitude Valley nightclub – was burnt down,' he said in his firm voice. 'No one was hurt. You may have seen the accused when he was arraigned. He was quite short. His name is – his nickname then and now, is Shorty. He, Peter Hall, Keith Meredith and Thomas (Tommy) Hamilton were hired to burn down the Torino. Hall and Meredith will tell you this is the case. Hall says that Dubois told them that Vince O'Dempsey arranged it.'

Meredith explained that the gang was paid $500 to do the arson job and that Hall and his fellow members of the so-called Clockwork Orange Gang had been regulation house-breakers before this 'one and only big job' came along. 'Eleven days after the Torino fire, on 8 March 1973, the Whiskey Au Go Go – another Fortitude Valley nightclub – was burnt down and 15 people died … James Finch and John (Andrew) Stuart were arrested a short time after the fire …'

From the outset, Crown Prosecutor Meredith painted a picture that went to the very dark heart of this saga. The jury could not know that a murderous rampage that had its making in a boy from rural Warwick, and a handful of recalcitrant teenagers from suburban Brisbane, could light the fuse that was the Whiskey tragedy, which in itself would trigger a domino effect of murders to protect those involved in that singular act in the early hours of 8 March 1973.

After canvassing possible motives of O'Dempsey and Dubois to kill Barbara – in order to silence what she knew about the Whiskey – Meredith told the jury that after four decades of silence, Peter Hall was finally prepared to come forward as a witness.

On day two of the trial, Peter Hall was called into the modern courtroom to give evidence. He was of average height, stocky, with a shaved head. His only concession to the 1970s and the era of the McCulkin killings was a bushy handlebar moustache. Hall looked uncomfortable sitting in the witness stand.

'Witness, can you tell us your full name, please?' Meredith asked.

'Peter William Hall.'

'Do you know the accused, Garry Dubois?'

'Yes, I do.'

'And how do you know ... what do you call him?'

'Shorty,' Hall said.

'Was he known as Shorty back in the early 1970s?'

'Yes.'

'And where did you grow up?' Meredith inquired.

'In Kedron.'

'Did you become friends with him after school?'

'Yes.'

Meredith asked if he knew Tommy Hamilton and Keith Meredith, and he agreed.

'Now, did you come to know a person called Vince O'Dempsey?'

'Yeah, I met him on a few occasions.'

'And how did you meet him?'

'Through Garry, Shorty,' Hall replied.

'Did you know what Vince was doing at the time, whether he had a job?'

'Yeah, I think he was a doorman [at the mock auctions in Brisbane].'

'Did you know a person called Billy McCulkin?' Meredith asked.

'I didn't know him, but I had seen him on several occasions.'

Hall told the court he was living with Carolyn Scully, Tommy Hamilton's sister, in Chermside, just north of the Brisbane CBD, in January 1974. He said he knew Shorty's girlfriend, Jan Stubbs.

Hall also said that on the evening that the McCulkins disappeared, Shorty turned up at the Chermside house and told Hall that he was going back to the McCulkins for drinks and 'to have sex with the girls' and asked Hall if he wanted to join him and O'Dempsey at Dorchester Street.

Hall said he declined.

'Now, you mentioned this group of [Keith] Meredith, Hamilton, yourself and Dubois who were engaged in some criminal activity ... did you know the Torino nightclub?'

'Well ... I knew it, yeah.'

'Right. Tell us about that.'

'We were engaged to torch it,' Hall admitted.

'Who asked you to do this?'

'It had come from O'Dempsey through Garry.'

'So how did you know O'Dempsey was involved?'

'Garry told us.'

'And what was the plan? It was an insurance job?' Meredith asked.

'We were to be paid $500.'

Hall also said the gang feared that they would be put under the spotlight following the inferno at the Whiskey Au Go Go less than a fortnight later.

He said the following year, just a couple of days after Barbara McCulkin and her daughters vanished, Dubois had allegedly confessed about the fate of the women. Hall said that Dubois and O'Dempsey had taken them for a drive on the night of 16 January 1974 in the bush near Warwick. Hall told the court Dubois told him that O'Dempsey had taken Barbara aside and strangled her, and then ordered him to rape one of the McCulkin girls, which he did reluctantly. He then alleged that O'Dempsey killed them all.

Just Little Girls

It turned out to be the very last act of their childhoods – a simple birthday party. Vicki McCulkin, 13, and her little sister, Leanne, 11, had been invited across the road from their home in Dorchester Street to celebrate with their friends Janet and Juneen Gayton. Juneen had turned 10 on that day.

The girls were close that summer. They played with each other every day and would take their skateboards down to a nearby garage to hang out. They often went rollerskating at the rink on Enoggera Terrace at Red Hill. The last night of their lives they were at a party with gifts, sweets and soft drinks – that staple event of every childhood – the birthday girl's face illuminated by the candles on the cake and the singing of good wishes. They could not know that within hours they would be violently torn from that childhood idyll and delivered into an adult hell that still hardly bears imagining four decades later.

By dawn the next morning the girls would be dead, along with their mother, Barbara, just 34. Despite all of the rumour and conjecture surrounding their disappearance – about what Barbara may or may not have known – it was never really understood why the two girls were also murdered. Why take the young McCulkin sisters? Who would kill two innocent children?

In late November 2016, the Supreme Court jury in the McCulkin case provided an answer to those elusive questions by pronouncing Garry Reginald Dubois, 69, guilty of the murder and rape of the girls, the manslaughter of Barbara and charges of deprivation of liberty.

Every trial of this magnitude ultimately evolves its own unique characteristics. The jury, the defence lawyers, the public gallery, the families of the victims and the accused enter as separate entities, and become familiar, bound by testimony and the rituals of the court.

Each day of Dubois's trial started the same – the gathering outside the court of tribes belonging to the prosecution or the defence, and a scattering of neutral observers. As the evidence unspooled over days, then weeks, Dubois sat staring straight ahead as if he were made of granite. A person young and vital when the offences were committed, he was now an old man in ill-fitting clothes, the tattoos on one of his forearms so aged they have morphed into a shapeless blur of dark ink.

During the trial it was difficult not to think of those little girls and their final moments. When sisters Janet and Juneen Gayton gave evidence to the jury during the trial, it was impossible not to look at these two middle-aged women who, as children, had gathered around that birthday cake with their lost friends in 1974, and not wonder what might have happened if the McCulkin girls had lived.

If so, they too would be in their early to mid-50s now. Barbara would be 76 years old. They might have had their own children, and those children today might be in their twenties or thirties. It was not inconceivable they might have had their own kids by now, too. And in the middle of all that life there would have been many, many birthday parties, strung like jewels of memory on a long necklace.

But it never happened. Dubois's sentencing was postponed until after O'Dempsey's trial, slated for 2017.

Silent Death in the Dock

At 10.02 a.m. on Tuesday 2 May 2017, Vince O'Dempsey was led into the dock for the start of his trial, also before Justice Applegarth. He stood charged with three counts of murder and one of deprivation of liberty. At his committal and in other court appearances prior to the trial, O'Dempsey appeared in his customary leather jacket and open-necked shirt. For his trial, he was attired in a charcoal grey suit. He walked to and from the dock with a slight pigeon-toed shuffle.

The Crown Prosecutor was again David Meredith. O'Dempsey was represented by Tony Glynn and Terry O'Gorman. O'Dempsey, 78, pleaded not guilty.

As the trial got underway, the court was told O'Dempsey had been charged with the alleged murders of the McCulkins along with Garry Dubois, but the trials had been separated. However, the present O'Dempsey trial, Justice Applegarth instructed, was the only one the jurors needed to be concerned about.

Meanwhile, O'Dempsey, in the glass and pinewood dock, had a habit throughout the day of rolling his tongue against the inside of his cheeks, or resting a forefinger lightly on his jawline.

On that first day, as the light faded outside, the court was shown a combination of photographs of the McCulkin rented home at 6 Dorchester Street, Highgate Hill, both recent pictures and black-and-white images taken shortly after the disappearance of Barbara and the girls in 1974. Two of Barbara's brothers – Graham and Neville – took the witness stand to tell the court when they last saw their sister and nieces. Graham was hard of hearing. Neville was slightly stooped.

As Meredith underlined in his opening address: 'This is an old case.' Subsequently, the jury was taken back to a Brisbane of the early 1970s, to Valiant Chargers, black-and-white television, photographs of pop star Elton John on the wall of one of the girls' rooms and records by Donny Osmond. It was also reminded of the great Brisbane floods of 1974, and the deluge that was building just as Barbara and the girls were swept away and murdered.

Throughout the trial O'Dempsey remained impassive behind the green-tinged glass of the dock. Occasionally he waved and joked with members of his family who sat in the public gallery behind him. Outside the court the two police officers most responsible for resurrecting this extraordinary case – Virginia Gray and Mick Dowie – came and went, milling with fellow police officers.

At one point a surprise witness was presented at the trial. A prison inmate claimed to have heard a gaolhouse confession from O'Dempsey. Prisoner X told police O'Dempsey began talking about the McCulkin murders in gaol while co-accused Garry Dubois was on trial in November the previous year. He claimed that during that time O'Dempsey remarked: 'I know they'll never find them, ha ha.'

The snitch also said he passed messages between O'Dempsey and Dubois in prison. He said he kept notes after having conversations with O'Dempsey, and in one he revealed that O'Dempsey had told him that Barbara McCulkin 'had to be dealt with', before she and her daughters went missing. 'Look, in those days you got a job, you got paid to do a job, you did a job,' O'Dempsey allegedly said to Prisoner X. 'I never laid a hand on the two kids, Shorty [Dubois] did.'

O'Dempsey had also said that historical sites were an ideal place to bury remains 'because they'd never dig them up'.

Prisoner X said he wanted no part in the $250,000 reward on offer to solve the McCulkin case. 'When I saw the picture of the two little girls with the mother, I knew that something wasn't right,' he told the court.

Shortly after midday on 26 May 2017, word was received that the jury in the triple murder trial of Vincent O'Dempsey had reached a verdict. Public observers, the families of both O'Dempsey and Barbara McCulkin, and the press, quickly assembled in Court 4.

At 12.10 p.m., O'Dempsey was brought into the court by two Queensland Corrective Services officers and took his familiar place in the glass dock. The accused sat quietly with his hands resting in his lap. At 12.27 p.m. the jury entered the court and stood in a single line facing Justice Applegarth. They quickly delivered their verdicts. Guilty on all counts.

At 12.30 p.m., O'Dempsey was asked to stand. Did he have anything he wished to say? After a short conversation with one of his defence team he said in a high-pitched voice: 'No.'

After some brief legal argument, Justice Applegarth adjourned the court. Dubois and O'Dempsey would be jointly sentenced in coming weeks.

With the court virtually empty, O'Dempsey then grinned broadly at his legal counsel, and turned to face his family who were sitting behind him in the public gallery. Still smiling, he cupped both hands upward and held them at waist height. Then he shrugged. It was a gesture that suggested – what can you do, you win some, you lose some.

At 1.04 p.m., O'Dempsey – amateur boxer, ballistics expert, farmer, pimp, thief, gunman and now murderer of Warwick, Queensland – was taken from the court.

A Deathbed Confession

Around the time of the murder trials of O'Dempsey and Dubois, and their flurry of attendant publicity on television and in the newspapers, police received a tip-off from a member of the public about the McCulkin mystery. The caller said that her elderly uncle had been a dairy farmer off Diggles Road, not far from the historic Glengallan Homestead just outside of Warwick, during the 1970s. Her uncle, now deceased, had decided to share on his deathbed the memory of something he saw early on the morning of Thursday 17 January 1974.

While out bringing in the cows before dawn, the uncle said he had witnessed a bright orange Charger, parked behind the ruins of the dilapidated Glengallan building. It was the morning after Barbara McCulkin and her two daughters, Vicki and Leanne, went missing in Brisbane. And the uncle knew, as almost everyone did in town, that the orange Charger belonged to Vince O'Dempsey.

Was this where the McCulkins had been taken?

Were they buried somewhere off Diggles Road, where the old Sparksman farm had once been? Where Vince's old school friend Brian Sparksman had grown up, under the guidance of SP bookmaker Jacob Sparksman, Vince's boss in the bad old days of debt collecting?

Was this where the McCulkins left this earth?

Letters from The Dodger

It appeared a satisfyingly peculiar coincidence that justice would catch up with both Vincent O'Dempsey and corrupt New South Wales detective Roger Rogerson. Both men had lived long lives of crime. The only difference was that for much of his career Rogerson had supposedly operated on the right side of the law. He would later be branded in the press as a 'psychopath with a badge'. Then in 2014, within months of each other, both old men were arrested for murder.

Strangely, too, it was Rogerson who had been rushed up to Brisbane with his police sidekick, Noel Morey, to help Queensland police investigate the Whiskey Au Go Go atrocity. And it was Rogerson who was present when Stuart and Finch were interviewed after their capture just days after the fire.

In June 2016 Rogerson, then 75, was found guilty, along with his co-accused, another former copper, Glen McNamara, 57, of murdering 20-year-old Jamie Gao during a drug deal gone wrong in May 2014. Gao was shot to death in a storage unit and his body dumped in the ocean. The jury took less than a week to reach its verdict. Both men were sentenced to life in prison in September 2016.

Rogerson had, of course, killed before. In 1981, as one of Sydney's most awarded detectives, he shot dead drug dealer Warren Lanfranchi in a laneway in the inner-Sydney suburb of Chippendale. Lanfranchi's girlfriend, the prostitute Sallie-Anne Huckstepp, claimed Lanfranchi was unarmed and murdered in cold blood. She demanded answers and accused Rogerson of being corrupt. She was later found dead in a pond in Centennial Park in Sydney.

Then in 1984, Rogerson was accused of attempting to murder a police colleague, Michael Drury, who said he had declined a bribe from Rogerson to alter evidence in a heroin case before the courts. Drury was shot twice in his home and was lucky to escape with his life. Rogerson was dismissed from the New South Wales police force and later gaoled for trying to pervert the course of justice.

Rogerson would later earn a quid touring pubs and clubs, telling stories of his life and career. He once did gigs with Melbourne criminal Mark 'Chopper' Read. In 2014, Rogerson sat down with Sydney journalist James Phelps and in his gregarious manner shared stories of his often inglorious police work. One of his career highlights, he said, was his involvement in the Whiskey Au Go Go case in Brisbane in March 1973. Rogerson explained to Phelps how he got involved in helping with the Whiskey investigation.

'The boss of the CIB sent me up,' he told Phelps. 'We had a Learjet chartered up there just for us. The bodies were still in the club when we got there ... anyway, we put surveillance on Stuart and he had a party and Finch turned up. We pinched them both.'

Then Rogerson explained how the Whiskey Au Go Go was torched. He said prior to the fire the nightclub owners had laughed at Stuart's extortion attempts. 'He [Stuart] had Finch by his side,' said Rogerson. 'The pair went to the bush in Queensland and started experimenting with accelerants, explosive devices. They would scare the clubs into giving them cash. They set fire to haystacks and farm sheds, to see which would work the best.

'Finch was the one that did the job. The nightclub had a mezzanine. Vince went to the stairs at the back of the kitchen and threw a Molotov cocktail in. Because it was downstairs the draught took it in and set the explosion rushing up into the club. Within seconds the whole place was on fire. There were 15 people in there. They were all killed.'

According to Rogerson, it was 'Vince' who went to the stairs at the back of the kitchen and threw a Molotov cocktail in.

But who was Vince? There was no mention of any 'Vince' in any part of Phelps's feature story.

In two letters from Long Bay Correctional Complex in Sydney in late 2017, Rogerson said not many police who worked on the Whiskey investigation all those years ago would be 'willing and able' to give evidence at any future inquest into the atrocity. He wrote:

> I suggest you look at the stories written by Brian Boulton [sic], the Brisbane journalist who alleged he was close to John Andrew Stuart and who wrote about his knowledge of supposedly hardened criminals being behind what eventually happened. You might say very flammable material.

When asked about the identity of the mysterious 'Vince' he had mentioned in the earlier Phelps story, Rogerson added:

> To start with, none of that is my verbage [sic], and to be quite truthful, it doesn't make sense and does not fit in at all as to how the fire started. I have never heard of anyone called Vince having anything to do with either Stuart or Finch. I can't help you with any new or secret evidence. There is none. I believe it was really a simple case.
>
> How is what you are attempting to do going to help the families of the Whiskey victims? I think it gets down to this.

When one psychopath cats with another psychopath you end up with mayhem. I think you are barking up the wrong tree.

Rogerson did not answer questions about who sent him and New South Wales detective Noel Morey to Brisbane on the morning of the fire. Nor about why New South Wales police would be in such a state of urgency that they would send their crack detectives north in a Learjet.

Given police and witnesses said that the bodies of the victims had been removed from the Whiskey by dawn on 8 March 1973 – or around 5 a.m. – how did Rogerson happen to be on the scene when 'the bodies were still in the club', as he told journalist Phelps?

To be a witness to that, Rogerson would have had to have been on the scene sometime after 2.30 a.m. (when the fire was deemed under control) and dawn (when the last bodies were taken out of the club).

Who was 'Vince'?

Out of Luck

On 1 June 2017, Justice Peter Applegarth continued his sentencing of Vince O'Dempsey and Garry Dubois. There was an edge to his voice. 'The two of you visited the McCulkin home at Highgate Hill on that evening. Barbara McCulkin lived there with her two daughters. She raised her two daughters with little financial support from her estranged husband,' he told the court. 'She worked hard to support her children and to give them a bright future. Barbara McCulkin cared for them in every way she could. The photographs of the home include a sewing machine which Barbara was using to make a dress for one of her daughters. A dress that was never to be finished.'

The picture showed a sewing table facing a fish tank that sat on a white metal stand, a hairbrush on the floor under the table, worn, patterned carpet, a clutch of floral material under the sewing needle, and the sewer's wooden chair pushed back and on a slight angle, as if Barbara had, only moments before, been interrupted and stood to greet her guests.

Justice Applegarth went on: 'The McCulkins were taken to bushland,' he said. 'They were tied up. At some stage Barbara McCulkin was taken by you, O'Dempsey, into bushland. Dubois stood guard over the girls. He may have thought that you were going to rape Mrs McCulkin. Instead, you brutally killed her.

'Dubois, you heard gurgling noises which seemed to go on forever. You aided the horrific attack by guarding the two daughters who, if they had not been tied up, surely would have tried to help their mother. You also encouraged the crime against Mrs McCulkin by your deliberate presence during that violence. You did not raise a finger in opposition or express any dissent. You must have known that Mrs McCulkin was being violently attacked. That is the basis upon which you were found guilty of manslaughter.'

Both O'Dempsey and Dubois remained impassive in the dock.

'O'Dempsey returned, having killed Mrs McCulkin,' Applegarth told the packed court. 'You, Dubois, knew at that stage that he intended to kill each of the girls. According to the evidence in your trial, O'Dempsey raped one of the girls and asked you to rape the other. You aided him to rape one girl and then, like a coward, did what you were told and raped the other girl.

'That evidence was admissible against you, Dubois, but not against O'Dempsey. As a result, and in the absence of other evidence that O'Dempsey raped the girls, it is you, Dubois, and only you who carries convictions for raping them.

'O'Dempsey, you murdered each of the girls. Dubois aided your crime. He restrained one or both of the girls and, by his active presence, encouraged you to murder them. He knew that was your intention, and he did nothing to stop it. The last hours of the lives of each of these three defenceless women must have been terrifying.'

Inevitably, Justice Applegarth returned to the firebombing of Torino's in February 1973 followed shortly after by the fatal torching of the Whiskey Au Go Go and its haunting legacy of 15 victims. These fires had glowed on the horizons of O'Dempsey's and Dubois's committal hearings and their trials into the murder of the McCulkins. Just moments before in court, O'Dempsey had made a direct denial of any involvement in the fires, particularly the Whiskey.

Applegarth continued: 'It is impossible to say for sure whether either of you was involved, along with John Andrew Stuart and James Richard Finch, in the bombing of the Whiskey Au Go Go nightclub. There is evidence that you, O'Dempsey, were so concerned about Finch returning to Australia in the late 1990s and implicating you in that arson that you told others that Finch would have to be "knocked": in other words killed.

'It seems that back in 1973 Barbara McCulkin knew something about who was involved in each nightclub firebombing. Each of you had a motive to silence her.' After summarising some of the evidence from key witnesses in O'Dempsey's trial, Applegarth declared him 'a cold-blooded killer'.

'Stand up O'Dempsey,' he said. 'On Count 1, deprivation of liberty, I sentence you to the maximum term of imprisonment for that misdemeanour, namely three years imprisonment. On each murder count there is only one sentence. I sentence you to life imprisonment for the murder of Barbara May McCulkin. I further sentence you to life imprisonment for the murder of Vicki Maree McCulkin. I further sentence you to life imprisonment for the murder of Barbara Leanne McCulkin. The sentences of life imprisonment are imposed pursuant to section 305 of the Criminal Code, as it stood at 16 January 1974.

'Sit down O'Dempsey. Stand up Dubois.'

Dubois raised himself to his feet with reluctance.

'Dubois, callous murderers like O'Dempsey are only able to commit horrendous crimes because they can rely upon the aid of fellow criminals like you, who will tie up victims or otherwise aid homicides,' Applegarth began. 'The evidence in your trial proved that you were prepared to aid the rape of one girl by O'Dempsey, and then rape the other when O'Dempsey told you to do so. Rather than stand up to O'Dempsey and protect a defenceless woman and two girls, you aided him and encouraged him. You showed no conscience at all.'

Dubois was sentenced to 15 years in prison for the manslaughter of Barbara McCulkin.

'As to the rape offences, fortunately we have been spared the details of the degree of physical violence which was perpetrated against those poor girls,' the judge said. 'It is hard to imagine a worse case of rape. The girls must have known that their mother had been killed. They must have known, as you did, that they were to be killed. The rapes were precursors to murder.

'The vulnerability of your victims and the mental terror which you inflicted upon them, when added to the physical violence, places these rapes in the worst category of rape cases. You have a past conviction for rape. You deserve the maximum penalty provided by the law, namely life imprisonment.

'On Count 1 on the indictment, you are sentenced to a maximum term of three years for deprivation of liberty. On Count 2, I sentence you to 15 years' imprisonment. On Count 3, you are sentenced to life imprisonment. On Count 4, you are sentenced to life imprisonment. I further sentence you to life imprisonment for the murder of Vicki McCulkin. I further sentence you to life imprisonment for the murder of Barbara Leanne McCulkin.

'You may sit down.'

With that, Dubois issued some mumbled protestations from the dock about an 'unsigned' record of interview he'd supposedly given to police when he was arrested in South Australia in 1980 and brought back to Queensland for the McCulkin coronial inquest.

'I said nothing to [Peter] Hall either,' Dubois said.

'You had your chance at the trial ...' Justice Applegarth replied.

Dubois then alluded to evidence in the trial that Billy McCulkin, Barbara's husband, had used a key to enter 6 Dorchester Street when he went looking for his missing wife and children.

'Where did Bill get the key from?' Dubois countered, implying that Billy had murdered his own family. 'There was only one key.'

Applegarth ordered Dubois to be removed. The prisoner was scowling as correctional officers led him through the wood-panelled side door. The judge continued his sentencing remarks in Shorty's absence. 'The life sentences which I have imposed upon each of you, your ages and your current prospects of being paroled, mean that it is likely that each of you will die in gaol,' he said. 'No decent citizen could have any sympathy that this is your likely fate. You spent four decades after 1974 at liberty in this community.

'Mrs McCulkin and her two daughters were denied the chance to live during those decades. Each was callously murdered. Mrs McCulkin lost the chance to live a happy and productive life, supporting herself and her daughters, enjoying the company of her friends and family, and finding new sources of happiness. Vicki and Leanne McCulkin lost the opportunity to pursue their education, possibly to pursue free tertiary education in the late 1970s, to pursue careers, and to share in the material wealth of our nation. They lost the chance to lead happy and fulfilling lives.

'When each of you dies, your family and friends will know where your body is buried or where your ashes are located. By contrast, the friends and family of your victims cannot visit their graves.'

He called Dubois 'O'Dempsey's fool'.

'Finally, Dubois and O'Dempsey, each of you escaped justice for decades,' said Applegarth. 'Luck was on your side. So was the fear you instilled in others. At least three things have ensured justice at last. First, the dedication of police. Second, the testimony of dozens of witnesses. Third, the conscience and courage of some key witnesses at each of your trials.'

One of the country's most haunting and brutal murder cases had finally concluded. The public gallery remained a little stunned. A set of emotional trials stretching over more than six months, littered with snapshots of horrific violence and depravity, of a criminal milieu capable of acts against other human beings, so ragged and debased, had concluded up to the final minutes with flashes of the same disregard for any societal order, or common decency, that had constituted these men's lives.

It hadn't been difficult, particularly on this day, to work out what went through the mind of 'Shorty' Dubois. He claimed the evidence against him was overwhelmingly circumstantial, or Billy McCulkin did it, or the cops had framed him. He shouldn't have been charged, shouldn't have been dragged through the courts since his arrest in 2014, shouldn't be in custody. The McCulkin case was old. Memories couldn't be relied on. Witnesses had made things up. Besides, crims were supposed to 'stay staunch'.

His rubbery, clown-like face remained downcast, except when he saw his wife and daughter in court. Now he was going away for good.

As for O'Dempsey, he was harder to read. Through his trial he had smiled at some witnesses as if to say – good to see you after all this time. He had spent most of his life avoiding this exact predicament – a lengthy stretch in prison for murder.

According to witness and former partner to O'Dempsey – Kerri-Ann Scully – he had once indicated to her that he had killed 33 people in total, which would place him as the country's most prolific killer. But in court he remained deadpan, only a trace of a shadow, in a certain light, imprinted on his face.

Now, at the end of proceedings, O'Dempsey turned and smiled sweetly at his family through a sheet of thick glass.

It was over.

Justice Peter Applegarth pushed his chair back, then motioned to rise. 'Adjourn the court,' he said.

That Indescribable Night

The day after O'Dempsey's and Dubois's sentencing, the *Courier-Mail* newspaper hit the streets demanding that the State Government finally reinvestigate the full story behind the historic atrocity of the Whiskey Au Go Go fire which claimed the lives of 15 innocent people. Given O'Dempsey's astonishing address to the court, and Justice Applegarth's rebuttal of the convicted murderer's claims of innocence, the newspaper planned to call on the government to act, and if not, it would initiate a rolling campaign of stories demanding action.

In the editorial on Friday 2 June 2017 it was reported that the revelation in the Supreme Court suggested there was evidence that O'Dempsey had been involved in the Whiskey mass murder. The newspaper said:

> For one, it draws into the murky Whiskey picture another potential suspect – a cold-blooded mass killer and ballistics expert, who, according to his trial evidence, probably organised and sanctioned the Torino's nightclub fire just 10 days before the Whiskey. Since the conviction of John Andrew Stuart and James Richard Finch for the Whiskey killings in late 1973, a lid was effectively put on the case.

The coronial inquest into the fire lasted less than two days and has never been reopened. Crucial documents in the case went missing, including substantial portions of the transcript of the trial of Stuart and Finch, pages that primarily dealt with evidence given by police who arrested and questioned both suspects.

On top of this, the Whiskey murder files have a 100-year non-publication order placed over them. They will not be able to be legally viewed until 2073.

The newspaper said the revelation that O'Dempsey may be a new suspect in the case could not go untested. 'While the truth behind the Whiskey has always remained blurred, this twist has the potential to rewrite our history and correct the past,' it added.

At around 11 a.m. on the same day the editorial was published, the Queensland Attorney General Yvette D'Ath announced a new inquest into the Whiskey. She hoped witnesses would now be willing to come forward and speak of the tragedy. 'There is no doubt there is significant public interest in getting answers in relation to the Whiskey Au Go Go firebombing in 1973 in which 15 people died,' she said. 'Given recent events, witnesses who have previously not been willing to come forward, might now be willing to provide new information that will give us those answers.'

Queensland Premier Annastacia Palaszczuk welcomed the inquest and said Ms D'Ath had been considering the Whiskey Au Go Go matter during the recent O'Dempsey court case. 'The Whiskey Au Go Go tragedy is etched in the memory of many Queenslanders,' the Premier said. 'We should take this opportunity to find any answers we can. I think a lot of people want closure and these are the right steps that the Attorney–General has made.'

The Whiskey inquest remained on hold throughout 2018 pending O'Dempsey's and Dubois's appeals against their convictions. However, on Friday 21 December the Court of Appeal finally released its decisions. The appeals were based on numerous grounds, including that the trial judge 'erred in admitting evidence of Dubois's motive', that the trial judge 'failed to provide adequate directions to the jury as to motive', and that the trial judge 'erroneously admitted the evidence of Billy McCulkin', among other arguments.

According to court documents, O'Dempsey submitted in his appeal that certain evidence should not have been led during his trial, including Barbara McCulkin's statement to her neighbour, Nisbet; her husband Billy McCulkin's knowledge with regard to the participants in the Whiskey arson; and Peter Hall's evidence that he, Meredith, Dubois and Hamilton were afraid of being implicated in the Whiskey massacre following their arson attack on Torino's.

The matter was over within seconds. The appeals of both Vincent O'Dempsey and Garry 'Shorty' Dubois were dismissed.

Many key players in the Whiskey drama have died, yet there are some crucial witnesses still alive who have been holding their secrets tightly since the fatal fire. With O'Dempsey's and Dubois's sentences upheld in late 2018, there is a sense among police investigators, survivors and the families of the victims that the essential truth behind the morning of 8 March 1973 could still be salvaged and bring clarity to the tragedy.

Many hopes rest with the next coronial inquest. It just may put to rest one of the most perplexing and haunting criminal cases in Queensland's history.

~

O, Almighty Father, in your great wisdom you led James and Johanna O'Dempsey from Ireland to these shores in 1855.

Through their faith in You and their labours, they prospered and were the forebears of many succeeding generations. Please grant them, and those descendants who have gone to join them, Eternal Repose.

We beseech You, in Your great mercy, to extend a Guiding Hand to we, the living descendants of James and Johanna, and future generations, so that we may avoid the evils and temptations of this World to enjoy the reward of Eternal Life in the Kingdom of God.

~

Author's Note and Acknowledgements

On 8 March 2018, about 150 people gathered outside the site of the former Whiskey Au Go Go nightclub at the corner of St Pauls Terrace and Amelia Street in Brisbane's Fortitude Valley to mark the 45th anniversary of the fire that killed 15 people all those years ago. It was a ceremony held in light rain, and present were Indigenous elders, government and council dignitaries, representatives of police, fire and ambulance services, former prison warders, family and friends of the victims, and a handful of men and women who survived that horrific night. Speeches and remembrances were offered around the brass plaque that remains embedded in the footpath outside the former club building. The circular plaque gives a short account of the tragedy. The unbroken perimeter of the circle is made up of the names of the 15 victims. It was a moving and emotional ceremony. For Kath Potter, this was the first time she'd been back to the entrance of the one-time club in Amelia Street. She recreated what happened that night, and she described what she saw, as if it had happened yesterday. Other survivors, like Donna Phillips and Hunter Nichol, were generous with their memories, despite the enormous trauma and health problems they suffered, and continue to suffer, from that night.

Throughout the research for *The Night Dragon*, it felt like there was an overriding collective will from those affected by the Whiskey tragedy, and many other Queenslanders, that the truth might finally be extracted. The full truth, after almost half a century, may never be known, but what was as equally evident as the goodwill around this project was a sense too that there were forces present that didn't want sunlight brought to the Whiskey mass murder. That remains the case.

I would like to offer my heartfelt gratitude to the likes of Donna, Kath, Hunter, Bevan Child, the Carroll family, the Palethorpe family, and all the families of the victims who were so generous in offering their recollections to me. Those 15 men and women who were lost will never be forgotten.

This book wouldn't exist except for the work of Queensland police detectives Virginia Gray, Mick Dowie and their colleagues. Their work in successfully solving the McCulkin cold case murders was without peer, and that in turn opened some windows on the Whiskey firebombing story. Thank you also to Keith Smith, David McSherry and Kingsley Fancourt.

Several men and women offered information on condition of anonymity. I thank you all for your enormous courage and trust. I have valued our friendship over the years and will continue to do so.

Thank you to Barbara McCulkin's brother, Graham Ogden, and his family, for being so kind and welcoming. And to Barbara's daughter, Jocelyn.

Thank you to my vibrant team of advisers, critics, friends, family, journalists, editors, sounding boards, former police and scratching posts who came on this journey, including: Nigel Powell; Jim Slade; Ian Alcorn; Hedley Thomas; Des Houghton; Christopher Dore; Trent Dalton; Lachlan Haywood; Sue McVay; Susan Johnson; John Shakespeare and family; Archie Butterfly; Ron and Karen Condon; Marsha and Phil Pope, and family; Gillian Morris and Geof Hawke; Gary Morris, Jo Gaha, and family; Mike Ahern; Sir Malcolm McMillan; Alex Mitchell and Judith White; and to the memory of the late Tony Reeves.

I would like to pay special tribute to writer Tom Clark for his invaluable assistance during research for this book. Several books were referenced, or directly quoted, throughout these pages, and I would like to thank the authors and publishers for permission to reproduce extracts in *The Night Dragon*:

The Prince and the Premier: Story of Perce Galea, Bob Askin and the Others who Gave Organised Crime its start in Australia by David Hickie, Harper Collins, 1985

'"Real Gone Town": Popular Music and Youth Culture in 1960s Brisbane' by Raymond Evans in *The 1960s in Australia: People, Power and Politics*, edited by Shirleene Robinson and Julie Ustinoff, Cambridge Scholars Publishing, 2012

Sydney Noir: The Golden Years by Michael Duffy and Nick Hordern, New South Publishing, 2017

The Whiskey Au Go Go Massacre: Murder, Arson and the Crime of the Century by Geoff Plunkett, Big Sky Publishing, 2018

Unbelievably, my odyssey of true crime books began more than nine years ago when I approached Madonna Duffy, publisher at the University of Queensland Press, with an idea for a volume on historic crime and corruption in the Sunshine State. Thank you, Madonna, and the team at UQP, for coming along for the ride which seemingly has no end. Thank you for your faith and expertise, your professionalism and your personal attention to detail. I also owe almost everything to my wonderful editor, Jacqueline Blanchard, whose magic and skill is on every single page.

Finally, as ever, I offer all my love to my beautiful family; my darling wife Katie Kate, and our children, Finnigan, Bridie Rose and Oliver.

THREE CROOKED KINGS
Matthew Condon

Three Crooked Kings is the shocking true story of Queensland and how a society was shaped by almost half a century of corruption. At its core is Terence Murray Lewis, deposed and jailed former police commissioner. From his entry into the force in 1949, Lewis rose through the ranks, becoming part of the so-called Rat Pack with detectives Glendon Patrick Hallahan and Tony Murphy under the guiding influence of Commissioner Frank Bischof.

The next four decades make for a searing tale of cops and killings, bagmen and blackmail, and sin and sleaze that exposes a police underworld which operated from Queensland and into New South Wales. This gripping book exposes the final pieces of the puzzle, unearths new evidence on cold cases, and explores the pivotal role that whistleblower Shirley Brifman, prostitute and brothel owner, played until her sudden death.

Based on extensive and unprecedented access to Terry Lewis and his personal papers, as well as hundreds of interviews with key players and conspirators, *Three Crooked Kings* is the first of three explosive books. Awarded journalist and novelist Matthew Condon has crafted the definitive account of an era that changed a state and is still reverberating to this day.

'Hailed as the most explosive book of 2013 — a riveting epic and unrelenting tour-de-force which will shock a nation. And it's all true.' —*The Chronicle*

ISBN 978 0 7022 3891 8

JACKS AND JOKERS
Matthew Condon

Continuing on from the bestselling *Three Crooked Kings*, *Jacks and Jokers* opens in 1976. Terry Lewis, exiled in western Queensland, is soon to be controversially appointed Police Commissioner. As for the other two original Crooked Kings, Tony Murphy is set to ruthlessly take control of the workings of 'The Joke', while Glen Hallahan, retired from the force, begins to show a keen interest in the emerging illicit drug trade. Meanwhile, ex-cop and 'Bagman' Jack Herbert collects the payments and efficiently takes police graft to a whole new level.

The Joke heralds an era of hard drugs, illegal gambling and prostitution, and leaves in its wake a string of unsolved murders and a trail of dirty money. With the highest levels of police and government turning a blind eye, the careers of honest police officers and the lives of innocent civilians are threatened and often lost as corruption escalates out of control.

Revealing more incredible facts and previously untold stories, award-winning journalist and novelist Matthew Condon once again exposes the shocking behaviour outside the law by the law. *Jacks and Jokers* is the gripping second instalment of the rise – and spectacular fall – of one man, an entire state and generations of corruption.

'*Jacks and Jokers* sprawls and appals in equal measure. Condon's true crime series is not just a compelling read: it is compulsory.'—*Australian Book Review*

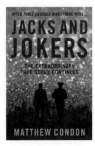

ISBN 978 0 7022 4996 9

ALL FALL DOWN
Matthew Condon

The gripping finale to *Three Crooked Kings* and *Jacks and Jokers* brings to a close Matthew Condon's best-selling true-crime trilogy.

In 1983, the soon-to-be-knighted Police Commissioner Terry Lewis continues to turn a blind eye to the operation of The Joke, a highly organised system of graft payments from illegal gambling, prostitution and illicit drugs. As the tentacles of this fraudulent vice network spread, the fabric holding together the police, judiciary and political system starts to unravel. *All Fall Down* offers an unprecedented insight into the Fitzgerald Inquiry and Lewis's subsequent years in prison, and explores the real story behind the dramatic exit of Sir Joh Bjelke-Petersen. Drawing from interviews with key players who have, until now, been afraid to speak publicly, *All Fall Down* celebrates the bravery of those unsung heroes who risked everything to expose the truth.

This epic trilogy provides the definitive account of an unforgettable period in Queensland's history. The devastating consequences of those decades of corruption still reverberate today.

'This is an excellent trilogy but, unfortunately for Lewis, it does not end with the dark knight rising.'—*Weekend Australian*

'*All Fall Down* is an exquisite finale to Matthew Condon's epic analysis of crime and corruption in Queensland.'—*Sydney Morning Herald*

ISBN 978 0 7022 5353 9

LITTLE FISH ARE SWEET
Matthew Condon

'We had a meeting and agreed that we would pay [Terry] Lewis. I paid [Tony] Murphy, who was then a sergeant and senior to me, on a monthly basis and extra for Lewis. I recall meeting Lewis on a number of occasions in company with Tony Murphy. I recall conversation getting around to payments of money with Murphy and Lewis. Lewis thanked me on several occasions and said, 'Little fish are sweet'. — Evidence of Jack 'The Bagman' Herbert to the Fitzgerald Inquiry into police corruption, 31 August 1988, Brisbane, Queensland.

Little Fish Are Sweet is Matthew Condon's extraordinary personal account of writing the *Three Crooked Kings* trilogy. When Condon first interviewed disgraced former police commissioner Terry Lewis, he had no idea that it would be the start of a turbulent six-year journey. As hundreds of people came forward to share their powerful and sometimes shocking stories, decades of crime and corruption were revealed in a new light.

Risking threats and intimidation, Condon tirelessly pursued his investigations into a web of cold murder cases and past conspiracies. What he discovered is much more sinister than anyone could have imagined.

'Now we owe a new debt to Condon for reminding us of our obligations as journalists and the consequences of ignoring them.'—*Walkley Magazine*

ISBN 978 0 7022 5410 9